Democracy in the Family

Democracy in the Family

Insights from India

Edited by
Joy Deshmukh-Ranadive

SAGE Los Angeles • London • New Delhi • Singapore
www.sagepublications.com

Copyright © Joy Deshmukh-Ranadive, 2008

All rights reserved. No part of this book may be reproduced or utilised in any form or by any means, electronic or mechanical, including photocopying, recording or by any information storage or retrieval system, without permission in writing from the publisher.

First published in 2008 by

SAGE Publications India Pvt Ltd
B 1/I-1 Mohan Cooperative Industrial Area
Mathura Road, New Delhi 110044, India
www.sagepub.in

SAGE Publications Inc
2455 Teller Road
Thousand Oaks, California 91320, USA

SAGE Publications Ltd
1 Oliver's Yard, 55 City Road
London EC1Y 1SP, United Kingdom

SAGE Publications Asia-Pacific Pte Ltd
33 Pekin Street
#02-01 Far East Square
Singapore 048763

Published by Vivek Mehra for SAGE Publications India Pvt Ltd, typeset in 11/13 pt Bembo by Innovative Processors, New Delhi and printed at Chaman Enterprises, New Delhi.

Library of Congress Cataloging-in-Publication Data

Democracy in the family: insights from India/edited by Joy Deshmukh-Ranadive.
    p. cm.
  Includes bibliographical references.
1. Family—India. 2. Women—India—Social conditions.
3. Democracy—India. 4. India—Social conditions. I. Deshmukh-
    Ranadive, Joy.
HQ670.D43   306.850954—dc22   2008   2008000577

ISBN: 978-0-7619-3631-2 (Hb)   978-81-7829-795-8 (India-Hb)

The SAGE Team: Rekha Natarajan, Samprati Pani, Anju Saxena and
                    Trinankur Banerjee
Cover photograph courtesy: Joy Deshmukh-Ranadive

*This book is dedicated to my mother
Ivy Prabhakar Deshmukh
who taught me the first alphabets of
'democracy in the family'
and why the word 'help' did not have
a place inside our home.*

Contents

Preface	ix
Acknowledgements	xiii

1. Introduction   1
   Joy Deshmukh-Ranadive

Section I: Experiencing the Family

2. Women Adjusting for Survival: Women Workers, New Economic Policies and Adjustments within the Family and Household   25
   Nandita Gandhi
3. The Light Shines through Gossamer Threads: Inside–Outside Political Spaces   55
   Sumi Krishna

Section II: Expressing the Family

4. Family in Feminist Songs: A Continuity with Women's Folk Literature   75
   Sonal Shukla
5. Resurrecting the Mother in *Mata Hidimba*   98
   Uma Narain

Section III: Seeking Justice

6. Sustaining Democracy within the Family through Family Courts: An Exploratory Analysis — 113
   Sita Vanka and M. Nirmala Kumari
7. Private Concerns in Public Discourse: Women-initiated Community Responses to Domestic Violence — 128
   Nandita Bhatla and Anuradha Rajan
8. The Shalishi in West Bengal: A Community-based Response to Domestic Violence — 151
   Shramajibee Mahila Samity

Section IV: Including the Excluded

9. Family, Gender and Masculinities — 183
   Radhika Chopra
10. Placing Gender Equity in the Family Centre Stage: The Use of *Kala Jatha* Theatre — 207
    Joy Deshmukh-Ranadive

About the Editor and Contributors — 226
Index — 231

Preface

The family constitutes the central locus of the beginnings of social life for the human being. Consequently, it has a place of great importance in the theory and research of all social sciences. Sociologists and anthropologists have for long researched the family as the primary unit of human coexistence and socialisation. In economics, the family has been subsumed within the understanding of the 'household' as a collective that consumes what is produced and sold in the market. In political science, conventionally, the family has largely remained invisible. The functions of the family are given attention in as much as they are necessary to maintain a stable political society, and attention is paid only when it malfunctions and results in the socialisation of children into 'deviants'. Women's studies, on the other hand, focus on the family as a site of power and discrimination along with being a locus of production, reproduction and distribution. It is within this discipline that researchers from various social sciences have broken academic norms and addressed the family in its complexity. The undemocratic nature of relationships within the family is complicated by the high emotive content that governs those relationships. Patriarchy as an ideology and value system cuts across cultures and societies. Feminist understandings of gender discrimination locate several of its beginnings in socialisation processes, a significant portion of which takes place within families and households. While it is important to identify power dynamics and seek countervailing solutions, it is also important to place those solutions within altered value systems. Unless value systems change to become democratic and intrinsically value women as human beings and not just for their instrumental worth, there will always be the danger of patriarchy being propagated by women as much as by men. On the other hand, it is equally important to have an inclusive framework wherein men are as involved in dialogues of democratising the family.

Public policies treat all that transpires within the bounds of families as sacrosanct and out-of-bounds for state intervention. In their aspiration to be gender-neutral, they ignore the implications of inherent gender biases that govern families. As a consequence, public policy often contributes towards intensifying gender discrimination, besides perpetuating injustices. There is a need for research to concentrate upon unpacking the family so that the links between intra-household dynamics and macro changes are understood. The interface between principles of democracy inside and outside the home should be highlighted. The political nature of activity within the family and the ways in which it impacts upon activity in public domains has to be focused upon. Issues of human rights and linkages with gender-biased understandings of duties need to be looked at. While discourses around human rights find platforms in macro contexts, it is equally important to question their validity and relevance in micro contexts of everyday living.

This book brings together a collection of papers, which revolve around the issue of justice in the family. The papers range from examinations of the institution of the family, the site of the household, practices of householding and relationships between members, the impact of non-democratic norms and attempts to seek justice in the face of domestic strife and violence to the advocacy of inclusive strategies that involve men and entire communities in democratising the family. The papers are revised versions of presentations submitted to the sub-theme, 'Promoting Democracy in the Family' at the Tenth National Conference on Women's Studies of the Indian Association of Women's Studies (IAWS), held at Utkal University, Bhubaneshwar, Orissa, India, from 17 to 20 October 2002, on 'Sustaining Democracy: Challenges for the 21st Century'. Seven of these papers, those by Radhika Chopra, Shramajibee Mahila Samity, Anuradha Rajan and

Preface

Nandita Bhatla, Centre for Advocacy and Research, Uma Narain, Sumi Krishna and Joy Deshmukh-Ranadive, were published in a special issue of the *Economic and Political Weekly*, 26 April–2 May 2003, guest edited by Joy Deshmukh-Ranadive.

Joy Deshmukh-Ranadive

Acknowledgements

Democracy in the Family is a milestone in my journey of investigating power and power relationships, which began way back in 1981 when I was working on my doctoral dissertation. However, this book would not have been possible without the encouragement of Dr Vina Majumdar who has been my mentor and guide for several years now. It was she who challenged me into seeking answers to power struggles within the domestic unit by posing questions around the notion of democracy. Thank you Vinadi.

My heartfelt gratitude to all my authors who bore with me right from the time of the Tenth National Conference on Women's Studies of the Indian Association of Women's Studies (IAWS), held at Utkal University, Bhubaneshwar, Orissa, India, from 17 to 20 October 2002 on 'Sustaining Democracy: Challenges for the 21st Century'. Most of them wrote papers at my invitation for the conference sub-theme 'Promoting Democracy in the Family' since they believed in it as a principle of life. My gratitude to the IAWS that provided a platform for such a deviant sub-theme.

I cannot forget the faith that several commissioning editors in SAGE Publications, New Delhi, (from Omita to Mimi to Anamika to Sugata) have had in me to bring this book to fruition. Their belief in the issues addressed, is one of the primary reasons why this book saw the light of day, or shall I say, SAGE!

Last but not the least, thanks to my families, both natal and marital, which have been my classrooms where I have learnt the meanings of justice in the family.

1
Introduction

Joy Deshmukh-Ranadive

The connection between the lives of human beings and their families is intimate and inseparable. The basic characteristic of the family is that members are tied to one another by relationships of kith, kin, birth, marriage or even adoption, governed largely by a set of culturally determined rules. These relationships within families, between spouses, parents and children, between siblings, and so on, are those that provide emotional security, material support, a sense of belonging, status, legitimacy and social identity. From being a shelter of protection and love to being a site of conflict and exploitation, the family has influenced the lived experiences of women and men differently. Women's lives are inexorably connected to the domestic environment they are placed in and the family is the locus as well as the instrument through which socialisation takes place. Gender socialisation allocates resources and work in such a way that women spend longer hours within this environment than men. Women also live more constrained lives. Further, these restrictions are justified by families in the name of protection and care.

There are as many kinds of families as there are systems of householding. However, the ideology of patriarchy seems to prevail largely, thereby resulting in hierarchies within which women as a group and as individuals, according to their placement within these hierarchies, find negotiations of justice difficult. Socio-cultural norms also differ across the world but, again, where patriarchy prevails there is less scope for voice and action. The lack of participation of all members in decision-making and the skewed distribution of resources and time, make for the lack of democratic principles in families and households.

DEVELOPMENT, HOUSEHOLDS AND FAMILIES

Development is the central pivot around which national and international policies revolve. Today, deve₁opment issues are inexorably connected to globalisation. Economic changes are structuring countries, and cultures are being irreversibly altered due to them. Of particular significance is the ideology behind globalisation, which is a move towards the liberalisation of markets, with privatisation and competition being both goals in themselves as also the means to achieve liberalisation. Policy packages like stabilisation and structural adjustment programmes are the measures through which these components are introduced into developing countries. Within these circumstances, dynamics between members of families and households alter in ways that impact upon the levels of justice within relationships. These dynamics are connected to the way globalisation and development policies play themselves out in fulfilling the requirements of production and distribution systems.

Production is no longer an activity or process that combines 'factors of production' like land, labour, capital and enterprise and which takes place within conceivable boundaries. The entire globe seems to be converting into a work site with the various stages and loci of production being spread across countries. The significance of this kind of production lies in its requirements in terms of 'factors'. Currently, the factor that is paramount is 'capital'. Different kinds of capital are required for production—physical, financial, technological, social and human capital. Technological capital determines the quantity and quality of physical, financial and human capital required for production. Social capital and human capital are interdependent wherein the development of individuals is dependent on their possession of social capital. When extended to the economy, positive

Introduction

social capital enhances development whilst negative social capital detracts from it.

The bottom line of this kind of production lies in the instrumentalisation of the human factor of production (otherwise known as labour). The owner is divorced from the service, wherein the service component takes the nature of capital, thus justifying investment in the owner of the service. Hence, the human being is valued in as much as she/he can contribute to the production process. Couched within the utopian desire of increasing human capabilities to lead worthwhile lives, is a primary requirement of enhancing human resources 'capable' of productivity. This requirement automatically puts the production of human beings, which itself is in the nature of capital formation, at centre stage. Human capital formation as a matter of necessity requires focused investment in habitat, in the provision of basic health and education services, as also investments in skill and training such as will allow for the formation of a labour force best suited to the altered structures of production.

The next reality to be faced, given this argument, is the importance of the household, and within it family structures, since it is the locus of the production of human resources. It is within the household that human resources are primarily reproduced and maintained. By and large, human beings are 'privately' produced within the household. Further, the woman plays an important role in this production. Due to biological reasons, the onus of reproduction lies with the woman. Additionally, due to a sexual division of household labour along gender lines, the maintenance of human resources also becomes her prime responsibility. As a whole then, within the household, the production of human resources is more the responsibility of women than of men.

Given the ideology behind globalisation, the household attains prime importance, and in the bargain so does the woman through her role in the production of human resources, to be used as human capital.[1] Fear has been expressed about adjustment programmes threatening the survival of poor households. We have been cautioned that there is a limit to women's capacity to adjust and it may so happen that a breaking point may be reached (Elson 1993).[2] An important fallout of reaching this breaking point lies in the effect it has on the production and maintenance of human resources (Cornia 1990). Elson (1993) points out how the production of human resources is different from the production of any other resources. The former has an intrinsic value besides having an instrumental value. If the demand or market value of a resource drops beyond a certain minimum, its production is abandoned or stopped for more lucrative options. But if the maintenance of children becomes difficult, mothers do not abandon them and consequently the pressure is absorbed by the women.

In India, the formal catalyst for the initiation of stabilisation and structural adjustment policies in 1991 was an economic crisis, when foreign currency reserves had plummeted, the annual rate of inflation was 17 per cent and the overall rate of growth was only 1.1 per cent. The policy changes (also labelled reforms/restructuring) spanned exchange and tax regimes, industrial policy, foreign investment policy and the financial sector. While the immediate objective of the policies was to stabilise the economy, the long-term goal was to raise the growth on a sustainable basis in the belief that if the economy takes off, there will automatically be a trickle-down effect due to which the poor will benefit. Sustained growth was thought to generate an environment congenial for the empowerment of the poor. However, with structural adjustment and globalisation, work for women within and outside the household increased. Worldwide, the 'feminisation' of labour has been recorded as a consequence of economic restructuring (Standing 1989).

The effect of economic policies on family dynamics and householding patterns is brought out in the first section, 'Experiencing the Family'. Nandita Gandhi, in her chapter 'Women Adjusting for Survival: Women Workers, New Economic Policies and Adjustments within the Family and Household', shows how existing hierarchies and non-democratic norms within the family and within householding make for larger sacrifices by women in food intake, education and other vital necessities, while coping with the effects of structural adjustment policies. Smaller gains through employment in terms of increased self-esteem do not alter norms, but work around them in interesting ways.

Introduction

Development interventions alter economic variables for families, thereby altering relationships between men and women. Gender relations in some *adivasi* (tribal) societies are relatively more egalitarian than among other communities, but enormous changes are now taking place in their resource base and livelihoods. In her chapter 'The Light Shines through Gossamer Threads: Inside–Outside Political Spaces', Sumi Krishna explores the process of change as a scattered semi-nomadic group of *adivasi* foragers come together to form a village settlement. Focusing on one family and one woman from it, the chapter reflects upon whether and how an indigenous democratic fabric and relative gender egalitarianism may be retained in the face of structural changes in the *adivasi* life-worlds. Using a personal narrative, shaped by different 'dialogical levels', it traces the dialogical stages through which the 'story' unfolds. It suggests that the narrative as a qualitative research tool may be used to interrogate women's political spaces and to bring the family into the development discourse.

UNDERSTANDING THE FAMILY[3]

The family as an institution and the household as a locus have often been romanticised as being the one refuge where conflict and confrontation are absent. However, over time, as has been pointed out by Moore (1994), there has been a move away from the folk ideology of the household as a 'haven from the heartless world', where relations between the family members are characterised by sharing, and are seen as essentially equal and cooperative. Feminist scholars have characterised the family/household as the site of women's oppression and as the locus of conflicts of interest between men and women.[4] A number of alternative models for the analysis of the household—based on contracts, bargaining and negotiation— have now been proposed by social scientists.[5] In such models, questions of power and ideology become prominent.

Feminist studies draw upon game theory to formulate bargaining models in order to explain intra-household power dynamics. At times, the 'negotiations' between members is cooperative, at times conflictive and at times a mix of both. Within a bargaining context, an important determinant of power is the 'threat point', that is, a person's fall-back position. Within dominating situations, the fallback position is indicative of the person's capacity to exist in the relationship and/or survive outside it. Social norms are particularly important in bargaining frameworks since they set limits on what can be bargained about, determine bargaining power, affect how the process of bargaining is conducted and constitute a factor to be bargained over (Agarwal 1997). Norms prescribe 'appropriate' behaviour within domestic units and, in doing so, ascertain the extent of voice that members should have. Kinship patterns, caste and class structures are important factors that shape norms and, consequently, it is more meaningful to consider socio-cultural rather than just social norms. Within a bargaining scenario, whether members cooperate or choose confrontation is determined to a large extent by the social sanctions they will face if norms are not adhered to. The normative pressure is a tremendous incentive for members to cooperate (Kabeer 1994).

Economics as a discipline is inadequate to holistically explain the reality of women's lives within domestic units. No doubt, instruments such as cost-benefit analysis, the rearranging of explanations via labour-time, the measuring of the value of women's work and a consideration of future benefits as against present advantage have been used to make sense of apparent paradoxes in household behaviour. For example, women often place the welfare of other family members above and before their own; in other words, they identify their welfare with that of the family to the extent of inducing self-damage. Or, women observably turn out to be the 'enemies' of other women, for example, daughters being discriminated against by their mothers or daughters-in-law being ill-treated by their mothers-in-law. The justification of such behaviour patterns can perhaps be found using one or a combination of the economic explanations discussed. However, there are paradoxes within household behaviour that go deeper than accounting and tabulating processes, for example, a woman choosing to stay within a household in spite of encountering violence and threat to life and limb. Here, undoubtedly the explanations have to take into account choices, the lack of them, the possibility of an exit, the exit, the extent of voice and the fall-back position. Economists could claim expertise

Introduction

in justifying such behaviour within their framework of bargaining theory, wherein a consideration of socio-cultural norms is enough to lend teeth to the framework and justify the paradox. However, I seek to point towards one factor that is of tremendous importance within familial dynamics and which is seldom spoken of, leave alone accounted for, in research attempts. I allude to the emotive nature of relationships within the family. The quality of emotions that exist within domestic units is of a different nature than those existing outside it. This is not to say that employees within a firm do not have emotions or any feelings towards one another. They do, but the emotional content within kin relationships and those that develop due to co-habitation are a strong force to 'fight' when decisions of exit have to be taken. The matter is further complicated by the fact that socio-cultural norms condition people into feeling certain appropriate emotions. Not only are behaviour patterns charted, but accompanying mental and emotional patterns are also chalked out. The primary emotion underlying families is one of loyalty. This is one of the primary reasons why data on intra-household conflict is difficult to ascertain. Ill-treatment by other members, especially the husband, may be hidden from investigative questions since it amounts to betrayal of family loyalty or, worse still, may be seen as warranted due to biased conditioning.

The experiences of living in non-democratic families and of being subjected to unfair social norms have been expressed through several artistic mediums—writings, films, television, songs and theatre. The second section, 'Expressing the Family', highlights the portrayal of the family through art forms. Two chapters investigate the use of songs and theatre to express the family. The chapter 'Family in Feminist Songs—A Continuity with Women's Folk Literature', by Sonal Shukla, discusses the use of folk tradition in feminist songs and how women's folk literature as well as feminist folk songs challenge undemocratic relationships within the family. These songs which have been created anonymously by women in the form of folk songs and stories show how women have not always considered family situations as private and sacrosanct—they have mocked oppressive in-laws, complained against their own natal family that chose such marital families for them and expressed their pain, fears and dreams through their creativity in oral traditions. The enormous popularity of feminist songs among women can be seen as being in continuity with the protest tradition in women's anonymous literature. These songs and those generated by the women's movement have been powerful tools for use in training in rural and urban areas. Women also sing of new norms of householding and family life where harmony is possible on the basis of equality, where housework is shared and where women participate in decision-making.

Uma Narain, in her chapter 'Resurrecting the Mother in "Mata Hidimba"', discusses 'Mata Hidimba' as an exemplary feminist play, written by a male playwright, that resurrects the image of motherhood from the *Mahabharata*, a mythological Indian epic. Focusing on Hidimba, Bhima's wife, who is largely invisible in the *Mahabharata*, it highlights issues of motherhood intertwined with race, caste and religion, affording a terrain for the overarching patriarchal power play.

DEMOCRACY AND GOVERNANCE IN THE FAMILY

Given the fact that families are inherently hierarchical, the question that springs to mind is whether democracy as a concept is relevant at all within the family. The word 'democracy', as well as the concept it represents, can be traced back to the region surrounding the Mediterranean Sea. The beginnings of democracy can be credited to the Greeks of 6th century BC. The word comes from two Greek words: *demos*, meaning 'the people', and *kratein*, meaning 'to rule'. These two words are joined together to form 'democracy', literally meaning 'rule by the people'. Over time democracy has become unanimous with the ideas of participation, freedom, governance with voice to the people and a relatively pluralistic distribution of power.

The idea of democracy is central to all notions of political activity and contains within itself the implication of being an ideal situation for humankind in general. Democracy is normally understood in the context of interaction in the public spheres of people's lives.[6] The family, on the other hand, is supposed to fall within the realm of the 'private', absolving it of scrutiny from the point of view of jurisprudence. However, the political spaces accorded to a person are spread across both public and private domains. It is the private political spaces that allocate status and position to members of a

Introduction

family. It is these spaces that determine the placement of an individual within a structure of power in the family. Questions of rights, responsibilities and duties within the family may not usually be the topic of public discourse, but their outcomes impact upon the lives of individuals in serious ways. In as much as a family is removed from democratic principles, members that are low in the hierarchy, as are women and girl children, face the repercussions. When people are subject to violence and neglect, issues spill over from these supposedly 'inner' worlds, with repercussions for the 'outer' world at large. The ultimate understanding of the intrinsic value of human life and human existence calls for the collapse of all such barriers that allow for the perpetuation of injustice behind walls of 'privacy'. It is as much necessary for the notion of democracy to prevail within homes as it is necessary for it to govern public life.

The idea of democracy is closely linked to the system of governance that it plays itself through. Just as there are systems of governance within nation-states, there are informal systems of governance within families and households. Governance is usually understood as the decision-making processes within organisations. Similarly, within families, decisions are taken according to socially acceptable systems of role allocations. Social norms take the place of laws, and behaviour is regulated as desirable and undesirable according to them. Informal systems of jurisprudence that are regulated by family and community networks influence people's lives. All the elements of political behaviour that can be observed in the public arena are evident within the private domain of the domestic unit.

Participation by members of the family in householding decisions; the freedom of expression and movement that they are allowed; a pluralistic distribution of power among men and women and also between women themselves—all of these factors depend on the level of democracy within the governance of the domestic unit. For instance, let us take into consideration the following types of families. A nuclear family represents a typical male-headed family of husband, wife and their children. The father, as the head of the family, is placed at the top rank.[7] The head generally controls decision-making, can issue commands and trains subordinates. He is also supposed to protect and provide for others and disburse resources. In return, he receives obedience, deference and service. The intermediate ranks include the service position occupied by the mother. In this type of a family she is an economic dependent; she bears, nurtures and protects children who in turn obey her and give her affection. In the service position, the mother also has to serve the father. This service may be different from that provided to children, but the service position also caters to the top ranks. Children and the ill or incapacitated members occupy the bottom ranks, while adult children are not included as they move on to set up a separate domestic unit, given the definition of a nuclear family. The family structure, within a patriarchal understanding of power, automatically has to legitimise the use of force, reprimand and violence in order to train and ensure compliance. All these are also meted out in the guise of 'protecting' the lower ranks, sometimes from the supposed harm they may do to themselves and sometimes because of real or perceived threats of harm from outside, for example, violent protection of women's honour.

Similarly, a typical, unilateral kinship-based, patrilineal South Asian extended family consists of several men, women and children. Its hierarchy will generally consist of three tiers, with the father as the head of the family in the top rank. Intermediate ranks, consisting of training, training-cum-service and service positions, would be occupied by the oldest adult son who may be promoted to the top rank if his father dies or becomes too old or ill to function. A younger adult son is generally unable to become the head if he continues to live within the same extended family. However, if and when the oldest brother becomes head, he may move up in the hierarchy *within* the training positions. Training-cum-service positions could also be occupied by adult daughters while they live in their natal families and they could subsequently move into training positions in their marital households when they get married. New daughters-in-law find themselves in training-cum-service positions as they train in the ways of the new family. The service positions are held by the mother, older daughters-in-law, widows (for example, father's sister, aunt or daughter), divorced or deserted daughters and servants. There is a further sub-ranking within the intermediate ranks, wherein women with children are positioned higher than the issueless women, while women with sons are placed higher than are those who have daughters. Ranking at the intermediate levels is done on the basis of

Introduction

age and marital status. Children comprise the next measure for determining sub-rankings. The bottom ranks are occupied by children, where boys will move up to training and girls to training-cum-service positions on growing up. Sick people are temporarily in the bottom positions and move back to their places after recovery. Old people, incapable of service, remain in the bottom ranks. Guests, too, occupy the bottom ranks. This structure due to its lack of democracy has the potential for the use of violence to ensure obedience of lower ranks towards higher ranks.

Within a domestic unit there is another separate type of hierarchy—that existing *between* women. This is because in South Asian joint families, the world of women functions separately from that of men. Within service positions, there are those with authority and those without. The oldest daughter-in-law can move from a training to a service position with authority and even to the top rank after the death, illness or widowhood of her mother-in-law. Hence, in the world of men and women, the latter always remain in the intermediate ranks, but amongst women, there is chance of movement from the intermediate to the top rank in service positions. The sub-ranking mentioned earlier, with respect to the children that the woman produces, also holds good within these micro-dynamics. Thus, women who have produced male children have a higher status than those who do not. It is in this context that sex determination tests are conducted and, therefore, violence enters a woman's life while she is still at the foetal stage. A married daughter visiting her natal family may be treated well, but customarily she will have no authority and will occupy a bottom position. However, there are instances where married visiting daughters do wield considerable influence on other family members in their natal households. Sick people, after care and recovery, move back into their original positions, depending on their gender and age. Very old and unproductive members are ranked at the bottom since they are incapable of service and have no authority.

Again, in the hierarchy among women, which is governed mainly by age, there is ample scope for the use of non-democratic methods to gain compliance. When girls are married young, they tend to be more vulnerable, especially in the earlier years. Training is a legitimate reason for using force, threats and violence when a young woman is in a training position and when it is easier to subdue her. When girls are married into distantly located families, support from their natal families is limited. It is at such times that kinship norms give considerable authority to the older members of the marital family, both men and women, to 'train' the new bride into the ways of the family. Severe methods are then seen to be legitimate means of teaching her appropriate conduct.

The association of democracy with voice and participation is complicated when one applies it to the family. In patrilineal, unilineal kinship systems, as we have in most parts of India, men expect good services from women. Dissatisfaction is expressed in the use of verbal and physical violence, which then constitutes the voice of the man. Paradoxically, women expect this treatment and often rationalise it as a 'corrective' because they did not do what was expected of them.

It would seem that since violence should be a sign of a malfunctioning family, women would raise their voices against it; on the contrary, it is men who voice protest via violence about inadequacies in the domestic services provided. In fact, the 'normalcy' of domestic violence within families is worrisome since it is not seen as a sign of dysfunction, rather it is the 'normal' course of socialisation and training.

THE STRUGGLE FOR JUSTICE

It is only after violence crosses gross boundaries that women raise their voices. Changes in perception are addressed by organisations that work to bring about change in this scenario and particularly to combat domestic violence. They seek to help women raise their voices against injustices and address violence in their lives by articulating it. However, in order that voices be raised, several hurdles have to be crossed and the most significant of them is that of loyalty that women are supposed to have towards their husbands and families. Within a family or domestic unit, women often do not perceive violence as an injustice, instead they accept it as part of legitimate behaviour patterns. For example, inferiority in care, food or education, which translates into discrimination and deprivation, are seen as the 'fate' of women or are justified on the grounds that the requirements

Introduction

of women are less than those of men. These deprivations are no less violent than the more overt manifestations of physical abuse. It is only *after* discrimination or injustice is acknowledged that an attempt can be made to democratise the functioning of the family. If so, overt and covert steps taken may be interpreted as voice. In the case of families, both voice and exit on the part of women in the lower rungs of familial hierarchies are taken as signs of disloyalty. These often comprise reasons for further violence. For men and women in the higher rungs of familial hierarchies, however, violence is the manifestation of voice or, rather, violence is voice.[8]

Regarding violence, voice is the most important tool to protest against injustice. This voice, more often than not, cannot be an isolated one of the woman herself since the risk of aggravation and increasing violence stands. Outside intervention by organisations could clearly assist women to seek redress as collective strength always helps in raising voices against violence. Voice, however, comes at a cost, hence support structures and additional services are required if women have to be able to bear the responsibility of voicing protest.

The third section of the book, 'Seeking Justice', has three chapters. Sita Vanka and M. Nirmala Kumari, in their chapter 'Sustaining Democracy within the Family through Family Courts—An Exploratory Analysis', show how India has witnessed far-reaching changes in family relationships. Rapid industrialisation, education of women, legislation allowing divorce, changing perceptions about the role of women, and so on, have given rise to new stresses and tensions thus leading to newer agencies and forums for the administration of justice. Attempts have been made to introduce family courts only recently in India. The authors advocate that these should aim at resolving family disputes from the 'social' rather than the 'legal' angle and in a way which sustains justice and restores democracy within the family.

In the chapter 'Private Concerns in Public Discourse: Women-initiated Community Responses to Domestic Violence', Nandita Bhatla and Anuradha Rajan discuss findings of a participatory research study that sought to explore the dynamics of community-based responses to domestic violence across five sites in India. The study was intended to provide documentation of how women-led innovative responses have emerged, how they operate and how successful they are in addressing the needs of women subjected to domestic violence. Community responses to violence can open democratic forms of dispute resolution and operationalise an objective process through a feminist perspective, incorporating a strong element of preventive justice.

The Shramajibee Mahila Samity, in the chapter 'The Shalishi in West Bengal: A Community-based Response to Domestic Violence', shows how traditional community/village level dispute resolution systems still coexist with formal processes of justice and administration. The 'shalishi' is one such method of arbitration in West Bengal that has been used by non-governmental organisations (NGOs) to intervene effectively in settling domestic violence cases. Shalishi scores over the more formal legal avenues of dispute resolution because of its informal set-up. But deriving its legitimacy as it does from the conventional norms and values of the community, shalishi works in favour of keeping the family intact, often compromising feminist notions of empowerment.

AN INCLUSIVE FRAMEWORK: THE RIGHT TO BE HUMAN

While the struggle and quest for justice through systems of jurisprudence is necessary in order to devise sustainable strategies for bringing democratic principles within families, it is also necessary to understand the world of men. An inclusive framework is required in order to understand the positioning of women in families. It is not enough to only focus on the constraints faced by women. This in some way tends to see men as necessarily the villains. In the context of values of democracy and the challenging of existing discriminatory social norms, feminist ideology should attempt to change the understandings of power and empowerment towards one where men are not isolated in the exercise towards equality. There is tremendous advantage to be gained by both men and women when gender discrimination is lessened. Patriarchy is unjust and may seem to benefit half the population, but this is not true. Injustice and its effects are as detrimental to the overt victims as to the supposed perpetrators. In the case of patriarchy, both men and women are victims. As pointed out by Batliwala (1994), the psychological gains

Introduction

for men when women become equal partners are important. Men are freed from negative roles that see them as oppressors and exploiters. They also escape from gender stereotyping, which limit the potential for self-expression and personal development in men as much as women. Furthermore, experiences worldwide have shown that men discover an emotional satisfaction in sharing responsibility and decision-making. They find that they have not only lost traditional privileges but also traditional burdens. If attempts are made to change values towards justice and democracy, it will be mutually beneficial. The instrumental and intrinsic value of such exercises far surpasses the effort and expense.

The fourth section of the book 'Including the Excluded' has two chapters both of which advocate the value of including men in gender sensitisation interventions and frameworks. Democracy not only involves participation of women but also of men in family and household dynamics in non-hierarchical and just ways. Radhika Chopra in her chapter, 'Family, Gender and Masculinities', brings into focus the way that men's support can be outlined and reflected upon in the context of gender equality and domestic democracy. Her chapter shows that supportive practices are more than an 'alternative' frame within which to place men. They enable us to hear an aspect of men's lives and expressions of their subjective positions in ways that have not been addressed so far.

The right to be treated as a human being is a constant struggle in the face of power and hierarchies. Human rights as are endorsed by the UN system of documents, covenants and conventions are a political exercise. The right to be human, however, is larger since it rests upon the philosophical premise that governs humanity.[9] The question to be asked here is that given the fact that the several forms of gender discrimination are enacted within the ambit of the house and within the family, is it relevant to talk of human rights within the household? The discourse on human rights and the right to be treated as a human being has always been within the realm of the public. Be it civic and political or economic, social and cultural rights, human rights of individuals, groups and communities are addressed within the domain of the interface between citizen and state. The responsibility of the state towards respecting, fulfiling and protecting human rights rests with the state. This locates the justifiability and realisation of these rights within the public domain. It is not usual for domestic strife to be translated as a crime against human rights.[10] Only when private discrimination enters public domains as, for example, when dowry violence is reported in a police station, justifiability is visualised. This is not to say that the state does not enter the household implicitly.[11]

Before examining why it is so critical that a just value system be institutionalised in the domestic arena, it is first essential to examine the philosophy underlying familial dynamics. This philosophy regards family life as sacrosanct and private and it works upon 'outsiders' like policy makers, researchers and social scientists, as also upon 'insiders', that is, members of the family. Issues of justice, ethics, right and wrong are not easily and overtly ascribed to the institution of the family. As highlighted by Okin (1989), in the most influential of all 20th century theories of justice, that of John Rawls, family life is not only assumed, but also assumed to be just. Most theorists of philosophy stress upon the importance of the family and its practices, for the wider world of moral and political life. However, the dichotomy between structures and practices of justice within and outside the family were not questioned. Rousseau and Hume, on the other hand, insisted that the notion of justice is not an appropriate virtue for families. According to Rousseau, unlike political society, the family need not be accountable to its members since it is founded on love.

Within a family, relationships are based upon dependencies. There exists an inherent vulnerability due to dependency since family members depend upon each other for the fulfilment of needs, physical and non-physical. This vulnerability can be mutual or asymmetrical. According to the moral philosopher Robert Goodin (1985), over and above the general moral obligations that we owe to persons in general, we bear special responsibilities for protecting those who are particularly vulnerable to us. The notion of 'protecting' is part of the emotive thrust within familial relationships. Parents are supposed to provide and protect their children, adult children are supposed to protect old parents, the sick have to be cared for by the able-bodied, and so on. Socio-cultural norms ascribe roles to various members as also establish hierarchies in the give and take of familial dynamics. By and large, men are supposed to be the providers economically

Introduction

and women the care-givers. The sexual division of labour within households is a much-debated area within feminist studies. The underlying ethos of this division of labour can also be traced to the emotion that forms the background of intra-domestic relationships. Goodin employs an examination of the respective capacities of the parties to withdraw from the relationship without severe cost as a test to distinguish acceptable relations of mutual dependency from unacceptable relations of asymmetrical vulnerability. The bargaining theory also considers the threat point and discusses possibilities of exit with minimum costs. However, what has to be remembered here is that there are economic costs, social costs and also emotional costs to the person since exit symbolises the breakdown of the relationship, especially in a marriage.

Some scholars have developed the notion of contractual relations between household members.[12] However, within a marital contract, what is important is not just the allocation of resources, but also the allocation of rights, need and duties. Rights and needs are intimately related. Women, for example, may have rights to pooled resources within the household, but their ability to exercise those rights is likely to be determined by various cultural and contextual evaluations of need. This ability depends upon the allocation of rights that is determined by socio-cultural norms. It is often implied that gender ideologies are just ideas, cultural beliefs and notions that are somehow attached to macro processes, but not constitutive of them. This kind of argument ignores the extent to which macro processes operationalise gender ideologies and other manifestations of difference such as race and class. These identities are reproduced at the level of the domestic unit and outside it. As has been argued by Moore (1994), rights and needs are differentially distributed between different sorts of people and the ability to define a social identity is the ability to assign appropriate rights and needs. Gender, class and race differences encode ideas about the rights and needs of the persons so differentiated. This process of differentiation privileges or disadvantages such persons in their capacity to make claims on resources, both material and symbolic, in the domestic arena and beyond.

The preceding discussion has focused primarily upon rights and needs. However, equally important are duties or responsibilities. It is the social identity of the person that ascribes roles, and roles are allocated duties according to socio-cultural norms. It can be said then that just as a citizen of civic society has rights and duties, similarly the members of domestic units also have rights and duties. When questions of ethics are posed vis-à-vis familial relations, it is these rights and duties that are the subject of examination. In the stereotyped visualisation of a family, the role of man is that of provider while women and children are dependent receivers. Women are further responsible for care services. It can be observed in reality (as the data of many earlier studies have shown and the current studies also corroborate) that men do not always 'fulfil' their duties as providers and women do not always get their rights as wives, daughters, daughters-in-law and mothers. *Experience shows us that whilst for men rights are actual but duties nominal, for women rights are nominal but duties actual.* To start with, it is in this asymmetry that injustices prevail. Injustices also manifest themselves in the fact that the understood rights and duties for men and for women are in themselves gender-biased and unjust.

Hence, while one can discuss the existence of human rights within the ambit of the public arena since the state is held accountable for the fulfilment of the rights, it is still relevant to talk of the right to be human in the context of the family and household. The right to be recognised as a human should come before the myriad roles that a person is expected to and actually performs in the domestic and public arenas. This right is closely linked to a life of dignity and well-being. Human rights as well as the basic right to be human are often violated and crimes are committed against these rights in both domestic and public arenas. The former are often out of bounds for formal addressals of justice and when they do enter the legal systems, it is after there is a breakdown in relationships. Yet there is a relevance to argue for a change in value systems towards justice and human rights through awareness building where every member of the domestic unit is involved. Awareness building which isolates one woman or even groups of women from men will not succeed as much in influencing ideologies or value systems as will those that involve the entire population under consideration. Value systems can be altered through transmitting information with the intent that it transit and then transform into knowledge which is assimilated into everyday living.

Introduction

The final chapter, 'Placing Gender Equity in the Family Centre Stage: The Use of *Kala Jatha* Theatre', presents an experimental intervention conducted through the use of folk theatre with the intention of altering perceptions of members of households towards more equal relationships between men and women. The author, Joy Deshmukh-Ranadive, argues that the everyday patterns of gender discrimination, which are accepted as justified and socially legitimate, have also to be questioned and placed centre stage. This can be done in an inclusive manner when entire communities address issues of gender injustice, recognising that men are as much victims of social norms and that hierarchies are actually detrimental to society at large.

NOTES

1. The argument can be carried out at two levels; one which maintains that it is important for the intrinsic value of the human being to be recognised and that converting her/him into a useful object is wrong. While this is true, we also have to consider the constraints faced by policy makers. Policies have to be justified, and the most effective justification is to show that they are economically rational. This is true of development policies too. The other level of argument takes its logic from this premise. If the instrumental value of the human being is placed as the pivot, then policies can be more focused and implemented faster. This may sound callous, but given the age-old dilemma of scarce means and many ends, it may seem a practical path to take.
2. Moser's study of an urban low income community in Guayaquil, Ecuador, shows just how difficult it has been for women to cope. Out of the 141 households surveyed, only 30 per cent managed to cope. In 55 per cent of the cases, the women were staking the lives of their children, especially daughters, to survive. And in 15 per cent of the households, the children were going astray and the family crumbling (Moser 1989).
3. Often, in development research, the terms 'household' and 'family' are used interchangeably since at a basic level both constitute a domestic unit. These are critical units of analysis since they constitute sites of the reproduction and maintenance of human resources, which are so vital to development. For purposes of this book, at a primary level, one could say that the household is seen as an arrangement of people that co-habit, co-reside, live under one roof and share a hearth. The family, on the other hand, whilst also comprising people, constitutes a set of cultural rules and values, and an ideology that governs a certain system of kinship. The 'domestic unit' considered is that of the family. This is not to say that the household has been bypassed or neglected

in the analyses, quite the contrary. However, since kinship systems, relationships and ideology are placed centre stage, the book focuses upon the family as the unit under investigation. Needless to say, household systems are governed by the norms of the family and hence also feature in the analyses in the chapters.
4. See Harris 1981; Mackintosh 1979; Barrett 1980; Whitehead 1981; Hartmann 1981.
5. See Folbre 1984, 1988; Fapohunda 1978, 1988; Jones 1983, 1986.
6. See Elshtain 1982.
7. Margolis (1989), in a discussion on gender and power, outlines the structure of placement orders. She shows how most placement orders are arranged into three major tiers. At the top is a set of higher ranks for adults. In the middle are the intermediate ranks which comprise (*a*) training positions and (*b*) service positions. The training positions prepare individuals for promotion to the higher ranks. The service positions are designed for system maintenance and providing services to the other members. These are intermediate ranks that are also held by mature adults, who by definition are barred from the top ranks, while the lower ranks comprise the immature and the biologically incapacitated. These positions may be ranked both according to age and the likelihood of entry into the intermediate ranks. Those in the highest ranks generally control decision-making, distribution of material resources and admission to all positions in the system. They may be obliged to protect everyone in the group and issue commands to those in the lower ranks and, in return, receive deference and services. What Margolis suggests is that power and placing systems are attached to positions in general, and their extent and limits are defined by the position in particular. Drawing upon, and modifying Margolis' formulation, I analyse placements within different kinds of families and show the systems of governance in the domestic unit. For a detailed analysis, see Deshmukh-Ranadive (2002).
8. For a detailed analysis, see Deshmukh-Ranadive (2006).
9. Renowned human rights lawyer in India Upendra Baxi has differentiated between human rights and the right to be human. This is done keeping in mind the involvement of the state in establishing human rights. According to him, the issue of human rights is coloured with existing power structures and exists for only some people. The human as a class versus the human as a species is placed before the researcher for questioning. Human rights concentrates upon the former whereas the right to be human on the latter. See Baxi 2002.
10. A 'crime' takes place when a non-state actor does not allow for the realisation of a right. A 'violation' takes place when the state does not fulfil its obligations.
11. The state, for that matter, enters households through several doors, one of them being population policies and policies around reproductive health of women. It is not within the scope of this chapter to discuss whether these constitute any violation of women's human rights or a protection of them.
12. See Jones 1983; Whitehead 1981.

Introduction

REFERENCES

Agarwal, Bina. 1997. ' "Bargaining" and Gender Relations: Within and Beyond the Household', *Feminist Economics*, 3(1): 1–51.
Barrett, Michelle. 1980. *Women's Oppression Today*. London: Verso.
Batliwala, Srilatha. 1994. 'The Meaning of Women's Empowerment: New Concepts from Action', in Gita Sen, Adrienne Germain and Lincoln C. Chen (eds), *Population Policies Reconsidered, Health, Empowerment and Rights*. Boston: Harvard University Press.
Baxi, Upendra. 2002. *From Human Rights to the Right to be Human: Some Heresies*. New Delhi: Oxford University Press.
Cornia, G. A. 1990. 'UNICEF's Views on the Experiences with Structural Adjustment Programmes', in *Structural Change and Poverty*, CDR Project Paper 90:2, Centre for Development Research, Copenhagen, Denmark.
Deshmukh-Ranadive, Joy. 2006. 'Spaces, Power and Empowerment: Interlinkages with Domestic Violence in India', *Asian Journal of Women's Studies*, 12(1): 63–100.
———. 2002. *Space for Power, Women's Work and Family Strategies in South and South East Asia*. New Delhi: Rainbow.
Elshtain, Jean Bethke (ed.). 1982. *The Family in Political Thought*. Amherst: University of Massachussets Press.
Elson, Diane. 1993. 'Gender Aware Analysis and Development Economics', *Journal of International Development*, 5(2): 237–47.
Fapohunda, E. 1988. 'The Non-pooling Household: A Challenge to Theory', in Daisy Dwyer and Judith Bruce (eds), *A Home Divided*, pp. 143–54. Stanford: Stanford University Press.
———. 1978. 'Characteristics of Women Workers in Lagos', *Labour and Society*, 3(2): 258–71.
Folbre, Nancy. 1988. 'The Black Four of Hearts: Toward a New Paradigm of Household Economics', in Daisy Dwyer and Judith Bruce (eds), *A Home Divided*, pp. 248–64. Stanford: Stanford University Press.
———. 1984. 'The Feminisation of Poverty and the Pauperisation of Motherhood', *Review of Radical Political Economics*, 16(4): 78–88.
Goodin, Robert E. 1985. *Protecting the Vulnerable: A Reanalysis of Our Social Responsibility*. Chicago: Chicago University Press.
Harris, Olivia. 1981. 'Households as Natural Units', in Kate Young, Carol Wolkowitz and Roslyn McCullagh (eds), *Of Marriage and the Market*, pp. 49–68. London: CSF Books.
Hartmann, Heidi. 1981. 'The Family as the Locus of Gender, Class, and Political Struggle: The Example of Housework', *Signs*, 6(3): 366–94.
Jones, Christine. 1986. 'Intra-household Bargaining in Response to the Introduction of New Crops: A Case Study from North Cameroon', in Joyce Moock (ed.), *Understanding Africa's Rural Households and Farming Systems*, pp. 105–23. Boulder, Colo: Westview Press.

Jones, Christine. 1983. 'The Mobilisation of Women's Labor for Cash Crop Production: A Game-theoretic Approach', *American Journal of Agricultural Economics*, 65(5): 1049–54.

Kabeer, Naila. 1994. *Reversed Realities Gender Hierarchies in Development Thought*. New Delhi: Kali for Women.

Mackintosh, Maureen. 1979. 'Domestic Labour and the Household', in Sandra Burman (ed.), *Fit Work for Women*. London: Croom Helm.

Margolis, Diane Rothbard. 1989. 'Considering Women's Experience: A Reformation of Power Theory,' *Theory and Society*, 18(3): 387–416.

Moore, Henrietta L. 1994. *A Passion for Difference, Essays in Anthropology and Gender*. Cambridge: Polity Press.

Moser, C. 1989. 'The Impact of Adjustment Policies at the Micro-level: Low Income Women and their Households in Guayaquil, Ecuador', in *The Invisible Adjustment: Poor Women and the Economic Crisis*. New York: UNICEF.

Okin, Susan Moller. 1989. *Justice, Gender and the Family*. New York: Basic Books.

Standing, Guy. 1989. 'Global Feminisation through Flexible Labour', *World Development*, 17(7): 1077–95.

Whitehead, Ann. 1981. 'I'm Hungry Mum: The Politics of Domestic Budgeting', in Kate Young, Carol Wolkowitz and Roslyn McCullagh (eds), *Of Marriage and the Market*, pp. 88–111. London: CSE Books.

SECTION I

Experiencing the Family

2

Women Adjusting for Survival
Women Workers, New Economic Policies and Adjustments within the Family and Household

Nandita Gandhi*

In 1991, India introduced what was euphemistically called the 'New Economic Reforms' or the liberalisation policies, and shifted from its protected economic model towards an open, neo-liberal one. By then the impact of economic reforms on women in different countries had already become a dominant theme for academic research and issue-based struggles (Beneria 1992; Moser 1998; Nandraj et al. 1998; Deshpande 1999; Deshmukh-Ranadive 2000; Lingam 2001). The impetus for this study came from our dialogues with women workers, their deep concerns and adverse experiences of change in their lives and at their workplaces. I would like to highlight women and their labour within households, which tends to be invisible and neglected by policy makers and the public in general. In this chapter I perceive a relationship between a section of women workers as a group, the new economic policies, subsequent adjustments within the household and their right to security, dignity, equal gender relations, access to adequate health and education, and empowerment.

* This paper is an excerpt from the monograph 'Contingent Workers: Women in Two Industries in Mumbai' by Nandita Gandhi and Nandita Shah, which is part of their dissertation for the University of Amsterdam, The Netherlands submitted in November 2002.

Nandita Gandhi

WOMEN, THE CITY AND THEIR NEIGHBOURHOODS

Mumbai is a city of migrants. As the city evolved, it attracted migrants from all over the country who outnumbered its original inhabitants, the Kohli fisherfolk[1] and small farmers. The first wave came in the 19th century from the coastal regions and the western regions, and these migrants joined some of the first textile mills and the docks. Famines in Gujarat and Rajasthan drove many traders and small entrepreneurs to the city. In the 1950s, people displaced by the partition of India, migrants from Uttar Pradesh, Bihar and the southern states settled in the city. At present 40 per cent of *Mumbaikar*s speak languages other than Marathi, the local language. More than half of our respondents were migrants from the hinterland of Maharashtra, mainly from the Konkon region. Many were the daughters of the early textile workers. A large majority were Marathi speaking, living in Mumbai as some of the early residents of the worker's colonies.

Sixty-six per cent of the respondents stayed in the working class colonies of Borivili, Jogeshwari and Dharavi, which are large areas on the western and eastern suburbs of the city. Twenty-three per cent lived in tenements and 10 per cent in apartments. They narrated old stories about the origins of their neighbourhoods, which they had heard from their parents. Those who were from Devipada, the first working class colony in Borivili East, said that 55 years ago it was forest land inhabited by *adivasi*s, tribals[2] and a ghost on a white horse who kidnapped young women. Private landlords began leasing out land for building tenements in a piecemeal fashion, with little planning or concern for sanitation and hygiene. It began with 300 huts and the number of households has grown to 15,000. At first there was no electricity and water was drawn from a nearby well. It was considered *tadipar* or outside city limits and had a mix of criminals, tribals and workers. After Independence, the municipal authorities acquired some land from a charitable trust to rehabilitate families dislocated by development projects. The neighbouring colony consisted of milkmen from Bihar who had hired land for buffalo sheds. Illegal squatter colonies, with patronage from the local underground, had sprung up in many places.

Some distance away was Jogeshwari East with about 350,000 residents in an area of about 6 sq km. It was a mishmash of clusters of small huts surrounded by middle class high-rise buildings. Both neighbourhoods had a large Hindu population with some Muslim families and a sprinkling of Sikhs and Christians. Jogeshwari East has a history of communal violence and, after the 1992 communal riots, has remained a tense area. Dharavi's growth and composition is quite different. It used to be a marshy swamp until the early residents purchased plots of land, filled them up and built huts. Today, Dharavi has the dubious distinction of being the largest slum in the country. It accommodates 20 per cent of Mumbai's slum population or 500,000 people living in a congested area with a density of 7,000 persons per acre. Residential rooms and numerous small industrial sheds stand side by side. In 1997, a study done by Shramik Vidhyapeeth, a local organisation for skill training, estimated that there were 1,200 unauthorised and 500 licensed trades. It consists of different *pada*s or areas inhabited by different communities— potters, cobblers and leather workers, Muslim artisans and south Indian workers—with different political links, underground connections and police patronage. These communities, according to their squatter status and political links, have been able to procure electricity, toilets and water connections.

The haphazard development of these neighbourhoods is symptomatic of the chaotic growth of Mumbai, an island surrounded by the sea and an undeveloped hinterland. It is the sixth most populous city after Mexico, with a high density of population, which in some congested places like Bhuleshwar touches 0.4 million persons per sq km. Industrial development took place quite rapidly in the suburbs and outer suburbs whilst residential development followed the western and central railway lines all the way to Virar and Kalyan. There is an acute housing shortage in the city created by the natural boundaries of the sea, the Urban Land (Ceiling and Regulation) Act, 1976 and a nefarious nexus between politicians, builders and the underworld mafia, which created an artificial shortage and rise in land prices.

On the one hand, there are high-rise buildings in a Manhattan type skyline and, on the other, there are illegal settlements, *chawl*s (tenements) and dilapidated houses.

Unlike their rural counterparts, the women's urban working class household was nuclear with an average of four to five members. But their houses could not accommodate them. A typical residence would be a *pucca* (bricked) structure of about 12 ft by 12 ft room in a tenement or slum colony. In our sample, 57 per cent of women's households had *pucca* (concrete) structures and 10 per cent lived in *kutcha* structures (shacks) made from gunny bags, tin sheets, and so on. Seventy-eight per cent owned their own small homes. But ownership did not amount to much if the house was on illegally occupied land. The owners could be evicted as any other tenant or squatter by the municipal authorities. The difference between a poor and better-off worker would be the capacity to afford a loft to be used for sleeping and storage, tiled flooring and shelves full of kitchen utensils, a gas stove, water and electricity connection, a double bed, one steel cupboard and a TV. Seventy per cent did not have facilities like cooking gas or a refrigerator.

Eighty per cent of women workers in our sample identified the availability of basic amenities as the most important problem in their neighbourhoods. This included an inadequate supply of water, lack of sanitation and drainage, and lack of proper housing. For most households in working class colonies, it was a matter of pride to have a water connection within the house and not use the public tap with its long snaky queues. One survey estimated an average of 203 users for a tap and in some extremely congested areas, as many as 8,600 users. It was not surprising that the queues and water storage problems cut down the household's water consumption. Most households consumed as little as 15 litres per person per day while the government norm is 125–200 litres per person per day (YUVA 1997: 23). Water was a nightmare for most households, especially for the women, as it trickled through for an hour or so at any time through the day. Women in the colonies at Ghatkoper complained that they had to get up at three in the morning for the 'water time', fill the bins and catch some sleep before leaving for work. If women belonged to a colony which had an afternoon supply, they had to get a person to fill it when they were at work or buy water from a neighbour. Many women from the Vikroli area, staying on hills, had to bear the brunt of the wind and rain during the monsoons. Slopes meant carrying water from community taps located at a lower level to the top. During the monsoons, the Mithi river would flood the homes of the workers.

Most slum colonies had an average of 98 persons using one toilet, which was not only overused and dirty but sometimes had no water and broken doors or locks (YUVA: 1997). Other households did not even have this facility and had to use open spaces. A number of the better-off households pooled their money and built and maintained their own common toilets or were provided with such common toilets in the *chawl*s. Only 25 per cent of the women in our sample had such common but private toilets. Only a few of them in flats had their own toilets in the house. Garbage disposal was a huge problem. Municipal garbage vans could not enter the narrow lanes and so had to collect garbage manually every few days.

The presence or lack of civic amenities in these working class colonies was tied to electoral politics and parties. Political parties have developed links with communities along religious and caste lines and secured water, electricity connections or toilets for the favoured vote banks. Sixty-four per cent of the women reported that the Hindu right wing party Shiv Sena, which had taken over from the Congress and the Communist Party of India was the main party in their neighbourhoods. Both the latter parties had the minority Muslim votes, which were lost to the Muslim League or independent candidates after the 1992 communal riots in Mumbai and the demolition of the Babri Masjid in Ayodhya. Because of this peculiar tie of electoral politics and community identities, the parties play a dangerous dual role, procuring not only the needed essential amenities but also fanning communal tension and violence. The Shiv Sena *shakha*s or branches were part of the everyday life of people in these colonies. They sponsored community events like festivals, youth group activities and often also acted as 'protection squads' to extort money, or as 'big brothers' keeping the *ijjat* or honour of their women and community. Rightist parties have been known to use local, small events like a Muslim boy teasing a Hindu girl to incite communal feelings or to organise a *mahaarati* or roadside puja on the same day and place that the Muslim community uses for *namaz*. Thirty per cent of the women in the sample identified law and order problems like hooliganism and sexual harassment and 12 per cent were concerned about communal tensions in their neighbourhoods.

These working class colonies have a unique *Mumbaiya* culture and a dialect of a mixture of three languages. The variety of communities living side by side in a congested area, the latent violence, live presence of the underworld, the domination of political parties, unemployment and lack of amenities have given rise to a paradoxical existence. Hardships, corrupt policemen and a lethargic bureaucracy have forced people to rely on each other. At the same time, communal feelings and practices keep them away from each other. Economic hardships induced people to support each other but also produced jealousies and petty gossip. There is nothing private in these colonies. The thin walls and cramped quarters make every life an open book for others to glance through. Incidences of wife beating, alcoholism, status of employment, debt and links with the underworld are public knowledge. Young men hanging around street corners know everyone and their movements. Women especially get caught in the web of gossip as they are reported being 'friendly' with some man or coming home late in the night. There is a complex social code, which allows for a contradictory and uneasy mix of tolerance, control, communalism, violence, justice, indifference and care.

Nonetheless, the city has also been good to women. It is ranked as one of the safest cities in Asia.[3] There are not many cities in the country which can boast of young women walking unafraid and confident down the streets, training themselves for employment, sitting in groups in tea shops, seeking their own partners and opening their own bank accounts. We were amazed at the conspicuous clusters of young women in polyster *kameez*s (dresses) or *saree*s, with flashy buckles and plucked eyebrows, carrying large rexin bags, waiting for the early morning bus. Unaccustomed to working women in his own state, the Bihari watchman of the industrial estate called them 'heroines'. This new group had made a name and space for themselves in the city's workforce.

FAMILIES AND HOUSEHOLDS

The majority of the women whom we interviewed were young and from poor households. Fifty-three per cent of them were in the age group of 21–30 years, with some below but very few (4 per cent) in the middle age bracket. Forty per cent of these young women were married, 7 per cent were divorced or widowed and the remaining 53 per cent were waiting to be married. Marriage was not an option, given that for most Indian women it is considered natural and compulsory. Marriage used to be arranged immediately after menarche as a method of controlling women's sexuality. The men in the family were at pains to see that the 'good' name of the woman was unsullied as it affected the prospect of marriage. But there is an indication of the trend towards delay in age of marriage. Only 8 per cent of women were married before the age of 15. Education was one factor for this delay and the other seemed to be employment.

As soon as possible, parents sought out eligible boys or girls in their own communities and had their horoscopes matched. The prospective groom and bride were given a few bits of biodata about each other like the nature of their employment, their household background, whether the woman is expected to live in the city or village, personality traits, vices or rather the lack of them, and so on. An initial meeting of both the intended partners and their families is 'arranged' usually at the woman's house. If there were no objections from either side, the two sets of parents and other elders negotiate gifts, timing, venue and cost of marriage according to the community's customs of bride price or dowry.

Most women did not mind an 'arranged' marriage as they felt diffident and limited by restrictions on mobility as well as the social and family values to find their own partners. Even if a few of them do select their own partners, they feel bound to seek parental consent. Marriage is seen as a social contract between two families; so caste, community and village are important considerations. There is usually a strong opposition from parents if partners belong to a totally different religion or caste, with attempts to dissuade, impose house arrest and even inflict violence. Couples may decide to elope or get married the secular way through a court registration, with one side not attending the function. What happens if the marriage fails? Only 2 per cent of the women were divorced. Usually formal divorces were rare unless the man wanted to remarry, but desertions with the woman returning to her natal home were common.

Nandita Gandhi

Their households consisted of members of the immediate family and some relatives. The family, directly or obliquely, was involved in most of the women's life decisions and social identity. The acute housing shortage in the city and cramped, small houses usually restricted accommodation of only nuclear families of four to five members. The majority of households had more than one working member. Sixty-three per cent of the households had as many women as men in paid employment. And women headed 18 per cent of the households. They were honorary 'heads' or women who had lost their husbands or had set up independent urban houses with the rest of the family in the village. Generally older men, whether they were present or absent, were considered heads of the household by women, the community and the state. They were the main decision makers according to socially sanctioned patriarchal practices and they controlled the family members and their incomes. Traditionally, men are seen as the main earners and also happen to be so but the reality was that not even a joint income of several members was sufficient to support the entire family. Forty-one per cent of the households were at a subsistence level with a per capita income between Rs 421 and Rs 840. Twenty per cent of them had a per capita income of less than Rs 420 or below the poverty line as defined by official statistics. In the pooling of incomes, men's earnings formed the major proportion and women's incomes were complementary to them. 'I buy the *masala* (spices) and he buys the main foods', said one woman. Though women's income contribution was important, it did not in any major way change the patriarchal hierarchy of gender and age within the household. The gender division of labour did not change even to accommodate women's work or working hours. As many as half the women reported that men in their households did not even help occasionally. If men helped then they performed non-gendered tasks (23 per cent) in the household like picking up vegetables on their way home or dropping the children off to school. Only 2 per cent of the men did gendered jobs like cooking, washing vessels and clothes on a regular basis.

We asked women questions on what makes them feel secure. Some of our questions were: What would you like to have or already have which gives you a sense of security? What makes you happy?

Women Adjusting for Survival

One woman said, 'What does a person want ... basically *roti, kapda* and *makan* (food, clothes and a roof)... what else? But in order to get these, I will need a job.' Another woman agreed with her but added, 'I can tolerate anything except violence in the house. There should be no beating, no quarrelling or tension. Then it is possible to work together and get everything you need.' A third added, 'A happy family, a husband who has a permanent job, healthy children and a lot of luck.' Had we had more discussions, we might have, along with our women interviewees, checked the list of United Nations seven basic[4] securities. Their primary concern turned out to be their own survival and then that of their children. When we enquired if work was not important for them, the most common response was: 'Of course work is important but if there is no home and children, what are you working for?'

We asked women whether they believed that there should be equality between men and women in the family, they reacted with surprise, '... but in our family there is equality, men do what they are supposed to and women are respected.' For women it was important that the patriarchal contract and the sexually divided roles were respected and maintained by men. Women were 'in charge' of the household expenditure, the kitchen and the children. Most were ignorant of what their husbands or fathers earned and did not mind as long as they were given enough money to run the household. This non-interference on men's part was seen as respecting women's roles. This 'freedom' in fact placed the burden on women of making two ends meet under extremely adverse financial circumstances. As we shall see in the next section on household adjustments, they stretched their working hours, damaged their health and restricted their education or skill training.

ADJUSTMENTS WITHIN THE HOUSEHOLD

Studies have prioritised and grouped strategies used within households in different ways. Cornia et al. (1987) divided survival strategies into three types—for the creation of resources, for conserving and improving the use of existing resources, and extended family and migration strategies. Dreze (cited in Kabeer 1994) noted that one of the first household-coping strategies was austerity in consumption of food and in expenses on health and house repair. Agarwal (1992) in her study of poor agricultural families listed five survival mechanisms, namely, diversifying income sources, social relationships, adjusting consumption, and mortgaging or selling assets. Using different terms, Beneria (1992) and Moser (1998) followed the same lines. We have grouped household strategies into three divisions: expenditure reduction, income enhancement and tapping social networks. We had assumed that the most immediate step for a household would be to 'tighten one's belts' or try to reduce non-essential expenditure. The second or perhaps a simultaneous step along with the first may be to increase existing income by sending members of the household out for paid employment. But food, which was an ongoing expenditure, was a sensitive issue, and handled last after other expenses were considered. Labour deployment was not possible without tapping existing social networks or building new ones.

Economic rationales rarely function alone and are usually interwoven with the social, cultural and the political. During our field visits, a woman told us that her brother, the main earner in the family, had died. We were surprised that instead of looking for a job, she and her family were more interested in selling their room and moving to another place. From their perspective, the crisis provoked this Muslim household into shifting out of a Hindu dominated area to a Muslim one, secure from communal violence, before making other adjustments, even if it meant a loss of wages and depletion of savings. Our quantitative data showed us some trends, which we put along with our qualitative data in order to give us a better picture of the sort of adjustments being undertaken by households, namely, who in the household decides on them and how they involve and affect women. Most of the women workers we interviewed were part of these strategies, either at the decision-making level or the implementation of these adjustments.

Expenditure Reduction Strategies: Cuts in 'Non-essentials'

Ninety-two per cent of women in our sample said that their households had made some adjustments in different areas of their daily consumption patterns. The majority of them were in the areas of food and daily requirements, education and health expenses. The type of adjustments varied with the household's economic and social position. 'Non-essentials' like new clothes, outstation travel and big purchases came under review. Fifty per cent of the women said that they had been asked by their parents to cut down on buying new clothes. This was not an easy choice for the young women.

> I give my entire salary to my father and he manages the household expenses. But when it comes to buying clothes, he will buy them for my brother. Why? Because he works in an office but not for me because I work in a factory. I feel so ashamed going in the same clothes to work. Once I went and bought a dress with my friends but then I got such a beating from my father that I dare not do it again.
> We buy new clothes only during Diwali. This time we bought second hand clothes, as new ones were too expensive. My father and my mother did not buy anything.
> Earlier we used to buy clothes from near our house but now we go to the Parel wholesale market, where they are much cheaper and you have a good range. My parents accompany me to keep an eye and help me buy. My sister wears all my clothes so she is not bothered.

Generally women did not shop for their own clothes or for other big things like pots and pans or water bins as they were unaware of the locations of the main bazaars and wholesale markets. Many do not have the confidence to get a good bargain. Some of the workers had formed a network of friends who shopped together. Besides cutting down on new clothes, women were taking care of old clothes to make them last longer. Several women said they had switched to wearing clothes made of synthetic material even though the fabric made them feel hot and sweaty. They did not have to wash synthetic clothes every day, but could dry them or dip them in water, so that the fabric retained its lustre for a longer time. Several women had raised the demand for uniforms at their workplace. Uniforms would reduce the wear and tear of their own clothes and also eliminate buying in order to 'show off' new clothes to colleagues.

Outstation travel usually meant going to their hometown or village for a holiday. Mothers usually objected to small occasional family outings like going to the cinema or eating out. Cheap, second hand black and white TVs were purchased to cut down on cinema going. Every time our women workers made a request to go out for a meal, their mothers vetoed it by offering to make the dish at home. On the other hand, much to the ire of women, men continued spending money on cigarettes, *paan* (betel leaves), tea and an occasional drink, and sometimes gambling and drinking alcohol. 'Whenever I find out that my husband has been spending money on gambling, we have a huge fight. How can he throw money away, when the whole family is scrimping and saving?' For recreation, older women often went to *bhajan* or *kirtan mandal*s (religious singing and chanting gatherings) in their neighbourhood. Younger women would involve themselves in informal groups at the workplace. Women from subsistence and middle level households, rather than the better-off ones, were more active in religious and regional groups.

Reduction in expenditure also meant a delay in house maintenance or repair. Some of the houses the researchers visited were leaking like sieves into pots and pans kept all around the house. Women said that given a choice they would rather bear the inconvenience of water for one season than cut down on snacks or clothes. These were small but important pleasures, which did not cripple or damage health and happiness. These adjustments were not hard and fast rules for all households and often deferred till extra wages or bonuses came their way.

Expenditure Reduction Strategies: Allocations for Education

Sixty-six per cent of the respondents had young children who were mainly in municipal or subsidised state-owned schools. The state provides free primary education for all children till the seventh standard and till the 12th standard for girls. Working class households were withdrawing their children from municipal schools or shifting them out of private ones to municipal schools.

Financial costs, distance, children's learning potential, the tradition of education in the family and education as an economic requirement were factors weighed against each other by parents whilst making a decision to continue or discontinue their children's school education. When there was no financial crisis, the household seemed inclined to allow their children to continue at least till the seventh grade. However, a tightening of the household budget sent this decision into review. Besides cutting down the hidden costs of the free schooling system, withdrawal of children meant releasing the mother or an elder from the task of ferrying the children to and fro from school as well as a reduction in domestic tasks. The dropout child took over domestic tasks or engaged in income earning activities. Many of the women workers interviewed spoke bitterly of how they had protested when their parents had removed them from school to join work. Others were more understanding of their parent's problems and willingly withdrew from school. Partial cuts and withdrawal from education had the potential for a negative long-term impact on the future of the child and the family. Once withdrawn from the education process, most children do not rejoin school.

Expenditure Reduction Strategies: Unhealthy Adjustments

The women had this to say regarding their choice for healthcare:

> We used to go to the public hospital for all our problems. My relative worked as a ward boy, he would help us and it was free. But now even he is of no help, they are charging us fees and the queues are like snakes as the doctor is too busy. So we have shifted to the private doctor close to where we live.

> When you fall sick, what's your first reaction—let's go to the doctor. My mother says first try out home remedies. She gives us foul tasting turmeric and ginger pastes. It often works for colds and coughs. If it does not then she takes us to the local doctor. And if we are still unwell or for big operations, then the last resort there is the public hospital which is far away.

The women in our sample largely worked as diamond polishers or plastic workers—both categories complained of occupation related ailments. Forty-six per cent of the diamond polishers reported respiratory problems like asthma, tuberculosis and breathlessness. Twelve per cent of the plastic workers complained of fatigue and skin problems including burning and itching. Seven per cent of them had eye problems. Around 35 per cent of the workers complained about body ache and headaches. It was common for women to either not recognise symptoms or under report their illness. This usually led to a high percentage of workers delaying treatment. The oft-repeated reason for untreated illnesses in urban areas was not taking the illness seriously. Lack of financial resources was another important factor. Indirect financial costs of not earning for the day, taking someone along, paying for the transport and food were other considerations. Women did not seek treatment for illness, which was considered to be seasonal/temporary/not very disturbing. When it was impossible to deny illness, their financial capabilities decided the type of treatment. Four women from the plastics processing units reported that they had left their medical fate 'to God'.

Most households tended to approach private services for non-hospitalised/short-term minor illnesses and use the public services for major illnesses and hospitalisation (Yesudian 1988; Nandraj et al. 1998). But 30 per cent of women from the subsistence level households were going to public services for minor illnesses in spite of all its problems. First, visiting a public hospital meant the cost of travel for two persons, the loss of a day's wage because of the long line of patients, paying user fees and receiving a hurried substandard service. Second, people were not confident that they were being listened to or getting good treatment. The uncaring and brusque manners of the hospital staff were stark reminders to people of their poverty and dependency on free services. Most of the poorer workers were in the informal sector, with no medical benefits or casual and sick leave. Seventy-nine per cent of the women were not given a single day's paid sick leave. Only 20 per cent had maternity and other medical benefits.

Public hospitals were most commonly accessed for maternity services, operations, medical tests and specialised diseases like cancer. Suvarna, a young diamond polisher, had her hair caught in the rotating scaif by accident. Her father said, 'we had her cosmetic surgery done at the government hospital at Sion. We spent Rs 5,000 on medicines. If we had gone to a private hospital, the doctor's fees, bed charges plus the medicines would have cost us a lakh of rupees.'

Expenditure Reduction Strategies: The Last Choice is Food Cuts

Savitri and her husband had come to an understanding some years ago. Her mill worker husband purchased wheat and rice at the ration store in the mill shop. From her earnings as a home-based worker, she bought the vegetables and *masala*. She was afraid to tell him that as the prices had risen, she could no longer buy enough to feed the entire family. She and her daughter had stopped eating vegetables, so that her husband and son would not notice the fall in quantity.

To bypass the price rise, women from Dharavi would go to the wholesale vegetable market and pick up discarded vegetables.

These vegetables are not bad but they are a few days old and squashed in the transport. Of course we have to sort them out as they are mixed with rotten vegetables. Then we have to immediately use them, as they don't stay for too long. I go once in every two–three days. On other days, I make lentils and gravy in place of vegetables and *dal*. The problem has become acute because we cannot afford any meat or fish.

An analysis of the consumption expenditure data of the Central Statistical Organisation (*The Economic Times* 2002) showed that the overall consumption basket of the average Indian has changed. There has been a decline in food expenditure from 50.6 per cent (1993–94) to 46 per cent (1999–2000) and 42.8 per cent (2000–01). Except for fruits and vegetables, there had been a decline in expenditure for cereals, bread, pulses, milk and milk products.

A way to cut corners on food expenditure was bulk buying.

I, along with three other women, go to the Masjid market to buy coconut and chillies. You know how expensive it is. We go on

Sunday early morning and buy about 15 days worth of stuff. It is difficult to put in more money for the whole month and also it becomes too heavy to carry it back so I prefer doing two trips in a month than to hire someone to carry. I have requested my boss to pay me every 15 days and that helps in this bulk buying.

But not all women had the funds to buy in bulk and had to purchase small quantities on a daily basis, which cost them more. The alternative was to buy subsidised food grains from the fair price or 'ration' shops. The change in government pricing policy had dissuaded many from buying rations. Through the past 10 years, procurement prices had gone up and so had the price of subsidised grain. Women had this to say,

> Now the ration shop prices and the open market prices are more or less the same. Then why should I break my legs standing in a queue, missing a day's wage and waste my time cleaning twigs and stones from the wheat grains? Earlier it was worthwhile to buy from the ration shop because there was a big difference in prices. Now I only buy kerosene and sugar from the ration shop.

A third way was for the household to consume less food. The NSSO (1993–94) found that the lowest 20 per cent of the population consumed 1,500 calories of energy per day as opposed to an average requirement of 2,400 calories (Shariff and Mallick 1998). Some extra items were cut down so these cuts affected the entire household but more so women. As it was the married woman's responsibility to ensure that the household got 'adequate' food, she had to make some personal adjustments. It is a common practice in India for women to serve the family first, with the best and biggest portions going to the men. Women were sometimes left with the gravy or curry or the previous day's leftovers. Unmarried women did not have to face these food cuts, as usually there were other women like the mother or a sister-in-law who bore the brunt of the cuts.

Another option was to economise by cooking once a day. Women found the price of kerosene high and the quantity insufficient. But they could not use alternatives like wood or coal in their small, congested homes.

I just get up early and finish all the cooking in the morning. I don't want a fight with my husband as he wants his lunch box. My mother-in-law has not been keeping well so I can't leave anything on her. I tried to shift the cooking to the evening but the food got spoilt in the night. Once a rat ate up some of it and we had to throw away all the food.

DEVELOPING AND USING SOCIAL NETWORKS

Household members also employed the device of developing and using social networks. In the absence of a welfare state and social welfare policies, it was necessary for workers to develop a range of networks. Parents were expected to support their children especially during crisis.

After I had got the job in the diamond unit and I was earning quite well, his demands increased. My husband would beat me up to get the money. I could barely manage to make two ends meet with his constant requests. My parents like all parents were not very happy when I arrived at their door. Now I support my parents and my daughter. They are happy too and my life has changed.

There was more of a conscious effort on the women's part to maintain relations with the immediate and extended family and family by marriage through frequent visits, or attending family occasions, festivals and events. Most of the women had a rural-urban link, that is, part of their family stayed in the village. The relationship was strengthened by contributions, attending village functions and visiting each other for holidays. During the 1982 mill workers' strike, without the support of food, shelter and loans from their rural relatives, the strikers would have given in much earlier. This conscious attempt to forge family ties should not be romanticised as working class unity or solidarity as it was more an articulation of mutual dependency within a household and between its members and the extended family (Beneria 1992).

A different social relationship extended beyond the immediate and larger family circle to include community members. It is common amongst the Patel community of Gujarat in the diamond polishing industry to promote other Patels for employment or help each other out with loans. This served to strengthen community loyalty and identity so that individual members were reluctant to default or go against set norms (De Neve 1999). The larger community generally included those from the same village.

An informal non-kin network of neighbours, friends and 'designated kin' or those who are co-opted into being *rakhi* brothers (when a woman ties a *rakhi* [decorated thread] on the wrist of a man, he considers her a sister), mothers or aunts are sometimes important, especially when the issues involved the family, marriage outside the community and a different type of employment. Said a woman, 'My neighbour has been like my sister and helped me in many situations. She works as domestic help and gets clothes from her employer for my children. When she goes out of town sometimes then I cook for her sons and husband'. Neighbours have been part of the support system since the early stream of migration of workers into Mumbai. Mill workers have subsisted because their neighbours' wives or *khanawali*s (providers of packed lunch boxes) gave them meals at reasonable rates. In our sample, a large number of women had procured their jobs through their neighbours.

The extended family network plays an important role in the lives of women, which is probably why they and their households do not confront traditions but go out of their way to abide by them. When the balance between paid work and domestic tasks was under conflict, women workers depended on the women on their side of the family, that is, their mothers or sisters, to help out. In some of the households, women workers had called their mothers or mothers-in-law to come and stay with them to look after the children and help in the household work. Or they had sent their children to the homes of their relatives. The household maintains links with the larger kin network through contributions to the *Ganpati* festival, taking turns for puja of the community deity, or keeping fasts on a rotation basis. The social and other costs of being an outcast would be too high for women. Married women were considered critical for social links in the household and therefore had more responsibilities towards maintaining the kinship network. Unmarried women's link with the larger social kin network was mediated by their parents.

The employer often becomes a patron who looks after his worker in different ways. Loyalty is rewarded by emergency loans and day offs. Use of political patronage and charity, and help from the local underworld don were other support structures that the members of the household used for specific requests like school admission, health problems or death in the family. Most of the workers had vertical linkages with older workers and supervisors whom they asked for support in case of problems not only at the workplace but also at home. Women and other members of the household develop lateral and vertical linkages for their survival.

THE DYNAMICS OF HOUSEHOLD ADJUSTMENTS

'In a macro sense, India is back to the pre reforms days' was the analysis of *The Indian Express*, based on the Central Statistical Organisation's figures for 2001 to 2002. India had the lowest growth rate since 1986, overall investment levels were lower than that in 1991 and the fiscal deficit of the centre and the state governments was around 11 per cent of the GDP or exactly where the first finance minister had began in 1991 (*The Indian Express* 2002a). Maharashtra's agricultural growth, industrial development and employment had slowed down in the past two years (*The Indian Express* 2002b). At the micro level, households were struggling to make ends meet as their members pooled their incomes, and assisted each other through the changing and difficult times. The majority of women workers lived in working class colonies though their households belonged to the three categories of poor, moderately poor and better-off households. All of them reported that their households were making some sort of adjustments to cope with the new changes.

I do not know which member of the household first raised these 'common' strategies. They could have originated from the woman respondent, her parents, husband or brother but it was looked upon as a 'common' strategy meant for everyone and agreed upon by all members. The decision makers in the households were the men and elders but in many cases, the women reported that the adjustment strategies came from one of the women in the household. It is difficult to trace the origin because a father, embarrassed at his own inability to procure a family wage might have indirectly hinted at the deployment of another member, which would have then been taken up by the mother or brother of the woman respondent. Largely, women suggested making non-essential and food cuts whilst men were more concerned with economising through education cuts and deployment of labour. There seemed to be no priority on the basis of which decisions could be made about the particular sequence of adjustment strategies or whether these should be implemented simultaneously. The implementation of the adjustment strategy itself was often shrouded in secrecy. Many women said that it was embarrassing for them to tell anyone that their household was cutting down on food items. It was common to pass it off as observing weekly *upvas* (fasts), which meant cutting out meat items from the meal. It was difficult to assess if members of the households differentiated between short-term or long-term strategies. For example, the purchase of a gas cylinder for cooking was deferred not only because it was expensive but also because of possible hazards to small children who might use it wrongly.

It is not new for poor households to evolve strategies for survival in the context of low incomes and high consumer prices. They are well known devices used for basic subsistence, to stall a downward slide or to improve the status and lifestyle of households. Our data shows that the nature and implementation of strategies depend partly on the socio-economic location of the household, family ideology and its power hierarchy. They are influenced by the contractually defined gender roles, on the intra-family mutual support system and the nature of the household's social network (Bardhan 1990; Kabeer, 2000). These strategies could be passive, non-strategic, ambivalent, anti-strategic or even multi-strategic responses. They are the outcome of negotiations between different members of the household and each might accept the final outcome with willingness, resentment or anger. Given the nature of the gender and age hierarchy and traditional patriarchal practices in most households, the women's response was to appease the male hierarchy. They were afraid to negotiate with the more powerful family members. Confrontation was a rare response and was evident only when men had not kept their part of the 'patriarchal contract', that is, either refused to support the family or frittered away their income.

Household strategies affected everyone but in different degrees and they were taking a long-term toll on women that no one, not even the women, was aware of. The foremost but intangible toll was on women's health. The general level of calorie intake in poor households is deficient compared to the recommended levels. In implementing expenditure reduction strategies of food cuts, women were eating less or cutting down on specific items in favour of other members of the household. Most women suffer from 'nutritional anaemia' which lowered their resistance and advanced aging. The morbidity rate amongst women was higher compared to men. It has generally been observed that women are notorious in keeping their health requirements in abeyance whilst caring for the rest of the family. Outside of the export oriented units or formal sector units, none of the employers took any responsibility for the health of their workers, either financially or with paid leave. So the majority of the workers had to bear their own health bills.

Alongside these self-inflicted problems was the extension of working hours. Women's average working hours for paid and unpaid work came to anywhere between 12 and 14 hours a day. Rising prices had forced the women to take on extra tasks like going to wholesale markets, which involved getting up early in the morning (less sleep), walking, carrying loads, and extra cleaning and washing. Cutting down on what has been called 'non-essential' or on travel expenditure, deprived the women, more than men, of rest, relaxation and leisure. Men have their own ways of relaxation which are not available to women, like visiting their friends, spending time in a liquor den, playing cards, drinking tea with friends, and so on. Women rarely take adequate rest except when they sleep. Even while watching television, most of them work at chopping vegetables or doing home-based work. A break in the routine and change of air whilst visiting their native village was one way of relaxation. However, this was one of the first expenditure items to be axed. Household strategies were being implemented at the cost of the productive capacity of women (Agarwal 1990).

The sphere of women's paid work, from their entry into and continuing at the workplace, was an act of diplomacy, patience, negotiation and double work, almost always at the cost of mental peace and physical rest. The majority of women, 57 per cent, were engaged in domestic labour for about three hours; only 9 per cent of them did no domestic work. Most of these were unmarried girls who came from households with other women members. A large number of married women were doing domestic work for 3–5 hours. The burden of domestic work became obvious when the married women workers who were interviewed would compare their domestic work before and after marriage. 'Now I can't leave in the morning expecting my lunch box to be ready. I have to get up, cook and pack for myself and others before I leave.'

Seventy per cent of the women workers reported that men in their household did no domestic work on a regular basis. Those who did, picked only outside-the-house tasks like shopping and dropping/picking children from school. Some of them did women's work in the event of crisis, sickness or when women were not at home. Fathers and sons were more helpful than brothers and husbands. Mostly women arrived at an understanding between themselves, for example, the sister-in-law or mother took over the domestic tasks to release the younger women. A relative from their village was called in or neighbours were recruited for child care.

This was one area which both men and women found difficult to change. Though women were ready to challenge the sexual division of labour at the workplace by learning the so-called male skills like machine operation or shaping diamonds, they were reluctant to challenge it in the house.

> I would like my husband to help, but I live in a *basti* (slum) and everyone will laugh at me that I am making my husband work. The only thing I ask him to do is to fill water as my back aches with the weight. If I make him do more, he will say that it is better I don't go to work.

Men did not make it any easier by constantly stressing the neglect of home and children.

Aggravating the situation was women's overtime hours. Fifty-five per cent of the firms had compulsory overtime for their workers. They could request less overtime or no overtime on specific days.

But there were always subtle pressures, and without a valid reason, women could not always get out of overtime. Overtime meant extra hours at work plus travel time or about 10 to 12 hours out of the home. Willingness to do overtime earned women favours like time off, advance payments and a favoured status. On the flip side, declining overtime meant facing a threat of dismissal in a flexible labour market.

Conflict and apprehension at home came from a mix of fear of violence, character assassination and sulking by household members. Women reported that they had got used to hearing, 'If it means overtime, she should leave the job.' Women negotiated their way out by persuading their employers to convince their parents or husbands, coming home in groups or asking male relatives to escort them. But it was a mental strain to keep appeasing the males and the elders in the household through persuasion and extra efforts in cooking and cleaning. This non-cooperation in sharing domestic work, and the conflict on overtime reaffirmed the patriarchal privilege of men in controlling women's labour in and outside the household. The balancing of hours, work and stamina by women was reflected in their lacklustre involvement at the workplace to upgrade their skills and participation in collective functioning.

'I don't ever want to hear. Look at her just because she is earning, she has a swollen head. This is what my mother says if I ever have a fight', said one worker. Most of them or 68 per cent handed over their entire wage to their mothers/fathers or husbands. But women's earnings did not necessarily go into the common pool. In many extended households the male members' earnings were pooled together and a specific amount was given for household expenses. Women did not contribute directly but their earnings were spent on specific needs—extra clothes, tuition, and so on. Single women staying in their natal families were expected to pay a lump sum for their upkeep. In nuclear households, men took care of major expenses like food grains, rent, school fees, clothes, electricity bills and women bought smaller, daily items like vegetables and also paid for minor repairs. Many of the interviewed women contributed to specific needs like the medical expenses for an older member, buying fruits or meat on a regular basis or paying for the children's school tuitions. Some kept part of the money for their own expenses or put it away as savings. Women were extremely conscious of not projecting their income earning potential in a way that would alienate them from the rest of the household. They hardly spent money on purchases without some consensus from their parents or husband. However, this form of income contribution was largely invisible as the household absorbed it for its daily consumption needs. A woman felt proud of her contribution but neither she nor her wage had the status of an earner and a contributor to the pool.

'My parents say I will get married and go away or maybe later on there is no need for me to work outside. So it is okay to spend my money on buying things for the house and saving up for the future.' Married women too found that their wages were required in the household and used for daily consumption but their wages were not included in the household income pool. For men and the elders as well as women, paid employment of women was a contingent part of the overall adjustments that were being implemented in the household as a response to macroeconomic changes and the changing social values. Women were neither given the same identity of a worker/earner as that given to men nor did they expect it. Additionally, they were also not supported by a reduction in their duties in domestic work or in fulfilling the obligations of overtime and skill training. Rather the requirements of paid employment were held against them as impinging on their domestic work and gender roles, whilst their wages were absorbed into the general expenditure of the household. In the case of poor households, women's wages were an essential part of survival. By not supporting women's unpaid work and devaluing their paid labour by treating them as 'contingency workers', the men and elders in the household could control both their domestic and workplace labour. As the household's 'contingency workers', women were 'allowed' to work in paid employment as part of its adjustment plans for the overall welfare and survival of the household. But as they were, so to say, on lease to the workplace, their worker identity was devalued to their identity as a woman, mother, wife or daughter. The household saw no reason to make any shifts in gender relations or in the concept of patriarchal norms and heads. This is not to say that there were no changes at all in the households' gender ideology. Some patriarchal norms which restricted women were revised like their level of education was increased, marriage delayed, there was an increase in mobility and they were allowed limited employment. But the change did not encompass any fundamental shifts. Women carried with them to the labour market this ideological baggage, their own uncertainty, lack of education and training, gender subordination as well as the household's view of 'contingency worker'.

STRATEGIES FOR SECURITY

Women were no strangers to making adjustments or bearing the extra burden placed on them as they have often used these in case of crises afflicting the household like sudden unemployment, sickness and price rises. And as they were within the domain of the household, women were invariably expected to be responsible for implementation. Women rarely had the knowledge of the total income of the household nor did they have control over the distribution of household resources. They were hesitant or even afraid to initiate an open discussion on household expenditure or its reallocation.

> I do not know how much my husband earns but whatever he gives is insufficient. When I told him that he said he would borrow on his salary. That is no answer, where are we going to get the money to repay the loan?

Women felt obliged to stretch household resources by whatever means, using their ingenuity in cutting corners, in processing food, making their own clothes or through extra earnings. If adjustments within the household were painful, survival in the outside world was even more so, economically, culturally and socially.

Women's identity and sense of being was in relation to their family and larger kin group. Our women respondents' description of security was couched in terms of a 'happy family', material possessions and a violence free environment in their social relations of marriage and kinship. First, a married woman with an employed husband meant status and security. Single women did not feel 'legitimate' in their natal homes. Women with children were socially favoured and barren women pitied. Being a wife and mother gave women the acceptance, approval and support of their extended family, natal family, community and society. Second, but not in a hierarchical order, owning a home, that is, a permanent roof over one's head was security. But, in the space starved city of Mumbai, with the fear of eviction and high rentals, it was virtually impossible for most working people and especially women to afford legal ownership. Working class colonies could be extremely violent and intolerant to women. Finally, the other basics like food and clothes came with good and stable jobs, difficult to come by with women's lack of education, skill and contacts. The ability to economically stand on one's feet was seen as being less of a burden on family members and for use during emergencies. Usually, a woman had only her wedding jewellery and cooking vessels as financial backups.

The basis of women's social, cultural and economic living and their sense of security were intimately tied to the well-being of the family based household. It could well be that women themselves suggested some of the expenditure reduction adjustments or willingly endorsed the suggestions to stall any deepening of the crisis. And as the adjustments were within the domain of the household, they felt obliged to implement them even at the cost of their own well-being. However, women also discreetly counter strategised by finding alternatives and negotiating with men for a rational expenditure reduction plan. Some of the counter strategies were cheap alternatives like substituting *kirtan*s for holidays, home remedies for medicines and cooking fast food instead of buying them. One woman confided, 'I always eat some fruit in the train because I never get anything once they reach my family'.

Women's strategies within the household were discreet, sometimes invisible, never directly articulated and appearing to go along. They were not a conscious, well thought of, premeditated strategy on their part but unconsciously put into play.

Wages and savings was another story. The majority of women gave their entire wages to their family members or made substantial contributions to household purchases. But they also did not reveal their entire earnings or overtime wages. This was more common amongst the unmarried women.

> As soon as I get my pay, I go to the *sonar* (goldsmith) and give an instalment for my necklace. I don't even take the money home in case it gets spent in general expenditure. I cannot refuse if my

Women Adjusting for Survival

mother says give me some money. Or I am tempted to buy clothes or something. This way I save money.

The other method was saving through chit or rotating funds. This strategy was a difficult one for married women. One of them said,

> I kept some money away from my parents but they knew that I will not just spend it like that and the gold that I buy will only add to my dowry but with my husband's family, the mother-in-law keeps tab on my overtime and I am afraid that they will start doubting me in many areas if I get caught. So I give all the overtime money to my mother-in-law.

Some of them used their employer's help. One woman said 'My employer is quite good and he knows about my alcoholic husband. He helped me open a bank account so that I don't carry my money home.'

Why did women choose to continue with paid employment in spite of the physical stress, the balancing acts, constant negotiations, the appeasement of household members and loss of control over wages? The answer is that they felt an immense sense of self-worth. Some of the common responses with regard to this were: 'My mother takes me into confidence.' 'My brother talks properly to me.' 'My husband asks me to buy things.'

Without subverting the household hierarchy, they gained respect and empowered themselves. Women found that paid employment gave them self-confidence and increased their social networks outside of the kin circle. On the other hand, women were acutely conscious that they could not have procured jobs without the aid of their household members. That they were in paid employment because they are 'permitted' by the more powerful members of the household. They knew that they could be withdrawn from the labour market in case of any crisis in the household. They were conscious of their low wages, the unskilled nature of their work and non-inclusion in the household income pool. Women were acutely aware that their paid work was a negotiated space and it would be difficult to claim a right to paid work. But women were still attached to them because they weighed their employment not within the hierarchy and scope of the workplace but with their sense of security within the relations of the household. In the absence of any other tangible assets and social resources, paid employment was the only manner in which they could obtain some fall back position for household negotiations, and use in times of personal crisis or the breakdown of the household. In spite of the drudgery of unskilled and low paid work, with little control over wages and the constant guilt of neglecting domestic work, women felt a little less vulnerable and more empowered for the future.

CONCLUSION

It is difficult to analyse household adjustments as 'strategies' because they have been implemented over time and prioritised differently as short-term or pre-planned responses. But there were definite reactions from households, which were endorsed by the hierarchy of the household for implementation. Women were held responsible as the managers of the home and kitchen. Reared and living in a patriarchal society with hardly any independent backup systems and support, women were prone to resort to appeasement by executing adjustments at the cost of a long-term health toll on themselves. They followed the adjustments, in spite of knowing that men defaulted sometimes, by eating less, working longer hours, restricting their leisure and constantly balancing the paid and domestic work. Women were seldom supported by men in sharing everyday domestic work, the extra work caused by household adjustments or when doing overtime at the workplace. The male and elderly members of the household did not see the need for making any fundamental shifts in its gender practices or ideology as it perceived women's deployment in the labour market as part of its contingency plan for tiding over a crisis. Accordingly, women's wages were not included into the household pool but used for daily consumption. By treating women as 'contingency workers', household members trivialised women's work, devalued their contributions and deeply affected the development of their identity as paid workers.

Not many women had knowledge of the total income inputs by men or existing household assets, nor were they confident to initiate a dialogue on an overall restructuring of resources, labour and assets in the face of economic changes. They were, therefore, restricted to making adjustments with what they were most familiar, that is, at the household level. And in doing so they bore most of the burdens of adjustments. Households were also women's lifeline as they were restricted by patriarchal practices to function as individuals. Rather their entire existence was derived from their relations with their families, kin and community. They needed to look after their own security within the security of the household and they still nurtured the spirit to develop small alternatives to household strategies. The biggest and the most stressful burden of household adjustments was paid employment because of the constant balancing between domestic labour and requirements of employment. Women gave their wages to the household without demanding any status as earners and contributors to the household pool. They fulfilled their part of the bargain by giving their wages for household consumption but also surreptitiously saved in chit funds, jewellery and with their employers. In spite of the pain and stress, women were hesitant to give up employment because it was their only asset for a feeling of self-worth, as a backup for other negotiations in the household and empowerment for the future.

NOTES

1. Kohli fisherfolk were the first known inhabitants of the island city and still continue to do their traditional work.
2. *Adivasi*s and tribals differentiate themselves from urban and rural plains people on the basis of lifestyle and work.

REFERENCES

Agarwal, Bina. 1992. 'Gender Relations and Food Security: Coping with Seasonality, Famine and Drought in South Asia', in L. Beneria and S. Feldman (eds), *Unequal Burden: Economic Crises, Household Strategies, and Women's Work*, pp. 181–218. Colorado: Boulder Co., Westview Press.
———. 1990. 'Social Security and the Family in Rural India: Coping with Seasonality and Calamity', *Journal of Peasant Studies*, 17(3): 341–412.
Bardhan, K. 1990. 'Women's Work in Relation to Family Strategies in South and Southeast Asia', *Sammyashakti: A Journal of Women's Studies*, IV and V Centre for Women's Development and Studies, New Delhi.

Beneria, L. 1992. 'The Mexican Debt Crisis: Restructuring the Economy and the Household', in L. Beneria and S. Feldmen (eds), *Unequal Burden: Economic Crises, Persistent Poverty, and Women's Work*, pp. 83–104. Oxford: Westview Press.

Cornia, Giovanni A., R. Jolly and F. Stewart. 1987. *Adjustment with a Human Face*, Vol. 1, New York: Clarendon Press, Oxford University Press.

De Neve, G. 1999. 'Asking for and Giving Baki: Neo-bondage on the Interplay of Bondage and Resistance in the Tamil Nadu Power-loom Industry', in J. Parry and K. Kapadia (eds), *The Worlds of Indian Industrial Labour*, pp. 379–406. New Delhi: Sage Publications.

Deshmukh-Ranadive, Joy. 2000. 'The Adjustment Policy Programme in India and the Household in Shifting Sands', New Delhi: CWDS.

Deshpande, Sudha. 1999. 'Emerging Labour Market for Women in an Urban Slum: A Tale of Three Slums in Mumbai', *Indian Journal of Labour Economics*, pp. 651–674.

Gothoskar, S. 1992. 'Trends in Employment in Major Multinationals in India', unpublished paper, Mumbai.

Kabeer, Naila. 2000. *The Power to Choose—Bangladeshi Women and Labour Market Decisions in London and Dhaka*. London: Verso.

———. 1994. *Reversed Realities: Gender Hierarchies in Development Thought*. London and New York: Verso.

Lingam Lakshmi, Vrinda Datta and Maveen Sorres-Pereira. 2001. 'Hemmed in all Sides: Structural Adjustment, Urban Poverty and Gender', Paper presented at the workshop on Structural Adjustment Policies and the Social Sector, organised by TISS and Focus on Global South, 29–31 January, TISS, Mumbai.

Moser, Caroline. 1998. 'The Asset Vulnerability Framework: Reassessing Urban Poverty Reduction Strategies', *World Development*, 26(1): 1–19.

Nandraj, Sunil, Neha Madhiwalla, Rupashri Sinha and Amar Jesani. 1998. *Women and Health Care in Mumbai—A Study of Morbidity, Utilisation and Expenditure on Health Care in the Household of the Metropolis*. Mumbai: CEHAT.

Shariff, A. and A. C. Mallick. 1998. *Dynamics of Food Intake and Nutrition According to Expenditure Class in India, 1993–94*. New Delhi: National Council of Applied Economic Research.

The Economic Times. 2002. 5 February.

The Indian Express. 2002a. 'Editorial', *The Indian Express*, 4 February.

———. 2002b. *The Indian Express*, 23 March.

Yesudian, C. A. K. 1988. *Health Services Utilisation in Urban India*. New Delhi: Mittal Publications.

YUVA. 1997. 'Global Transition Local Democracy: A City Paper on Citizen's Participation in Local Governance', Mumbai, written for the project 'Volunteer Action Local Democracy—Partnerships for a Better Urban Future', UNIRISD, Geneva.

3

The Light Shines through Gossamer Threads
Inside–Outside Political Spaces

❖

Sumi Krishna*

INTRODUCTION

The family was for long the Pandora's box of development discourse, acknowledged to exist as an economic household but left safely untouched in other respects. Consequently, state policies and interventions were also premised on a public–private dichotomy with public institutional structures being distinct and separate from the politics of space and status within the family. This perspective began to change when the women's movement drew upon lived experiences and social anthropology to open up the family as a primary site of gender-power relations, and to bring the personal into the collective political domain. However, even those development interventions that aspire towards gender-neutrality are insensitive to the location-specificity and complex gradations of intra-family relations, and the transformations that are now taking place in families and communities.

Gender relations in many *adivasi* (tribal) societies are relatively more egalitarian than among other communities. In India, today,

---

* This paper also features in the author's *Genderscapes: Revisioning Natural Resource Management* (in press, Zubaan Books).

some small and very poor *adivasi* groups are experiencing a transition from semi-nomadism to a settled way of life.[1] They are interacting with several other social groups and institutions, including settled peasants, land-owners, employers, traders, the government, its agencies and non-governmental organisations (NGOs). What impact do these widening circles of interaction with non-*adivasi* institutions and agents have on gender relations? How do the enormous changes in their life-worlds affect the *adivasi* women's political spaces in the domestic and public spheres? Such questions have scarcely been dealt with by development researchers and practitioners.

Perhaps this is because practitioners are far more comfortable with using conventional social science tools, mass surveys and interviews for collecting and presenting quantifiable data. The development discourse is strewn with numbers (however suspect these may be)—so many hectares planted, so much savings made—as indicators of achievement or non-achievement. Even the newer 'participatory' research methods and focus group discussions are being used to generate quantifiable information rather than qualitative understandings of messy and complex social and human problems. Qualitative research skills, which derive from life experiences and sensitive responses to inequities, may seem more difficult to learn and teach. Yet, if we explore ways to do so, this could make research findings more accessible to wider social groups and perhaps help redirect the policies and practices of development.

One of the most effective and affective tools of qualitative research is the articulation of individual and group voices to 'tell a story'. Personal narratives have been widely used by the women's movement and feminist research. If, however, this is to be more than a 'confessional' exercise and provide insights to changes within a community, the researcher needs also to stand aside and reflect. A narrative has the accessibility of a fictional story with an actual setting, characters with whom one can empathise and actions which evolve towards a crisis that may or may not be resolved. Like other fictional devices, it allows one to depict the contingent, transient processes rather than simply capture the stationary junctures in the stream of our lives. But unlike fiction, the narrative as a research tool strives to make the leap from the particular to the generic, to clarify, explain and collate different strands of analysis. The narrative has rarely been

The Light Shines through Gossamer Threads

used in development studies, which have a disciplinary inclination towards the deliberately impersonalised social science 'account', sometimes illustrated by brief thumbnail sketches or 'case studies'.[2] This chapter attempts to extend the scope of development research and writing by depicting the gendering of political spaces through a personalised narrative of 'critical moments' in which the boundaries between life, work and research are blurred.[3]

This is the story of a small group of very poor and recently settled *adivasi*s in south-eastern India. It is also a story about one family and one woman among them. And it is a story of what one researcher learnt and unlearnt about gendered political spaces. Embedded in the specific context of this narrative are different levels of dialogue, as they take place and are represented by the researcher—among sections in the group; among different individual 'actors', the women, men and children in the story; between some of them and the researcher; between the researcher and peer reviewers (who are far removed from the immediate context); and also between persons playing several different roles, like myself, as a professional adviser-consultant, as a participant in the action and as a researcher-narrator. There are also 'hidden' dialogical levels in the unvoiced and the 'non-conversational' modes of communication between different actors including the researcher. Indeed, the narrative has grown out of these diverse, overlapping levels of dialogues and is unfolded through different dialogical stages.[4]

The narrative opens by 'setting the scene for dialogue', with a brief description of the community touching upon gender roles and relations. It then proceeds through three parts. First, the focus is on the actors and 'one-to-one dialogues' as one woman, tacitly acknowledged as the leader of the group, initiates and facilitates contacts between the *adivasi* settlement and an NGO working in the area. Next, the narrative moves to the action, 'dialogues in a group', tracing the seemingly democratic process by which the village (actually just a small hamlet) enters into the NGO programme even as conflicts begin to emerge within the community. This is followed by the crisis, the 'disruption of dialogue' with the distressing heightening of the conflict which engulfs the woman, her family and the rest of the community. Finally, the narrator-researcher reflects on the course of the story, her own part in it and the implications for development practice.

The story relates to a specific location but the actual setting and the identity of the persons have been deliberately left somewhat vague. This is the only way in which stories such as these can be shared without appropriating the lives of people for academic purposes.[5] It is a story of very recent happenings, but I will let it unfold slowly in the manner in which many *adivasi*s tell a tale, starting from a more distant beginning with single strands of the narrative and following the course of my own deepening understanding as multiple strands are gathered together.

THE NARRATIVE

These *adivasi*s are migrants from an adjacent state where a couple of generations ago they had lived a nomadic and foraging life. Living off wild foods gathered from the forest, small game hunting and occasional wage labour, they were probably not the self-sufficient, 'original affluent society'.[6] Life expectancy was low and their population may even have been declining. Whether from the pressure of coping with degrading habitats, the imagined promise of a better life elsewhere, or for some other reasons, they had migrated to a very different landscape. In the process they acquired a second language, other occupations and skills to cope with the new environment.

For several decades, the *adivasi*s continued to live in the new setting as they had in the past—as a group of semi-nomadic foragers in small scattered family-units, just a few families in one vicinity. Each family, usually consisting of a couple and their unmarried children, made a temporary camp on local plantations where they were employed as watch-keepers and labourers. They also continued to forage for wild foods, tubers, green fruits, leaves and seeds, keenly aware of the distribution and seasonal variation of useful resources in their new habitat. Some of the animal life was also different, so new ways had to be devised using their old skills of catching game with their bare hands.

None of the adults in this particular group of *adivasi*s are literate and till recently none of the children had ever been to school. The families are all equally poor because foraging, the sale of foraged produce and intermittent wage income are insufficient to keep them out of indebtedness to the non-*adivasi* plantation owners or the tradeswomen in the local market. The *adivasi* women are in daily contact with the market women who buy their foraged game or other produce and loan them money for necessities, illnesses and emergencies. Despite being peripherally linked to the plantation economy the *adivasi*s have retained much of their old way of life including the relative autonomy of each family, as in each family's separate interactions with employers and market women. Yet, the *adivasi*s also form a kin group who may come together for foraging and on ritual occasions such as marriages and festivals.

Viewed from the outside, gender relations appear to have been relatively egalitarian. Descent is traced through the male line but does not seem to affect personal autonomy. Both women and men may choose their marriage partners or divorce a spouse. A couple may deal jointly with employers to negotiate the family wage, and even if a plantation owner paid out the wage to the man, he would hand it over to his wife and they would jointly take decisions about how to spend the money. Since they have had almost no tools and no property, except for the few cooking vessels which the women control, questions about inheriting property do not exist.

The division of labour has been flexible. In the spectrum of daily and seasonal activities, those surrounding the hearth—cooking and feeding of young children—are women's responsibilities while the traditional panchayat is all-male. Almost all other activities are undertaken by women and men together or by either as the situation may demand. Women have a subsidiary role to men in the *adivasi* rituals. But since these are still conducted in the first language, which some women have retained to a greater degree than the men, the women are consulted during the process of a ritual, for instance, to supply the words of a prescribed chant. In practice, therefore, the women often direct the course of a ritual.

THE ACTORS: DIALOGUES ONE-TO-ONE

From what I had read, heard and seen of them, it had seemed to me that many of these *adivasi* women have all the characteristics of solidity, strength and decisiveness stereotypically associated with masculinity in other communities. If feminism is 'resistance to invisibility and silencing',[7] they are feminists. Like other *adivasi* and peasant women, who depend on physical labour for a livelihood, they too carry their bodies with grace and pride. For years they have been living in close proximity to a town near a frequented tourist route and have interacted with non-*adivasi*s in the local market. They have witnessed visible signs of development in the nearby villages and also in one recent *adivasi* settlement. Some of the *adivasi* women envisioned a different future, articulated this and planned to lead their people in alternative directions.

One such woman, let us call her Ira, was tacitly acknowledged as the leader of the group. Ira, along with her husband, had taken the initiative to convince each family living in the scattered camps among the plantations that the times of semi-nomadic life were past. Settling down all together in one permanent location would be to their advantage. A site was staked out near the first *adivasi* settlement in the area. As Ira's small family (she, her husband and daughter) and other families began to put up their huts in the new settlement, a hamlet took shape. With an eye to the future it was named after the leader of a major political party.

In the past, the *adivasi*s were always disadvantaged in their necessary dealings with plantation owners, tradeswomen and the occasional junior government official (usually from the forest department). Like other *adivasi* groups elsewhere, they were wary of outsiders. This began to change when a new player, an NGO, entered the local scene a few years ago. Ira had watched the NGO staff (almost all of whom were men) scout the neighbouring *adivasi* settlement and interact with the people on friendly terms. She had seen activities being started and visible changes in the settlement. Perhaps viewing the NGO as a new 'forage-able' resource in the environment, Ira then took a remarkable step. Maybe it had been in her mind all along when she and her husband were persuading their people to settle down in one place. Ira sought out the NGO staff. She asked them to 'take up' her village too. The NGO was at first reluctant. Ira persisted. She visited them in their office in town. She reasoned and pleaded. They finally agreed and set out some conditions. The NGO was not a charitable organisation. It was engaged in the business of restoring and managing degraded environments for conservation and to improve people's livelihoods.

THE ACTION: DIALOGUES IN THE GROUP

The first step was to determine whether the entire village agreed to take on this activity. Discussions were held in the shade of a tree in the sandy ground near the village. Ira's enthusiasm carried the group and, of course, they agreed. The NGO staff then explained that they would help the *adivasi*s with technical inputs and some financial support, but first a village 'development committee' would have to be formed. This would have to be done in a participatory, democratic fashion, with an 'executive' consisting of a president, secretary, treasurer and other members. A bank account would also have to be opened in the town. The discussions continued. The children, including Ira's daughter, were excited by all the activity. They would stop playing catch around the trees and listen to the elders' discussions. Soon the English language words 'committee', 'meeting', 'president', 'bank' became familiar even to the young children.

The recently settled *adivasi*s continued to discuss all this among themselves without coming to a point. They knew that the committee would be given a grant which would be deposited in the bank and that the committee would then pay out wages to the women and men who were engaged in the restoration work. The NGO staff was eager to get on with the important decisions, the formation of the committee, opening the bank account, fixing the wage rates for the men and women who would do the labour of digging, carrying, planting, and so on. The staff had to fulfil project schedules and other requirements set out by their headquarters and meet commitments made to the foreign donor agency.

The first issue to be decided was the daily wage rate. The *adivasi*s informed the NGO staff that they had all agreed that the men would be paid, let us say, rupees 'x' and the women half of that amount. They had worked this out keeping in mind a 'fair' familial wage of roughly rupees one and a half 'x' a day. The NGO team leader felt the difference between the male and female wage rate was too much. A meeting of the *adivasi*s with the NGO staff was arranged to reconsider this.

At that time I was visiting the area and went along to the meeting with the staff. It took a long while for the women and men to gather under the tree; there were some older women; then the men came in twos and threes forming separate little groups; it was mentioned that the women were busy cooking the evening meal; some of the young men got bored as nothing seemed to be happening, got up and left. Ira did not come at all. Eventually, there were enough people to start the meeting. The *adivasi*s seemed to feel there was nothing to discuss. An elderly man said this was the prevailing wage rate for men and women in the local contract labour market. One of the staff said to me that the official daily wage rate for unskilled labour in the state was also different for men and women because they did 'different kinds of work'. So, what was the problem?

At this stage, I suggested to one of the NGO staff that he might like to initiate a discussion on broader lines—on the differences in the life-worlds of the *adivasi*s and the local non-*adivasi* communities, moving on to the strengths in the *adivasi* way of life. This discussion led to identifying the relative gender equality among *adivasi*s as one of their strengths. Why did they want to change this in the new matter of daily wages, I asked. The women remained silent through most of the meeting. The men agreed, almost too quickly, that the women should be paid more even if the work they did was different (carrying and transporting rather than digging), but said that their own wage should not be reduced. Someone then pointed out that the funding could not be stretched to pay both women and men rupees 'x' a day. This was a difficult knot to untangle.

The knot was ingeniously untied. One of the men said that the women should be paid according to the number of hours they would work. I asked why the women would be working fewer hours than the men. Because they would have to cook and bring the meal for them at the work site, the men said. At this point, some of the women spoke up to say, yes, this was true, they would be working for fewer hours than the men on the site. By this time it was dusk and the NGO staff did not want to go back to the town without a decision. So, it was agreed by consensus that the principle of equality of wages would be recognised but that women and men would be paid in proportion to the number of hours they spent actually working at the site. This would increase the group's daily expenditure on wages only marginally. Everyone seemed satisfied with this outcome.

I got up, searched for my sandals and bent down to put them on. Suddenly the women were clapping and singing. They had formed a circle around me and were dancing. It took a little while for me to figure out that the song and dance were in some way related to me. I did not understand the words (which seemed to be in their first language), nor could I fathom the emotions being expressed—laughing one moment, sad the next. I did not know how to respond and was embarrassed. When it was over and the circle broke up, they crowded around me; there was a lot of touching, holding hands and hugging but nothing much was said to me. What was it all about, I asked one of the women staff, and learnt that it was the song sung when a girl gets married and leaves the group.

Why had a middle-aged woman, whom they had never met before, been adopted (apparently spontaneously) as one of their own and bidden farewell as a bride? At that time I thought this was perhaps the women's way of acknowledging my interest in them. On reflection, it seemed possible that they saw me as some kind of 'authority', since I was an older city person who was being treated with respect by the young NGO staff. A few of the *adivasi* women had asked whether I was the NGO's 'teacher'. I do not know whether the episode signified fellowship or strategy on their part, or both. It is easy to romanticise *adivasi* emotion; one need not, however, swing with the pendulum to the other extreme and read tactics into every friendly gesture.

THE CRISIS: DISRUPTED DIALOGUES

The following day, we set out again to the *adivasi* settlement carrying the cheque. For the NGO it was imperative that the formalities of organisation be completed, that the president and other important members of the executive committee be chosen that very day. I learnt that the staff had earlier suggested that the *adivasi*s choose Ira as president. They were impressed by her initiative, energy and leadership and her selection to the top post would reflect the NGO's own gender sensitivity. The *adivasi* women and men were agreeable to this. Ira was well-respected and liked. But the suggestion had caused considerable disquiet because Ira's husband had felt slighted by this public recognition of his wife's informal status as the leader of the group. This was perhaps why he had also vigorously opposed increasing the women's wage rate on the previous evening. Ira's absence from that meeting now seemed ominous.

When the *adivasi*s gathered, once again, Ira was not present. She had sent word that she did not wish to be the president. The women who had sung for me the night before were subdued. I learnt from them that the relations between husband and wife had deteriorated so much that 'the hearths had been separated'. The NGO staff said it was not good that the couple's domestic differences should 'spill over' into official work. Their view was that these spaces should be kept separate.

The staff insisted that Ira be called. She then came with extreme reluctance, almost being dragged by some of the women. She looked frightened and sat among the group only after her husband had nodded permission. There was nothing about her bearing when I saw her that day to suggest the strong woman I had been told about. The discussion began. When it was her turn to speak, without looking at anyone, drawing circles in the ground with her forefinger, she said let him be the president—meaning the husband. Many of the *adivasi*s agreed. The matter seemed to have been nearly decided. But there were some rumblings and a few of the NGO staff were also not satisfied; it was felt the husband would not make a 'good' president.

At that point, one woman began to speak quietly. She was identified for me as Ira's friend. A little later I learnt that she was also Ira's sister-in-law, the husband's sister. She spoke of her anguish at the separation of the hearths, of how this had divided the village with people taking sides, something unprecedented in the life of this community. She mentioned the eight-year-old daughter, an only child, now with the mother who was separated from the father. She retold the story of how the group had been living in scattered camps, how Ira along with her husband, the two together, had worked so hard to bring all the families to settle at this place. She said the village owed everything that they had now to this couple. Bringing her fingers and palms together as in a *namaste*, she said, 'the husband and wife were like this. What had happened now?'

The gesture of placing her palms together stirred a thought in my mind. I asked the NGO team leader whether there was any rule, of the bank, the NGO or the donor, that the executive should have only one president. Why not joint presidents? Indeed, this was roughly how Ira and her husband had functioned earlier. Why not formalise that instead of pushing the two of them around one chair, a game in which one would have to take a fall? The idea quickly caught on. With the exception of Ira herself, everyone was pleased at the seeming resolution. It was formally accepted, recorded and witnessed. Other posts were swiftly filled. The cheque was handed over. The work was soon to begin. There was relief all around.

It was quite dark before we could leave. The women knew that I would not be back. There was warmth in the leave-taking but no dancing and singing. In the darkness, Ira took me aside. She was nearly in tears. 'Where are you going?', she asked. I told her. 'Take me with you', she said. I misunderstood her, thinking she wanted to visit. I told her that I would be glad to welcome her to my home. In fact, I would soon be moving south and then it might be arranged more easily. She said she was not talking about a visit; she wanted to come away permanently. 'What about the village and what about your daughter?', I asked. Clinging to my hand, she said it would never be the same again. I could make no response.

Soon after that, for unconnected reasons, my own relations with the NGO changed and I had no way of knowing how things had turned out. A year later, I made discreet enquiries and learnt that the work had progressed very well. What about Ira? She, her husband and daughter had moved their hut to the adjacent village because the relations between the husband and the rest of the group had worsened. They did not like his style of functioning, and Ira did not intervene. The joint-presidentship was only in name. The 'naming' itself had become the problem.

I knew that among some other *adivasi* groups conflicts are traditionally avoided; when things get really bad they are dealt with simply by one party moving away to ease the tension. There is no elaborate discussion. Perhaps this was the way among these *adivasis* too. Ira and her husband still belonged to the village that they had dreamt about and set up but they no longer lived in it.

That year the NGO's published reports stated that women's empowerment in the project villages had been substantially increased by their greater participation in the executives of the development committees.

REFLECTIONS

In life (as in narrative) the task of gathering together single threads into multiple skeins, without getting them entangled, is fraught with difficulties. As another year passed and I reflected on the course of the story—from one-to-one dialogues to dialogues in the group and the crisis of disrupted dialogue—I continued to be troubled by my own part in it, my presumptions, complicity and eventual helplessness as an 'outsider' unable to help the NGO staff or the village beyond circumscribed limits. It is also disturbing that none of the persons involved, with the possible exception of Ira herself, realised how things would unfold.

In Ira's life, and in that of this *adivasi* group, the public and private worlds were closely intertwined. The political spaces both within families and the group were relatively gender egalitarian. This enabled her to act in the new public political spaces opening up for a community in the process of transition from a semi-nomadic to a settled way of life. Yet, her confident assertion of a vision for her people had repercussions which were deeply disrupting for herself, her family and the community.

The well-meaning NGO staff were constrained by the inflexibility of project schedules and formal procedures, and did not have the imagination, experience or skills to deal with the cascading impacts. Yet, the reasons why they were so constrained lie at the core of many developmental interventions which are instrumentalist in approach and may even undermine women's existing rights. Furthermore, their (and my) inability to perceive and anticipate the tensions between the prevalent *adivasi* decision-making systems (the overtly informal and individualistic and yet democratic structures and processes) and the attempt to incorporate new activities and institutional mechanisms shaped by our particular conception of democracy reflects our collective misunderstandings. I do not know whether in such a case a conventional NGO could set the right pace and direction simply by more sensitive facilitation.

The 'feminist' strengths, autonomy and decision-making power, of the *adivasi* women in this small 'face-to-face' community seem to have been garnered within a framework which maintains (or is seen to maintain) men's pride (*ijjat*) and their socially sanctioned role and position (*maryada*) in the political and ritual spheres. In terms of political strategy this has some resonances with the manner in which middle class women, in urban milieus of vastly different scales and levels of interaction, negotiate paths by skirting around the rocks of male *ijjat* and *maryada*. The *adivasi* women, however, are not seeking to establish democratic norms in the family but to prevent the loss of relative equity and existing democratic strengths. Ira herself was not blind to the complex linkages between gender-power relationships in the privacy of the family and the quick sands of the public democratic domain—the spaces between which this impoverished *adivasi* community were caught.

I do not want to idealise a 'traditional' *adivasi* way of life, imagining the collapse of inner and outer spaces, an open, free-flowing, undifferentiated fluidity. Such a perspective would only be the obverse of the view that sees no linkages between intra-household dynamics and the public domain. When a household is marked by just a few palm fronds in a coconut grove, when there is no door to shut, no yard to cross, there can be no sharp physical boundary between the worlds of home and work. Yet, that does not mean that there is no division at all. In an *adivasi* community, such as this, the swaying threads that separate 'inside' and 'outside' spaces are gossamer thin; there is a certain translucency through which the light shines. When we attempt to wind these threads on a spool, weave a democratic cloth in looms of our making, in patterns set to our conventions, the threads do not hold.

Yet, the problem is not only one of the 'master's tools'.[8] The question is 'who wields them and to what purpose?'[9] One can venture to suggest that the narrative is a tool that may be used collaboratively and creatively to bring the family into development discourse. The understanding gleaned from the particularities of this narrative may enhance our comprehension of the impact of modern democratic institutions on the inside–outside political spaces of similarly placed *adivasi* women elsewhere. Many such *adivasi* groups have an indigenous conception of democracy, which is relatively gender egalitarian, and of processes by which this is realised within the community. This indigenous democratic fabric, however, may be frayed by various forces of change, by the people's own needs and aspirations for wider social integration and by developmental interventions inspired by other conceptions of democracy having different institutional processes. The problem for *adivasi* women and men, and for those who work with them, is to find innovative ways to accomplish the transformation from semi-nomadic foraging to a settled way of life and new processes of formal collective decision-making, while retaining the autonomy of individuals and families and the relative gender egalitarianism that seems connected to this.

Perhaps this could all have been handled differently. Perhaps ... if Ira and the other *adivasi* women and men had been freer to devise their own institutional processes, in the light of their own lived experiences, and at their own pace, then...the complexity, fluidity, translucency of the linkages between their private and public political spaces might not have been rent asunder. The gossamer threads might have been unravelled with a gentler, defter touch.

ACKNOWLEDGEMENTS

An earlier version of this paper was presented at the Tenth National Conference of the Indian Association for Women's Studies, Sub-theme 2:'Promoting democracy within the family', Bhubaneshwar, 17–20 October 2002. Thanks are due to Joy Ranadive-Deshmukh for inviting me to contribute a narrative; to her, P. Thamizoli, Sanghamitra Misra and G. Ajay for their perceptive comments; and to Maitreyi Krishnaraj for her encouraging support. I am also grateful to the staff of the NGO who first introduced me to this *adivasi* community.

NOTES

1. The major shifts from nomadism to settlement were completed in the pre-colonial period, as is borne out by Indian sociology and ecological history. However, even today there are some small, semi-nomadic *adivasi* groups scattered in pockets along the coastal and hill-forest regions of the country. They are gatherers, hunters, animal-trappers, 'non-gear' fishers or any combination of these who did not hitherto practise any form of cultivation. Despite their small numbers, their significance for action-research is that they are now choosing, or being propelled by circumstances, to settle as farmers, fishers or wage labourers.
2. A very early attempt in this direction was Kusum Nair's (1961) *Blossoms in the Dust: The Human Element in Indian Development* whose content and methodology marked a shift from conventional economic research and writing. When development studies in India grew as a bounded discipline, however, it adopted the more 'objective' and impersonalised approach of orthodox social science. Among the few recent examples of a different kind of writing is 'Becoming a Development Category', the moving story of the Nepalese-born US academic Nanda Shrestha (1995); and the 'travelogue' by Subhash Mendhapurkar (2003), of the NGO Sutra in Himachal Pradesh, which winds its way with remarkable frankness through the fluid interfaces between the professional, personal, institutional and methodological.
3. There are many 'messy, unspoken, complex and disturbing moments' in qualitative research which Horsfall, Higgs and Byrne-Armstrong (2001: 4) call 'critical moments'. As Mulligan (2001:141) says 'We can consciously blur the boundaries between life, work and research when we look for overlapping interests, projects and discourses. We can learn to love the creative chaos that this involves. But we will also experience frustration and despair when we are torn apart by competing priorities or overcome by a sense of failure. We might reconceive life and work as artificially constructed conceptual categories, but we all know that they often seem to collide with such force that sparks fly, leading to heated arguments or smouldering tensions. In the chaotic interaction of conflict we may discover the spark of a new idea or we may even find that our lives reemerge in a new form like a Phoenix rising from the ashes.'
4. The idea of dialogical stages of narrative in this paper was inspired by P. Thamizoli who also drew my attention to Mannheim and Van Vleet's (1998) study of the dialogical levels of the oral narratives of the southern Quechua (Andean Inkas). Their work integrates narrative analysis with ethnography by distinguishing four different (and simultaneous) dialogical levels. An earlier work, *The Dialogic Emergence of Culture* (1995) edited by Tedlock and Mannheim shows how narrative (from field research to publication) is the product of social interaction. Recognising the resonances between this approach and the course of my narrative, as it was first presented, I have framed the story through consecutive dialogical stages and briefly drawn attention to its different dialogical levels.

5. Some have questioned why I refused to identify the main protagonist of the narrative, and said that this may take away its authenticity. My answer is that if it were a story of an educated middle class woman (such as myself) I would wish to ensure the privacy of the individual. I believe that the same principle needs to be applied in research with poor illiterate women.
6. The notion of the 'original affluent society' put forward by Sahlins (1971) has fostered the widespread assumption that the low-energy subsistence lifestyles of gatherer-hunters satisfied their 'basic needs' and was a consciously chosen way of life inspired by ecological wisdom. Many, including myself, have disputed this; as I have written elsewhere (Krishna 1996: 89–92): 'Although nature may be bountiful in the humid tropics, it is simplistic to presume that the population was somehow always in happy equilibrium with the food supply, and that painful and desperate choices were not necessary.'
7. Feminism is variously defined but the concept of feminism as resistance suggested by Karleen Faith (1995) provides a common denominator to strategise women's political articulation against subordination in different cultural and socio-economic contexts.
8. Contrary to the feminist Audre Lorde's (1984) precept, 'The master's tools will never dismantle the master's house', I would suggest that we do need the 'master's tools' to dismantle patriarchal epistemologies, but feminist and gender studies also need other kinds of tools to build other kinds of houses. Innovative action-researchers could break new methodological ground by fostering dialogues in particular local contexts between different ways of knowledge construction, different institutional practices and forms of representation (see also note 9).
9. In the context of the 'unacknowledged tribes' of California, Field (1999: 193) asks 'How do these [anthropological] tools change depending upon who wields them and to what purpose? Are there other kinds of intellectuals who have other tools at their disposal? In the hands of other such intellectuals, might anthropology's tools prove useful for undermining the foundations of the master's house?' Drawing upon Gramsci (1971), he suggests the possibility of collaboration between the leadership of the tribes (indigenous intellectuals) and 'the academics who wield the master's tools' (traditional intellectuals).

REFERENCES

Faith, Karleen. 1995. 'Resistance: Lessons from Foucault and Feminism', in H. Lorraine Radtke and Hendrikus J. Stam (eds), *Power/Gender: Social Relations in Theory and Practice*, pp. 36–66. New Delhi: Sage Publications.

Field, Les W. 1999. 'Complicities and Collaborations', *Current Anthropology*, 40 (2):193–209.

Gramsci, Antonio. 1971. *Prison Notebooks*. New York: International Publishers.

Horsfall, Debbie, Hillary Bryne-Armstrong and Joy Higgs. 2001. 'Researching Critical Moments', in Hilary Bryne-Armstrong, Joy Higgs and Debbie Horsfall (eds), *Critical Moments in Qualitative Research*, pp. 3–13. Oxford, UK: Butterworth-Heinemann.

Krishna, Sumi. 1996. *Environmental Politics: People's Lives and Development Choices*. New Delhi: Sage Publications.

Lorde, Audre. 1984. *Sister, Outsider, Freedom*. California, US: Crossing Press.

Mannheim, Bruce and Krista Van Vleet. 1998. 'The Dialogics of Southern Quechua Narrative', *American Anthropologist*, 100(2): 326–46.

Mendhapurkar, Subhash. 2003. 'From Subjects of Change to Agents of Change: A Travelogue', in Sumi Krishna (ed.), *Livelihood and Gender: Equity in Community Resource Management*. New Delhi: Sage Publications.

Mulligan, Martin. 2001. 'Sparks Fly When Life, Work and Research Collide', in Hilary Bryne-Armstrong, Joy Higgs and Debbie Horsfall (eds), *Critical Moments in Qualitative Research*, pp. 136–43. Oxford, UK: Butterworth-Heinemann.

Nair, Kusum. 1961. *Blossoms in the Dust: The Human Element in Indian Development* (Indian edition 1971). New Delhi: Allied Publishers.

Sahlins, Marshall. 1971. *Stone Age Economics*. Chicago: Aldine Artherton.

Shrestha, Nanda. 1995. 'Becoming a Development Category', in Jonathan Crush (ed.), *Power of Development*. London and New York: Routledge.

Tedlock, Dennis and Bruce Mannheim (eds). 1995. *The Dialogic Emergence of Culture*. Urbana, US: University of Illinois Press.

SECTION
II

Expressing the Family

4

Family in Feminist Songs
A Continuity with Women's Folk Literature

Sonal Shukla

Family is the first patriarchal institution that socialises women and men and prepares them for their expected gender roles. This institution reflects and perpetuates the patriarchal norms of the society. Constructed as women are by the family, they internalise these norms. The various other social institutions reinforce the early indoctrination of gender roles. While this is basically true, in its reductionist form, this view tends to see women only as passive recipients who do not perceive the unjust and oppressive nature of patriarchal values or the contradictions within them. Accounts of individual women's struggles, of their challenges and triumphs as well as the subversive elements in Grandma's tales and protests expressed through women's folk songs tell a different story.

This chapter argues that not only have women traditionally made attempts to create space and legitimacy for articulating their protests, but also the widespread acceptance of songs from the women's movement and their popularity have a basis in such spaces created by creative but anonymous women. Women who composed and sang these songs challenged family norms and the power of certain categories of men and women within the family. The chapter illustrates this with examples from Gujarati folk songs and Hindi and Gujarati songs from the women's movement that are in folk style.[1] Almost all information has been accessed through conversations, personal letters, observation and participation and from small booklets published by women's groups. The chapter first deals with folk songs as anonymous literature of the powerless. It then goes on to discuss *khayana*s and *garba*s, the two poetic forms in which women in Gujarat have expressed themselves. The third section of the chapter talks of the impact of urbanisation, emergence of the middle class nuclear family and commercialisation of folk music. The fourth section goes on to discuss the songs that have emerged from the women's movement, their continuity with folk songs, and the use of new songs and their popularity. The last section notes that women enjoy and accept the political content of 'feminist folk songs' even if they do not have the scope to change their own lives accordingly or would not want to disturb the present equilibrium in a major way. It also notes that the women's movement songs have not been targeted by the patriarchal forces so far and makes conjectures about the possible reasons.

FOLK SONGS AS ANONYMOUS LITERATURE OF THE POWERLESS

The more restricted definition of a folk song is that the author or the authors are anonymous and that it is passed on orally, that it is well known or has been well known at one time and it is common property. There is no copyright over the notes or words of a folk song. Another characteristic of folk songs is that they are written in certain common metres with common musical compositions. However, there are many songs written more recently by certain poet-composers which follow the folk tradition and are 'folksy' in mood. They become popular precisely because they sound like folk songs. Most people forget their origin. Some songs and *garba*s by the poet-composers Avinash Vyas and Ninu Mazumdar and several others written a few decades ago are already in popular anthologies of folk songs in Gujarati. This will continue to happen because copyrights are not observed strictly and people have an easier access to songs in folk tradition, although only through unscrupulous or ignorant publishers. In one convention, songs of a particular genre are all called folk songs, for instance, Caribbean folk songs of Harry Belafonte in the 1950s.

Family in Feminist Songs

If a folk song has, by definition, to be by anonymous author/s and preserved in oral tradition long before it is written down and published, the implication is that when literacy, printing and copyrights are available to all, there shall be no creation of folk songs (or folk literature) any more. Songs of the powerless have necessarily been in the oral tradition. How else would they be preserved when their creators had no wealth, status, literacy or patronage? It was not until researchers in literature and social sciences began to look at them or when the interests of the ruling classes and community leaders so required, that they were recorded. Individual authorship would hardly be assumed by people who had no right to individuality and very little individual property. Compare this to the care with which presumably Brahmin scribes would add their names even when they had merely copied some great literary or religious work in a particular manuscript. Authorship has been given only to royal personages or to gurus and writers who had patronage in ancient and medieval times. The only exceptions have been the saint-poets who, apart from Meera and a few others, usually came from the 'common stock'. In the songs available to us, the saint-poets almost always put their names in the last verse addressing the final lines to God or to an audience of disciples and fellow *bhakta*s. People have preserved these songs in oral tradition with the inevitable updating of the language, but the names have survived along with the poetry. Perhaps stating their names was also an act of courage and defiance and not merely one of claiming authorship. We have a Kabir taking on vested interests in *masjid* and *mandir* alike in his poetry, a Meera defying restrictions placed on a widowed Rajput queen and, much earlier, Mahadevi Akka accepting only Shiva as her lover and husband and not covering herself with clothes. They did not conceal their own identities. Ordinary people have refrained from attaching their names, perhaps because they were vulnerable. And possibly also because they were humble and modest and did not wish to be credited with authorship. This seems to have become a custom not just for songs of protest or songs with subversive content but also for songs of joy and happiness. People often added lines to *bhajan*s or wrote new ones but credited authorship to well respected saints and gurus, by saying in the end *Kahat Kabira* (Kabir says) or *Bai Meera kahe* (Meera Bai says). The verses are called interpolations now and deleted by the purists.

KHAYANAS AND *GARBAS*

If anonymity was necessary for the security and protection of vulnerable sections of society like peasants, artisans and others, it was even more so for women who lived in close and intimate relationships with people who had absolute power over them before and after marriage. When married they would be under scrutiny at all times. Yet they managed to express their feelings in songs while fetching water, doing daily chores, performing pooja, going on a pilgrimage and celebrating special occasions and festivals.

Women's folk songs are created around family events. There are songs celebrating pregnancy, child birth and weddings and there are also laments and dirges. Songs praying for a child and celebrating the first pregnancy or child birth are usually in relation to a male child. Lullabies are also more often for putting a male child to sleep. However, there are other songs where women take the opportunity to mock people with power over them. Songs sung at weddings give scope for that. Until the marriage is solemnised, women from the bride's family can joke about people who are related to the bridegroom. A *phatana*, a Gujarati verse formed to mock the other side, says a railway train has come from Mumbai bringing all kinds of stuff. For example, it says, the train has brought a lot of *ringana* (eggplant) and along with that all these fellows who are *thingana* (very short). Women from both sides sing *phatana*s against each other and also against members of their own families, especially about the husband's younger brother and husband's sister's husband, men with whom a certain flirtatious or joking relationship is possible. Once the marriage ceremony is over, the bride's side accepts a permanently lower status and treats the other side respectfully.

Dalna and *khayana* are triplets in which the third line may not necessarily rhyme with the other two. Women sing them while performing tasks like grinding and pounding grain and spices. Usually called just *khayana,* they express pain and humiliation suffered by women. Due to the commonality of experience, singing these songs has a cathartic value for all women. They have often been request numbers on radio programmes and women's organisations are known to have *khayana* competitions. *Kunwarbainu Mameru*, a medieval *akhyan* (a long story in verse, based on side themes in ancients texts such as the *Mahabharata*) in Gujarati by Premanand, includes many popular *khayana*s that describe the pain of a motherless daughter. Looking at the mother–daughter relations in gestalt terms one of them says:

> *Bedu phute ne razale thikari*
> *Tevi Ma vinani Dikari chhe*
> *Aa sansarma*
>
> (When an earthen pot is shattered, a shard lies abandoned.
> Such is the condition of a motherless girl
> In this world)

Another *khayana* mentions a daughter's chance meeting with her mother. Both have gone to fetch water. Chance meetings with the woman's mother or brother are a recurring theme in women's songs with tragic themes. The husband's family often expressed its power by not permitting a daughter-in-law to visit her parental home. The intensity of pain felt is anonymously articulated in a *khayana*:

> *Ma ne dikari sarvar kanthe malia*
> *Dhruske dhruske radia*
> *Ke Sarvar bharai gaya.*
>
> (Mother and daughter met at the lakeside
> They sobbed and cried
> And the lake filled up with their tears)

Fantasising an ability to fight back is also part of women's songs. One *khayana* says:

> *Sasu ne vahu malia*
> *Ke samsaama ladia*
> *Ke dugra dolia*
>
> (The mother-in-law and the daughter-in-law met.
> The confrontation that followed
> Made the mountains tremble.)

*Khayana*s are rendered while working at home. Wedding songs are also sung when women come together to make preparations for the event, completing tasks like cleaning grain, rolling *papa*ds and making sweets and savouries prior to a wedding and while the ceremony is on. However, most women worked in fields too. Fewer songs of women in agricultural or other occupations have been documented. One of them is an open song of protest against the husband. In most Gujarati folk songs set in domestic surroundings, there is usually no reference to the husband or he is seen as a romantic lover. In this particular song, a *garba*, a landless woman complains about her husband who is lazy and jealous of her capacity for hard work. She says:

Savva bashernu maaru datardu lol, ghadyu olya Laliye luhar munja Vahalamji lol
Haave nahin jaun vidi vadhava re lol…

(My sickle weighs two pounds and a quarter; it is made by Laliya, the blacksmith
O' my friend I shall not go harvesting [with my husband].)

The man she has married, she says, reaps only five bundles and earns a quarter of a rupee a day whereas she reaps 20 bundles or more and gets one and a half rupees. She is given a large quantity of good wheat for her labour and he brings home only some coarse millet. The end of the song describes how she lifts his load and helps place it on his head, but he walks away without helping her in return. So she requests a traveller to help her place her bags on her head. She takes this man, who is like a brother she says, home and cooks sweet *seera* for him. Use of the term *vahalamji* is a little vague here. It means dear or darling with reference to a man. Women have used it for their husbands generally. It is unlikely that an angry wife calls her husband *vahalamji*. Is she addressing her lover and complaining about her husband or addressing a woman friend, as women do when a line ends with a *lol*, and referring sceptically to her husband as a darling? We shall never know for certain. The point is that she has proudly described her capacity to work hard and earn better wages than her husband, protested against him and taken action and mentioned all of it in a song.

*Khayana*s are rendered in slow wailing tunes whereas *garba* songs have a faster rhythm. Although known as a folk dance of Gujarat, *garba*s can be rendered as songs without the accompanying dance.

The term *garba* is said to be derived from the Sanskrit word *garbha* meaning the foetus. It refers to the sacred earthen pot symbolising the mother goddess during the *Navaratri* festival in autumn as well as to the songs and dances dedicated to her. It also refers to other similar circular dances and the songs that go with them. *Garba*s were meant to be performed outside women's quarters in courtyards and in streets. Men performed their *garba*s separately and more vigorously. Men sang prayers to Devi Ambika, songs of Krishna and romantic songs but seldom of their family life. Women sang similar songs but they also sang a great many other *garba*s that expressed their pain and sorrows, their joy, aspirations and fantasies. These *garba*s are addressed to the mother goddess, to one's own mother, to a sister or to a woman friend. Occasionally they are addressed to the husband or a lover, the latter, usually the rare non-family man that women came in contact with, such as a bangle seller, a *banjara* who comes with his caravan, a drum beater in *garba*s or Krishna, the divine lover.

The family relationships described in various *garba*s are both happy as well as sad or hostile; they are about whether or not the author gets along with women in her husband's family—the mother-in-law and the sisters-in-law. There is sometimes a suggestive reference to the young bride's friendship with the husband's younger brother. He is younger than the husband so she does not have to cover her face in his presence. She can talk to him and even joke with him. Marriage to him is a possibility in many communities if the husband should die. One of the most famous Gujarati *garba*s has a line that says, 'The young brother-in-law is a dear one. He brought a *mehendi* (henna) plant. He picked the leaves, ground them and brought cupfuls of *mehendi* to me saying, *bhabhi* do put henna on your palms.' The woman hints at her commitment to her own husband saying, 'Whatever should I colour my palms for when the one who should see (and appreciate) them is travelling in distant lands?'

The mother-in-law is usually seen as oppressive. Even though *garba*s express common experiences of women and they are collectively rendered by women, somehow there is no song that has all daughters-in-law (wives of the husband's brothers) together against the mother-in-law. It is always about one woman alone. In some *garba*s, a woman fantasises about giving back as good as she gets, about punishing her mother-in-law. She says:

Sonal Shukla

Baijie lidho dhoko mori sanglala
Mein lidhiti ees mori sanglal
Baijini dhoko tuti padyo re sanglal
Ees padave cheece mori sanglal

(During a confrontation—
The mother-in-law picked up a wooden club, my friend.
I took a wooden plank from the bed, my friend.
Her club broke in to pieces, my friend.
And the plank got a scream out of her, my friend.)

Family relations are in a joint family setting. The father-in-law or his father is the head whereas the mother-in-law or grandmother-in-law wields power directly over younger women. Since the patriarchal joint family functioned through a hierarchy in which a woman never deals directly with men older than her husband, there is hardly any expression of anger against male elders in the matrimonial home. If at all, her own grandfather is blamed for choosing a husband for her from a cruel family. In one song a woman sends a message to her grandfather that she is going to throw herself into a well because she can no longer work constantly from early morning to late at night as dictated by her unkind mother-in-law. The song ends with the grandfather getting her back to the parental home even if it is only for a visit.

There is a song directed to the grandfather, in which the girl describes to him the kind of husband she wants. 'Neither too fat nor too thin, neither too dark skinned nor too fair. Instead get someone who is slim and somewhat darkish, actually the one who has been described and praised by my girl friend.' Here one can see the playful relationship she has with an indulgent grandfather though she maintains the etiquette and decorum by not actually naming the man she has in mind. This is how a girl has learnt to deal with the centre of family power from an early age. She has no independent choice but enjoys a certain amount of indulgence through her direct relationship with the male head of the natal family.

After marriage, a woman has empathy from her mother who has no power to help her. They are both victims of a system and they both cry when they meet at the village well or the river or the lake. One such song describes the power hierarchy in a joint family.

Family in Feminist Songs

Ghaamma Sasaru ne gamma piyariyu lol
Dikri kejo sukhdukhni vaat jo
Aa kavala sasariyama jivavu re lol

The woman's natal family and her in-laws lived in the same village. When they met at the well, the mother asked her daughter how she was since she was living with difficult people. Further in the song the daughter says that the days of happiness for her were over and that pain and problems had sprouted all over like small plants. These are the opening lines of the song. The rest of it describes how the husband's sister overheard this and reported the conversation to her mother, the woman's mother-in-law. The mother-in-law reported it to the father-in-law and the latter repeated the incident to his eldest son. The eldest son went to his brother and told him that his wife, the family's daughter-in-law, had spoken against the family and had adversely affected its reputation. Without wasting a moment the younger man rushed to the local shop and bought a large quantity of two kinds of poison. He mixed them and offered the cup to his wife saying either she drank the poison or he would. She did. Returning home from her cremation the husband cried saying he was the one condemned to be lonely and unhappy for a lifetime now.

This song seems to have been based on experience in a rich *bania* or Brahmin family since in most other communities women were married to men outside their own village. The song describes the family hierarchy in which a young husband is just one step above his wife. In this case, his personal feelings and affection had to be subservient to what was seen as the family honour. That may be one reason why there is seldom a complaint against one's husband in a *khayana* or a *garba*. It was also considered sinful to speak against one's husband. Apart from the song of a landless woman peasant described earlier, one hardly comes across songs that are directly critical of the husband. The woman's own father is also a relatively young married son, which is the reason why the woman addresses her desires and demands to her grandfather.

The story of the woman poisoned by her husband is immortalised through a long *garba* that elders do not like women, even those in their 70s and 80s today, to sing. The fact that it survived over generations shows that women empathised with the victim, saw something of themselves in her and expressed their own protests by rendering the song.

URBANISATION AND THE COMMERCIALISATION OF FOLK MUSIC

Women continued performing *garba*s when they entered the modern city life. One of the main activities of the earliest Gujarati women's organisations was *garba*s that were performed on stage for an audience. Women's journals published new *garba*s written by women and men. Working towards the construction of a new woman, reformers wrote *garba*s to put across their messages. Dalpatram, the first modern Gujarati poet, wrote *garba*s to promote women's education in the mid-19th century. In the first part of the 20th century, nationalists wrote inspiring *garba*s for women. There is a *garba* with the story of Jallianwala Bagh, a khadi propagation *garba* and several against the British. None of these songs carried women's own experience and feelings though the form and the composition were traditional. Women did feel excited by the nationalist *garba*s and are known to have performed dances to these with great zeal. But they hardly ever wrote any themselves.

On stage, the participatory dance became an item to be viewed and reviewed. Women's organisations were managed by upper caste members from educated and wealthy families. This was reflected in their choice of songs. They selected songs by literary writers who were men. Educated upper class men had stopped performing *garba*s whereas women of the same class had taken up that activity on stage. The lines between private and public spheres were becoming clear in the newly emerging society and talking about the family was considered gossip that good women did not indulge in. Pain or bitterness was not to be expressed in public and, therefore, they were no longer the themes of songs on which *garba*s were performed on stage. In the newly emerged and expanding middle class, women were becoming one half of a couple and getting divided by nuclear families, losing live daily contact with other women. This author is not arguing for the joint family system. However, it has to be noted that women's creativity suffered in the new set-up. Women, especially

Gujarati women, did not use modern poetic forms successfully until the last decades of the 20th century. Women poets in Gujarati emerged in any sizable number only in the last two decades of the 20th century. Very few have acquired visibility and stature. Some old songs sometimes surface in school text books in the mandatory lesson on folk literature. The traditional songs still survived in the *garba* festivals in neighbourhoods and on the streets until the 1970s or even later, though there has not been much creation of new *garba*s collectively by women in which they talk of their own new experiences.

By the end of the 1960s, the *garba*s emerged in a new form as *disco dandia*. The strict segregation of sexes was loosened to let young boys join girls in the community *garba*s in building compounds and streets. These boys were from educated families where men had stopped dancing in public for some generations. They were also not from the westernised background with exposure to ball room dancing. In any case, the formal ball room dancing was being replaced by the more casual and individual disco variety. This element was introduced in *garba*s, and the drum beats became faster. The *raas* with *dandia* sticks, earlier the last item on the list, replaced the *garba*s which are performed only through claps and snapping of fingers. Very soon *garba*s became a youth activity and *Navaratri*, a youth festival. Audio cassettes and professional singers replaced older women who knew *garba* songs. The old songs could not now be transmitted directly to younger women. Some fast *garba* songs have remained popular. Every year new *garba* cassettes are produced that have old and new numbers. The new songs are usually imitative and fake ethnic. *Garba*, like the *Ganesh* festival of Maharashtra, has become a big business with commercial and political interests.

There has been comparable vulgarisation of folk culture in other parts of the country also. Commercialisation of Punjabi folk music is most evident because of television advertisements for it and their presence in Indipop countdowns. Addition to folk songs and other kinds of change are not only natural but also necessary ingredients of growth for a folk culture. However, the impulse for the new *garba* song does not come from common experience of women and women's articulation but from a commercial angle where glamour is emphasised. Similarly, there are new *mehendi* songs in Hindi after the more recent American fad for 'temporary tattoos'. The new generation accepts this as tradition. It has become a tradition, not by growing within a cultural milieu but, by replacing a tradition of women's creativity with profit motive.

SONGS FROM THE WOMEN'S MOVEMENT

It would appear that women's music has come to a dead end, that women have been successfully silenced, and that they have lost the space and the tradition they had created for giving expression to their protests. The fact that this has not quite happened is due to some feminist women claiming their collective foremothers' inheritance and using the folk medium to reach out in solidarity to other women.

The women's movement groups that were formed in the 1970s and 1980s wrote three kinds of songs. Many of the women had come from Left parties and groups. They rewrote some revolutionary songs to introduce women's issues and perspective in them. Some of these original songs were great musical compositions since the radical Indian People's Theatre Association (IPTA) had some great composers as its members. However, the music was often very militant and also tended to be in western style. Not having the trained choirs that IPTA did, women's groups and now even representatives of Communist parties find these songs difficult to render. Of the more successful attempts in this genre is Vibhuti Patel's version of a song originally dedicated to Paul Robson. Here the word *hamari* (our) along with strength, collectivity, and so on, is replaced with *nari* (woman) as a prefix so that it means women's strength, and so on. One verse is:

Unhe dar hai hamari shaktika
Unhe dar hai hamari sangathanka
Unhe dar hai hamari ekataka
Unhe dar hai hamare sangharshka
Unhe dar hai hamare viplavka

(They are afraid of our strength, our coming together, our unity, our struggle, our battle)

Family in Feminist Songs

This could be applied against patriarchal authorities as much as against other ruling classes. This author once changed a few words in the first stanza of a popular people's song keeping the same metre. The original is:

> *Ruke na jo, zuke na jo, dabe na jo, mite na jo*
> *Hum voh inqilab hain*
> *Zulmka jawab hai*
> *Har shahid, har garib ka hameen to khwab hain*

(We are freedom fighters that do not stop, do not bend or can be pressurized or destroyed.
We come in response to all repression
We are the people that the martyrs and the poor have dreamt of.)

The women's version is:

> *Ruke na jo, zuke na jo, dabe na jo, mite na jo*
> *Hum voh narivadi hain*
> *Zulmki virodhi hain*
> *Har shahid, har garib ki hameen to sathi hain.*

(We are the feminists who do not bend ...
We oppose all repression
We are the supportive friends that the martyrs and ...)

The original had a line that said that we fight so that love survives so that '*aadami ka khoon koi aadami na pi sake*'. Used metaphorically here, the words literally mean: We fight so that no man can drink another man's blood. When the metaphor was changed to say we fight so that no man can drink a woman's blood there was an uproar and the words were later changed to '*auraton ki jaan koi aadami na le sake*', that is, we fight so that no man can kill a woman.

There are some well known songs based on film lyrics and tunes. Until the *Indipop* music cropped up and gained popularity, beginning with the urban middle class youth, film songs were comparable to western pop songs in glamour and popularity. The tremendous outreach of Indian film songs and their catchy melodies were used for expression of women's messages. The problem with this genre is that the music composition has been created to arouse or express feelings and emotions that are at variance with what the new words aim at expressing. Besides that, the tunes conjure up images of romantic love songs and the hero and the heroine dancing around trees or whatever it is that they do during a certain period in film history. Can the new words override these images and be appreciated in new spirit? Can even a *lavni* dance song—a form of erotic folk dance performed traditionally by professional women dancers—with its sexual innuendos and direct attempt to please a male audience, be used for conveying women's solidarity? *Lavni*s have generally very attractive tunes and rhythm. They are written in the old folk style. The *lavni*s that have featured in films have become tremendously popular among Marathi speaking people. Some have been used for writing new women's songs. One of the best known songs from women in Shahda in Dhule district is *Ug Venubai, kashala rahte dabun dabun chala morchavari* (O' Venubai, why do you remain so suppressed? Come, join us in the *morcha*) is based on a *lavni*. However, when another such song was selected as the lyrics for a cassette of songs produced by Vacha, a Mumbai based group, two Maharashtrian women among the singers refused to render this song because a dance full of suggestive gestures was associated with it. Position on this issue needs to be clarified given the much greater outreach of the music industry and the easy access to film music, on the one hand, and the decline in the awareness of women's songs of self expression and protest, on the other. There is also a limit to the number of folk tunes available. The repetitiveness in a folk tune and the similarity among many is a limiting factor though folk tunes from different regions are used to create more melodies by women. Film songs have been rewritten as *bhajan*s and this version is pushing out great *bhakta* poets and traditional temple music from *satsang*s of different kinds. Women's groups are not likely to be out of this influence.

At times the mood of a film song matches with the spirit of a radical song. One of the best examples of this is a song by Kamla Bhasin based on the famous song *Mera joota hai Japani, yeh patallon Englishtani, sar pe lal topi Rusi phir bhi dil hai Hindustani* from the film *Shri 420* made by Raj Kapoor in the 1950s. The song features Raj Kapoor as a cheeky tramp who laughs at the establishment, and symbolises the goodness and self-respect of ordinary people. Kamla Bhasin, who is a pioneer in building a network of women's groups in South Asia, wrote the new song at the height of General Zia's dictatorship in Pakistan, in the midst of talks and preparation of war and an atmosphere of suspicion and tension on both sides. It is considered part of women's songs since peace and democracy are also women's issues. It says:

> Yeh adharmi Pakistani, Yeh hai qafir Hindustani
> Neta yun nafrat phaylaye
> Yehi unki hai shaitani
> Jungoka dar phaila karke
> Tanashah ban jate
> Dushaman aya
> Kahake fauj badhate
> Deshmein fauje mojon karti
> Aam Janata Bhookhe marti
> Neta yun nafrat phaylaye, yehi unki hai shaitani

(This is the Pakistani without a good religion, this Hindustani is a *qafir*, a non-believer
Such is the hatred spread by leaders and this their devilish way.
Creating a (false) fear that the other side is preparing for war,
They become dictators.
They say the enemies are on the way
They create bigger armies.
The armies are well looked after
While the common folks starve
Such is the hatred...)

Of the three—revolutionary songs, film songs and women's folk songs—the last perhaps is the most authentic expression of women's voice, since these are based on the legacy of women's ways of documenting their experiences and articulating protest. When based on a folk song, the new song is very well received by women from all strata of society. The music composition is a known one as is the general mood of the song. The known aspects seem to create a receptivity for the new words. As it is one folk ditty can carry many songs in folk tradition. One more is then easily accepted. Because of a common music tradition in much of north India, folk tunes of one area appeal to people from other areas as well. Bhasin has written prolifically, often choosing tunes from women's folk songs from Punjab, Rajasthan and Uttar Pradesh (UP). Her song *Tod todke bandhanoko dekho behene aati hain* has become a women's movement anthem, joyously sung by groups of women workers, teachers, students and activists in most unexpected places. Bhasin (2002) says:

> *Tod tod ke bandhanon ko*, was the first song I wrote. I remember I was conducting a South Asian workshop. We were all in Bangladesh. There was tremendous energy in our South Asian togetherness. The song just sprang out of me. I was the author of the song, but the women around me were the authors of my feelings and sentiments.
>
> *Tod tod ke*, is based on a Punjabi folk song, inherited by me from my Punjabi fore mothers. In this song the woman is complaining about her difficult life in her marital home. Even the crows there, are out to make life difficult for her. She works from morning till night, but in spite of that her husband quarrels with her during the day and during the night. Fed up of this life she threatens to leave and go to her natal home. Her final words to her husband are—'if I leave, you will sit and cry helplessly'.

> *kut kut bajra main kothe utte paani aan*
> *hai maa aange kaag uda jaange*
> *saahnu doona pawada paa jaange*
> *dine wee ladha hai*
> *raati wee ladhda hai*
> *hai maa meriya oo dine wee ladhda hai*
> *paani shareekyaan da dhonwenga*
> *peke tur gayee te bai ke rowenga*

Apna din ham manaayen is based on a UP folk song, taught to me by women living and working in the *basti*s of Kanpur, during a workshop. In this folk song, the women are venting out their anger and frustration against their male in-laws: father-in-law, brothers-in-law and husband. They are hoping to see bad things happening to these men. The protagonist in these songs says it will be wonderful to see these men cry.

That song was:

Nathaniyaan daiyya haale to bada maza aaye
nadiya kinaare sasurji ka dera
saasu ko le gaye chor
sasurwa daiyya rowe to bada maza aaye

Here the woman fantasises that the mother-in-law has been kidnapped and the father-in-law will cry in public and what fun that will be. Finding the protest potential of the song irresistible, Bhasin wrote a song that mocks not just individuals but the whole system that creates an unequal situation where men are privileged. Initially talking about the family, the song touches many issues in a holistic way. It says:

Apana din hum manaye to bada maza aaye
Use tyohar banaye to bada maza aaye

(What fun if we celebrate our own day and make it into a festival!)

It goes on to say:

Paisa camane naukariya ko jaaye
Thak kar jab ghar vapas aaye
Balam khana khilaye to bada maza aaye

(We go to our jobs earn money
And when we come home tired in the evening
How nice if the beloved man feeds us [what he has cooked]!)

What appears to be said in jest, for instance, when it says what fun if the beloved man also observes the *karva chouth* and fills the parting in his hair with *kumkum*, finally turns into legitimate demands and dreams of a better and just world. Then step by step the song talks of the daughter also getting her share in the family property and there being a world where there are no impediments to a daughter's right to live or her development, and they grow and bloom. The continuity in all this is the repetition of the words *sang sakhiyan*—together with my women friends—in almost every verse and each has one dream woven into it. This song arouses mirth even among women who seriously and devotedly observe *karva chouth* and other comparable fasts meant for a long life for the husband, longer than her own. It inspires women who have not heard of Women's Day. The singer and the listener share the longings and dreams. Since the lines are rendered and repeated in many folk songs, the listeners become participants.

Used during training for trainers (TOTs) and other training programmes by Jagori and other women's groups, Bhasin's songs have become well known in various parts of the Hindi belt in the country. Booklets of songs published by Jagori contain her songs for all occasions ranging from lullabies for the girl child to a critique of globalisation, arousing joy or tears depending on the content.

In Gujarat, songs by Sarup Dhruv, Meenal Patel and Vibhuti Patel have become new folk songs for many women. Meenal Patel and Vibhuti Patel also write songs in Hindi. Many of their songs are produced in the form of cassettes by Vacha, a Mumbai based women's group. One of Meenal Patel's new version of old songs in which a woman tells her husband *Sahyaba hunre trambani hele paaninda nahin bharun* is one of the most popular songs in gender training programmes. In the original song, a woman says she will not fetch water in a copper pot. She longs for a silver pot. She longs for a joint family so that she can cover her face in presence of male elders, and is required to speak softly and touch her mother-in-law's feet. The new version is:

Sahyaba ekali hun vaitaru nahin karun
Sahyaba mune sarakhapanani ghani haam re sahyaba!
Sahyaba munthi jagna samachar vegala
Sahyaba mane chhapa vanchyani ghani haam re sahyaba!

(My dear, I shall not tackle the daily chores/drudgery alone
My dear, I long for equal sharing, yes, I do my dear.
My dear, I feel too far away from what is happening in the world
My dear, I long to read newspapers, yes, I do my dear.)

Family in Feminist Songs

Sahyaba is from the word *Saheb* meaning master or lord but *Sahyaba* in Gujarati and Konkani is used colloquially to mean lover/beloved husband.

From a dream of an idealised joint family life in an idyllic setting talked about in the original song, Meenal Patel creates the reality of women's felt needs and demands in modern nuclear families.

Vibhuti Patel has written a *garba* on the significance of *garba* in a mother–daughter relationship.

Naani dikari mane poochhe, 'garabo kyaanthi aavyo jee'.
Maa boli, 'garabani paachhal moto maram chhupayo jee,
Dharati Maata dhaan ugade; Maa baalakne poshe jee
Garabo gaataa kehti beno vaato honshe honshe jee'.

(A young daughter asked her mother, 'where has the *garba* come from?'
The mother said, 'There is much significance underlying the *garba*,
Mother earth gives us grain; a mother gives nutrition to the child
Women sing and happily share their stories through their *garba*s.)

The first new *garba* that stunned everybody was Sarup Dhruv's song written in the 1980s. Women activists grabbed it as their own.

Sarkhi saheli ame saath saath ghumashun sheriman saad kari kahishun re lol
Ketala jamanaathi vethi chhe vedana, aavado julam nahin sahishun re lol.

(We women friends will move together and cry out in the streets:
For so many generations have we borne the pain,
No longer shall we tolerate such oppression.)

By the beginning of the 1980s, Sarup Dhruv was in the process of acquiring critical acclaim from the Gujarati literary establishment that no woman poet had received. However, she chose to drop out of the mainstream and became a people's poet. During a certain phase in her writing she created *garba*s that have now become classics. *Sarkhi saheli* now has verses added by other women as they sing along and Dhruv welcomes this without claiming ownership and copyright to her song. 'Copyright is right to copy!', says Kamla Bhasin jokingly but sincerely, in reference to the use of her songs by the women's movement groups.

The powerful voice of Shubha Mudgal can be heard in the album *Manke Manjire* but no one can hope to imitate her song. A new all women pop group has also come up with interesting themes in their songs. These songs can be heard and enjoyed and they are valuable from that point of view. Meenal Patel now writes songs that are meant for individual rendering, for example, her Hindi song:

Maine sapana suhana ek dekha
Mujhe baandh sake na koi rekha.

(I saw a beautiful dream in which no boundary could hold me back.)

However, this is still a collective 'I' as also in Vibhuti Patel's *Sati* song in which a woman gives witty but firm answers to patriarchal powers like the family head, the *pandit*, the trader and the politician that want her to commit sati. *Mein achhi hoon Ghabarau nako, aisa khatmein likho* (Write in the letter that I am fine), a song written by Shahnaz Sheikh and Geeta Mahajan in a type of Urdu spoken by rural Muslim women in Maharashtra and set in folk rhythm, is in the form of an illiterate woman asking someone to write to her husband who is employed in a gulf country. The bitter humour directed against the man who tries to control her life from long distance and the narration of her reality here is representative of the experience of many poor women whose husbands are abroad. These women have the responsibility of managing the family home and fields without any important decision-making powers.

BEYOND FAMILY RELATIONSHIPS AND FEMINIST SONGS

What makes these openly feminist songs so popular among women? What makes various powerful agencies of the establishment ignore and even sometimes support these songs? One obvious reason why women love them could be that we still have a live tradition of singing which is not professionalised and commercialised. The new women's songs fit into it. Poor women may be deprived of formal schooling and literacy but they have as much love for poetry and music as anyone else. They enjoy feminist songs that come to them as folk songs with new content. But possibly the fact that this content is not entirely new also makes them more receptive to them. The new song is put in the musical forms that were in any case used for more traditional messages. The messages in old songs also contained articulation of pain and dreams of emancipation but the creative expression had only a cathartic value. It might have made the oppression tolerable and helped women survive emotionally. The new songs are part of a political struggle to change gender equations in the family as well as outside and to create a fair and just society for all. They may be spontaneously created but the spontaneity is within a certain worldview or a range of worldviews. The new paradigms are not concealed from women recipients of the new music. They are put across in a variety of ways using several mediums including sharing and discussions.

Apparently something very important happens when women who observe *karva chouth* laugh when that very festival is made fun of. Unlike zealous reformers, these song writers and others who sing and pass them on do not ask women to give up various superfluous symbols of patriarchal power. They merely share a different view of what these symbols stand for. They do not maintain that throwing off *mangalsutra*s and non-observance of fasts will usher in a revolution. They do not treat women as objects or followers to preach to but as sisters and friends with common problems, goals, hopes and desires. It is possible that the enthusiastic welcome that the songs receive has roots in this aspect of the songs.

Yet another reason for the popularity may be that women can add to the feminist songs as they wish. Often the new songs arouse the original creativity of women. *Beti hoon mein beti mein tara banoongi. Tara banoongi mein sahar banoongi* (I am a daughter, that I am; I shall shine like a star. I shall be a star and also a strong pillar of support) is a song that has emerged from workshops with rural women in Bihar. *Chet sake to chet jamano aayo chetanko* (Beware, the times are such that we have to careful of them) is a powerful song of awareness that was created by women in Rajasthan. Here women talk of having to unite and find remunerative work, otherwise the children would starve.

In the new songs, family relationships are viewed with a new perspective. In Vibhuti Patel's song about the origin of *garba* featuring a mother and her daughter, a daughter seeks knowledge from the mother instead of both of them helplessly experiencing pain as in earlier songs when they meet at a well or a lakeside. In *Apna din hum manaye* and the *sahyaba* songs, the issue of the husband sharing housework comes up whereas the earlier complaints usually used to be against the mother-in-law. The picture that emerges in many songs is that of a nuclear family whereas in the earlier songs the complaints were often against the mother-in-law. Oppressive situations in a nuclear family have rarely been confronted in folk songs even though joint families had begun to break up in some way or the other for decades. Even songs created in rural areas now rarely mention the mother-in-law and brother-in-law.

Songs of the women's movement are part of a large scale and relatively silent revolution that is taking place to change the present gender equation. Development projects, women's empowerment programmes, activities of women's movement groups and their networking, introduction of women's studies courses in colleges, gender training of police and other government personnel, and 33 per cent reservation for women at the panchayat and municipal level are some of the other elements supporting the new and far reaching changes.

Feminist songs have been broadcast on radio and television. They have been published in women's journals and sung when government officers are present. It is not a secret that women sing *tod tod ke bandhanoko* or *sarkhi saheli* thinking of their liberation. Women farmers continue singing the new *sahyaba* song even after they return home from training programmes at their credit societies. How is it that the songs escape criticism when women's liberation or feminism is otherwise a target of hostility? How is it that the male *sarpanch*s and caste panchayats have not declared a fatwa against them? It cannot be that they do not take women seriously, not when women are already making their presence felt through panchayats and development projects. This is where one feels that 'benign negligence' or 'tolerance' is due to the space women had originally created for expression through their protest and subversive songs. They have proved that women will sing and continue singing in protest; that they will sing joyfully and in pain; and that they will make complaints and raise issues. The women's movement is expanding that creative space and also adding new dimensions to the work initiated by their foremothers, together with women from different sections of society.

NOTE

1. A rough translation of Gujarati and Hindi songs is provided by the presenter.

SELECTED BACKGROUND READING, OTHER RESOURCES AND INTERACTION

Bhasin, Kamla. Personal letter (1 October 2002).
Jagori. 2001. *Aao Milzul Gaayen* (Hindi). Delhi: Jagori.
Joravarsinha, Jadav. (ed.). 1975. *Lokjeevannan Moti* (Gujarati). Ahmedabad: Gujarat Rajya Loksahitya Samiti.
Kamgar-Karmachari Parishad. 1978. *Juni va Navi sphoortigeete* (Marathi). Mumbai: Kamgar-Karmachari Parishad Prakashan.
Mehta, Rajul. Discussions on women's folk songs, interactions for training and recording.
Nari Kendra. 1988. *Agni phoolanchi Gaani* (Marathi). Mumbai: Nari Kendra.
Patel, Meenal. Try-outs in metre and flow of folk songs, discussion of sentiments expressed.
Shukla, Sonal. 1987. 'A Women's Festival Hijacked—the Gujarati Navaratri', *Manushi*, 34: 10–13.
Vacha Women's Resource Centre. 2001. *Geet Vacha*. Mumbai: Vacha Women's Resource Centre.
Zaverchand, Meghani. 1973. *Radhiali Raat* (Gujarati). Ahmedabad: Gurjar Prakashan.

5

Resurrecting the Mother in *Mata Hidimba*

―――――•◆•―――――

Uma Narain

Theatre's recent dalliance with characters from the *Mahabharata* is an interesting phenomenon in terms of a subversive reading of the popular myths. *Mahabharata* is a tale of timeless distillation. It offers us the closest mythological reflection of our own times. Every possible human situation can be found in this text and 'what is not in the Mahabharata is nowhere'. The characters are so eternally alive as if they are members of any family today. Also, the epic makes no attempt to idealise its characters and does not hide anybody's faults. No wonder playwrights return to this plot time and again to contextualise the chronic social patterns of 'family'. Much has already been said about the major characters of *Mahabharata* but Chetan Datar[1] in his recent play *Mata Hidimba* turns the focus on the hitherto invisible character of Hidimba, and brings out issues of motherhood intertwined with those of race, caste and religion and affords a terrain for the overarching patriarchal play of power within the family. Chetan Datar's treatment of the female protagonists in this play highlights the 'family' as the locus of exploitation and oppression and attempts to address it in a manner that is at once transforming and liberating.

The play refers to an early episode in the *Mahabharata* where the Kauravas attempt to decimate their cousins, the Pandavas, by encindering them in a combustible palace. Sensing foul play, the

Resurrecting the Mother in Mata Hidimba

Pandavas foil the plan; trick Kauravas into believing that they are dead; and escape to the forest with their mother Kunti. One day during a night halt, they arrive on the territory of the *rakshasa* Hidimb. While Bhima goes to fetch water, he is challenged by Hidimb for trespass. A fight ensues in which Hidimb dies but, ironically, his sister Hidimba who had watched the combat falls in love with valiant Bhima. The story of their love and marriage, the birth of their son Ghatotkach (the firstborn of Pandavas) and the subsequent claims of 'family' form the plot of the play.

Chetan conceptualises this play as a dance-drama—a style that opens up various threads of interpretation. The two classical art forms, dance and drama, are the heirs of this style. Dance is a kinaesthetic art—its appreciation is grounded in the entire body of the performer and the relationship of the performer to the performance space. Julia Kristeva's (1984) *Revolution in Poetic Language* sets forth a theory of representation—a semiotics of art that provides an excellent framework to analyse the feminist angle of this play. Since the body of the performer also constitutes a text in a performance, the Brechtian convention of 'gestus'[2] employed by the dancer playing Hidimba is a powerful way to re-inscribe the epic from a feminist point of view.

Drama is both literature and theatre, and the narrative is constructed through parallels, contrasts and binary opposites. For deconstructing a popular legend, the playwright can invent scenes, confront characters who have not met in the original story and allow them to plumb their own depths and reach at their private selves. The world of this great epic can thus be reconstructed and contemporised by the collective dynamics of theatre and dance.

Thus, the performance of the play is a statement by itself and can be employed to decipher and understand the dynamics of 'family' beyond the written text.

On a bare stage with just a red panel on the back wall, the play opens with a narrator who engages the audience in a dialogue about man's favourite preoccupation—*war*. 'What are the most potent weapons of war?' he asks. Not bombs or bullets or AK47, but young men in the age group of 14–24, fed on hollow ideology, anger and hatred as was Hidimba's son Ghatotkach. But the play is not about the son, it is about the mother and the family structure that perpetrates and directs the outcome in the play. Then appears Hidimba in an energetic dance movement and we are informed that she is a non-Aryan born in a *rakshasa* family; she despises the divide between Aryans and non-Aryans; and is 'violent yet refreshing like a waterfall, wilful yet a woman of mind and intellect'. She and her brother Hidimb reign the forest where one day the Pandava brothers arrive along with their mother Kunti. Taking them to be trespassers, Hidimb challenges Bhima to a fight and gets killed by him. At this point his sister Hidimba falls in love with his killer. During the romance, Bhima tells her that he cannot marry her unless his mother Kunti agrees to the match and Hidimba readily agrees to plead her case.

What takes place now is a highly dramatic scene of power-play between Kunti and Hidimba that can easily be identified in any contemporary matrimonial negotiation where the caste and status of the two parties is not compatible. Kunti obviously is averse to her son marrying a *rakshasi* woman. The ensuing dialogue is a gradual build-up of a power dynamics where Hidimba surprises us by matching Kunti blow by blow with uncanny deftness—a stance any modern woman would envy. The senior woman is clever in setting the context for this negotiation—'What is the objective behind this marriage proposal?'

- To sanctify her honour by marrying the victor. (Hidimba is Bhima's 'captive'. By defeating her brother, the sister becomes his prisoner-of-war and in such cases, the rights of the victor over the 'spoils' are absolute.)
- To appeal to their mercy as an 'orphan' in order to find shelter (with the brother dead, there is no one else to take care of her).

In both cases, little help is possible as the Pandavas are nomads themselves. Then she reminds Bhima of his princely commitments and duties—an assault has just been made on their lives. This is not the time for the indulgence of marriage and domestic bliss. These are troubled times, they have a crisis at hand and Bhima ought to direct his undivided energy for the imminent war with the Kauravas.

It is a reminder of familial obligations that is at once understood by Bhima but not Hidimba. She sees it as an unnecessary deflection and tells Kunti that she is neither saving her 'honour' nor seeking protection. She can look after herself as she comes from a matrilineal society and stands to inherit the entire forest. If Pandavas are wanderers, she can adjust with them as well since she is not averse to a hard life. Here, her body language is enough to convince the audience that it is so. Also, she loves Bhima enough to not come in the way of his family obligations. Kunti then throws doubt at the sincerity of love and romance of the young—unstable and short-lived like the rains. Besides, matrilineal societies require the husband to move to the abode of the wife and Bhima would never leave the Pandava household. Hidimba does a little arm-twisting by telling Kunti that if she were to accompany them unwed, the Pandava honour would be highly compromised! The matter is referred to Yudhishthir, the eldest Pandava (the 'family' structure), who agrees to the marriage on the condition that Bhima would return home every evening to serve their mother and once a child (a Pandava heir) is born to the couple, he would relinquish his wife forever. Nothing could be more outrageous than the appropriation of a wife's conjugal rights! Hidimba concedes to this unreasonable demand for now as she has other plans for the future. But Bhima has cold feet and succumbs to the patriarchal pressure and changes his mind about marrying Hidimba; maybe this is not an opportune time. What shocks Hidimba is Bhima's lack of protective instincts towards her. If he cannot be relied upon to support her now, what hope can she pin on him later in marriage? At the same time she feels committed to him because she loves him. It is again a typical dilemma of choice that Hidimba handles like any contemporary woman. She tells Bhima:

> **Hidimba** (squatting)[3]: By renouncing me you wish to show your right over me. But to love is my exclusive right—I loved you at first sight. Now if you deny me, I am surely not going to end my life for I have glimpsed love in your eyes. I will bide my time and wait till you discharge your family obligations. I will patiently wait.[4]

This is how Hidimba responds to an attitude typical of the Pandavas—the true progenitors of India's patriarchal society—regarding a girl of inferior race. It is well known that the lives of women in the *Mahabharata* have entirely been in the hands of others: 'men act, men direct and women suffer' (Karve 1991). It is what follows that is remarkable. Hidimba and Bhima marry; as agreed, Bhima returns to the Pandavas every evening but as soon as Hidimba conceives Ghatotkach, she turns the tables on him by renouncing him for ever. She denies him the right to meet his child and frees him from the responsibility of its up-bringing.

> **Hidimba**: Bhim Sen, I was even ready to give up my kingdom and come to you but you trapped me in your conditions. I thought my love could transform you—but you could never forget those conditions. If you think you can send me away once the child is born, I pre-empt this by asking you to leave now. I do not need you to bring forth this child into the world. I am capable of rearing him on my own (*Mata Hidimba*, Act 1).

Here, I see Hidimba as a woman in repossession of her body as a mother. She breaks free from the general patriarchal marginalisation of motherhood that treats the female form as a territory to be exploited and a machine producing life. She is what Mary Wollstonecraft (1999: 70) was to applaud as 'few extraordinary women ... male spirits confined by mistake in female frames'.

The story of Kunti who also brings up her sons as a single mother contrasts with that of Hidimba. Iravati Karve (1991) sees Kunti as the driving force behind the crucial events in the *Mahabharata* and links her scarred adolescence to events in her brief married life and the long years of widowhood. First, she is given up for adoption to a close friend of her father, who is childless and needs a daughter to play hostess to sage Durvasa during a religious ritual. The sage is pleased with Kunti and gives her an unusual gift—a *mantra* which can summon any god to beget a child. Curiosity makes the young girl test the gift and she becomes an unwed mother of a son. Kunti has to give away her son, as under patriarchy there is no sanction for a child outside the confines of the institution of marriage. Later, she gets married to Prince Pandu who is impotent and yet desires heirs. Using sage Durvasa's mantra once again, Kunti obliges by bearing for her husband three sons and facilitating Pandu's second wife to bear two (together, the five Pandavas). Patriarchy once again controls her sexuality and appropriates her reproductive function into an essentialised motherhood. When her husband dies, she is left with the task of bringing up the five sons as a single mother but with a difference. She is not independent and must co-exist with the Kauravas in the patriarchal joint household. It is a tough alternative because the Pandavas not only have to put up with the sibling rivalry of the Kauravas but also one day wrest their right in the kingdom from the same cousins. Kunti also knows that she needs to keep her sons united and well trained for the inevitable war of succession.

Hidimba, on the other hand, has had a wholesome childhood and adolescence in the matrilineal, eco-friendly ambience of the forest. She is strong and confident—marries for love and possesses the courage to bring up Ghatotkach on her own. She does not compromise her self-respect when she finds that the man she loves is so tied to patriarchy that he cannot be relied upon to share parental responsibility. Kunti, on the other hand, may have suffered at the hands of patriarchy as a young woman but for Hidimba, she becomes a part of the same oppressive power structure. As a mother-in-law, she perpetrates the control of Hidimba's sexuality and does nothing to check the politics of power. Here, she only wants a son from Hidimba so that the hands of the Pandavas may be strengthened in the eventual war with the Kaurava cousins. She might have allowed their romance initially, but in reality she is not likely to give any 'space' to Hidimba in marriage. Feminists would agree that the reproduction of subordination by the older women is a well-known tool of exploitation for their younger counterparts. By bringing the two mothers as binary opposites, the playwright locates Hidimba as a stronger woman of the two and a radical feminist who goes on to bring up Ghatotkach as a 'single parent'. Kunti stands for motherhood with its connotations of power and autocracy; Hidimba for autonomy and motherliness.

ASSERTION OF PATRIARCHAL FORCES

The second act opens with the narrator informing the audience that the Pandavas have been collectively married to Draupadi at the behest of Kunti. It is not a mistake; Kunti has strategically done this to weld her own and Pandu's second wife's sons into an unbreakable whole for the inevitable war with the Kauravas (Karve 1991). Ghatotkach, meanwhile, has grown into a strong young man. Curious to meet his father, he pesters Hidimba to take him to the capital of the Pandavas. The indulgent mother complies on the condition that after meeting Bhima, Ghatotkach would return with her to the forest for good. But patriarchy has already woven an imperialistic design for Ghatotkach and 'chance' obliges. While taming a wild elephant, Ghatotkach is spotted by Krishna. Like Kunti, he can foresee that the Pandavas would need brave allies in the war. So he approaches Hidimba and reminds her that Ghatotkach as the eldest Pandava son owes an obligation to his paternal family. Accordingly, he should start receiving military training in preparation for the war. Hidimba understands the patriarchal trick but Ghatotkach, the young enthusiast (as already mentioned by the narrator in the beginning) is soon won over. Ghatotkach is claimed by the patriarchal family and dispatched to Dronacharya, the erstwhile teacher and now the general of the army, for training. It is a highly dramatic scene that at once brings to mind a terrorist camp today.

In the play, the actress playing Hidimba doubles up for Drona; and the two characters form a triangle with Ghatotkach in the centre against a red panel (suggesting violence and bloodshed). The triangular blocking of actors on the stage represents the conflicting stance of state (patriarchy), motherhood (matriarchy) and the youth (the tool of war and the victim). When Hidimba dominates the argument, she moves to the central red panel with faster dance steps to the rising tempo of drum-beats. The choreography and scene construction highlight her agitation further. The transformation of the same actor into Hidimba and Dronacharya is a powerful theatrical device, linking the producer, nurturer and trainer roles. One of the chief concerns of feminism has been to deconstruct gender assumptions in general and theatre in particular. Theatre had been a male bastion right up to the 17th century. Since women were not supposed to act, the female roles were performed by male actors. In fact the test of good acting used to be how well an actor played a woman's role. In *Mata Hidimba*, when the actress playing Hidimba unsexes herself and also plays Drona, the teacher warrior, the reverse cross-gendering becomes a critique of the arbitrary construction of gender in society. It is important to convey the feminist perspective in cultural

Resurrecting the Mother in Mata Hidimba

discourse in order to change the way society thinks not only about gender but also about sexuality, race and class. The following parts are alternately played by the same actress—as Drona, she is ruthless and harsh; as Hidimba, she is gentle and kind.

> **Drona:** Ghatotkach! Remember three things—soldier, bravery and war. We are always just and ethical. Every opponent is an enemy to be vanquished. No one is related to you. Kill! Revenge! Kill and the world is yours.
> **Hidimba**: Son! Remember that we along with plants, animals, the river-water, air and sky are all part of the same ecological system. We are the children of Mother Nature. When forced to kill a man-eater lioness, do not forget that you kill a mother.
> **Drona**: Listen carefully! Bring utmost cruelty to mind when you hold the weapon. Concentrate and go for the kill.
> **Hidimba**: Son! Kill only when hungry. Never strike a scared or wounded animal. When you mount the weapon, be most serene (*Mata Hidimba*, Act II).

Clearly, the two approaches of Dronacharya and Hidimba echo the concerns of humanity on the brink of any war. The 'masculine' principle of patriarchy favours war, the 'feminine' principle of motherhood desires peace. One destroys, the other nourishes. The essential 'male' identity is based on an all pervasive violence fashioned out of political expediency. Its rhetoric of power is so familiar and finds resonance every time a superpower threatens a small nation. The 'feminine' approach, on the other hand, is rooted in the eco-friendly motif of 'motherhood'—it is caring, nurturing, emotional, and linked to the cosmic order and believes in peaceful co-existence. In the play, when the actress plays Hidimba and Dronacharya together, the playwright perhaps hints at an integrated approach—a message that life should imitate art. Confronted by the opposing forces of patriarchal power and matriarchal gentleness, Ghatotkach is naturally confused. The lure of power is tempting as it is newly found, yet something withholds him. But obviously power is mightier—the young boy is dispatched for rigorous military training as the scene ends.

The last scene takes place on the battlefield of Kurukshetra. The war is at its peak—warriors are dying on both sides and the Pandava camp is tense. Ghatotkach, meanwhile, has completed his military training. Now is the time for Krishna and Arjuna to approach him for the final sacrifice. Surprisingly, it is not Bhima who asks his son for participation in the war but Krishna who reminds Ghatotkach of his paternal debt. The boy's internal conflict is still unresolved. He barely listens to Krishna's argument; he already has a premonition of his end. His heart pines for his mother whose warnings he now understands. But the trap of patriarchy is laid; Ghatotkach cannot get out of it without repaying the debt of birth with his life. The dancer enacts a cosmic world turned upside down; the smell and sounds of the animal world pervade the living world, foretelling death and destruction. Hidimba too senses this omen but she can do nothing at this point. She might have withstood the injustices of the Pandava household all her life but through her son, they finally win.

The all too familiar strategy of the Abhimanyu plot[5] is replayed except that Abhimanyu's 'chakravyuha' was a military configuration whereas Ghatotkach is caught in the 'chakravyuha' of arguments of selfish elders who do not hesitate to commit the sons to war. Ghatotkach is sent to confront the great archer Karna in the battle. Filled with the battle cry, the young boy's arrogant challenges so enrage Karna that in a fit of rage, he uses the rare weapon on Ghatotkach that he had all along saved for Arjuna. Ghatotkach's death fulfilling the Pandava's purpose and Krishna's soliloquy rejoicing his death, form the crux of the play.

The play shows Krishna as an imperialist. He is not the 'god' of our collective consciousness remembered for childhood pranks or the exotic lover of Radha or the great preacher of *Bhagavad Gita*. He comes across as a shrewd statesman, using his diplomacy to uphold the patriarchal might of the Pandavas as superior Aryans—a diplomacy that neither protects nor gives 'space' for the rights of individuals and the minority.

> **Krishna:** Though Ghatotkach was the eldest Pandava son, he was a non-Aryan like Jarasandh—and all those who oppose the brahmins and threaten religion, must be killed by me. So if Karna had not killed him today, I was bound to finish him off one day. Religion demands it (*Mata Hidimba,* Act II).

This speech of Krishna comes as a shock and reveals how close the manipulations and connivance done in the name of strategy border on fundamentalism and racism—a sentiment that finds multiple followers all over the world today. The play needs to be applauded for this new slant.

Hidimba's lament, fraught with hurt and loss, closes the play. In Ghatotkach, she has lost a son and a friend while his so-called brave father Bhima still lives. Fie on him! A patriarch who uses his young son for the greed of power is no husband to her. Bhima is finally renounced as a husband. The play brings out another irony of fate. Ghatotkach, the firstborn of the Pandavas is killed by the eldest Pandava, that is, Karna, Kunti's illegitimate son. The playwright has juxtaposed Karna and Ghatotkach to bring out a buried discourse of the Pandava family. Ghatotkach, though brought up in the matrilineal tradition, still belongs to the patriarchal order for he was born within the confines of the family. Karna, on the other hand, was not only abandoned by Kunti at birth but also born outside the sanctity of marriage and thus marked for life (Krishnan 1990). Karna never forgave his mother for abandoning him at birth and for consigning him to a life of shame as a man of no parentage. Ghatotkach, on the other hand, always adored his mother for bringing him up as a single mother. He gave the status of 'father' to his mother by desiring to be buried by her—a right that the thesis of the play upholds.

GENDER IN PERFORMANCE

Mata Hidimba made an enormous impact in performance because of the powerful portrayal of Hidimba by Rajshri Shirke, a dancer par excellence. Her choreography offers the spectators a new kind of meaning and demands from them a new way of seeing the story of the 'feminist' Hidimba. Feminist theorists of dance and drama consider the 'body' of the performer as the text of the performance and also the ground of perception. In dance, the communication between the spectator and the performer is not just a simple transfer of meaning through representation of images. It is a process of communication, which consists of two inseparable and simultaneous realms: the symbolic and the semiotic. At the symbolic level, the words of the play operate in a way that is linear, logical and syntactical; on the semiotic level, meaning is imprecise, fluid and underground, yet it is communicated more powerfully. In dance, the meaning is derived by both the symbolic and the semiotic practices but the subversive element occurs when a performer is able to rupture the symbolic by the semiotic—that is, a performance capable of bringing about new social relations. This is the 'revolution' which Julia Kristeva refers to in the title of her book, *Revolution in Poetic Language* (1984). A revolutionary performance need not be obviously political but it demands a new way of perception on the part of the spectator. *Mata Hidimba* is a triumph in this regard.

At the semiotic level, Rajshri Shirke performed Hidimba not as a delicate nymph but with the 'goodness of the whole body', depicting the abundant figure of motherhood. For feminists, the 'goodness of the whole body' is as much a part of the women's movement as the demand for voting rights. Her dance is not an external objectification of the body; it is a form of a woman conscious of motherhood and empowerment. She dances with her whole body and not with chest or pelvic movements. Her portrayal of Hidimba's persona becomes a signifier, signifying an empowered 'mother of us all' confidence. The performer's body and its meaning as well as the nature of display changes the power equation. Even in the scene where Hidimba woos Bhima, there is no sexual display or any attempt at seduction. Shirke's Hidimba is not intimidated by powerful men, be they the Pandavas or Krishna, or by Kunti or by the difficult choices in her life. Her decisions entailing hardships do not deter her. She lives her life on her own terms with strength and commitment. She could easily use her son to get even with the Pandavas but her bringing up of Ghatotkach has no selfish agenda. Such awareness at the personal level is a necessary element of social change. And this performance is not merely reflective of social change but productive of social change. Hidimba's final comment on Bhima and all the Pandavas makes the audience think—think really hard.

Another concept related to this performance and to feminist theatre is that propounded by the German playwright Bertolt Brecht. Women writers have often conjoined socialist and feminist politics by using the Brechtian style of dramaturgy that works for social

Resurrecting the Mother in Mata Hidimba

change by creating a historical allegory for contemporary issues and events, and by using the convention of 'gestus'. Brechtian convention of 'gestus' refers to a singular, symbolic gesture associated with a character that controls and articulates the audience's relation to the actor-as-character. For Brecht, 'gest' 'is not supposed to mean gesticulation: it is not a matter of explanatory or emphatic movements of the hand, but of overall attitude—it is an artistic principle. The social gest is the gest relevant to society, the gest that allows conclusions to be drawn about social circumstances. It is the social gest that breathes humanity into it' (Willett 1964: 104). In this play, Rajshri Shirke's portrayal of Hidimba as a self-possessed and confident woman becomes a 'gest' that succeeds in reclaiming the story of *Mahabharata* from a woman's point of view. She externalises the emotions of Hidimba and develops them into a gesture that tells the audience what is going on inside her. In this way, Rajshri's performance becomes a discussion with the audience about social conditions and a feminist transformation of her situation against the repressive social environment of patriarchy. The scenes of Hidimba with Kunti, Dronacharya and Krishna show her empowerment in the private and public arenas. She is equally at home in public space, challenging the opposition of private and public domains.

Written by a male playwright, *Mata Hidimba* is an exemplary feminist play that resurrects the image of motherhood from the story of the *Mahabharata*. While the feminist theatre emerged as a cultural form out of the women's movement of the 1960s and the 1970s, many women playwrights and directors today resist the title 'feminist' for fear of narrowing their audience. What is encouraging is that more feminist statements are being made by male playwrights. Chetan Datar deserves full credit for his script and production that places Hidimba in the subject position to deconstruct, negotiate, transform and re-inscribe patriarchy.

NOTES

1. Chetan Datar is a well known Marathi playwright of Mumbai whose theatre technique is firmly grounded in traditional Indian dramaturgy. Four of his plays are inspired by the great Indian epic—the *Mahabharata*—with strong feminist angles: *Shyam Sakhi* (on the unique relationship between the dynamic Krishna

and the intense Draupadi); *Dvanda* (on gender issues of two individuals—one soul of Amba and Shikhandi); *Niputi Mata* (on Karna and Kunti separated by destiny) and the recent play *Mata Hidimba* (on the single mother figure of Hidimba). Chetan has 25 plays to his credit. He is also an actor and a director.
2. A gesture of the performer that is identified as a signature of the character being portrayed.
3. Squatting is a powerful dramatic posture on the stage suggestive of a protest, a kind of 'dharna' (sit-on).
4. The manuscript of the play *Mata Hidimba*, Act I (translation is mine).
5. Abhimanyu is Arjuna's son who is ruthlessly used by the Pandava elders in the Great War. He is dispatched to break the unique military configuration but is trapped and killed by the enemies (the Kauravas).

REFERENCES

Karve, Iravati. 1991. *Yugant*. Hyderabad: Disha Books.
Krishnan, Prabha. 1990. 'In the Idiom of Loss: Ideology of Motherhood in Television Serials', *Economic and Political Weekly*, 25(42–43): 103–115.
Kristeva, Julia. 1984. *Revolution in Poetic Language*, (trans) Margaret Waller. New York: Columbia University.
Willet, John (trans). 1964. *Brecht on Theatre*. New York: Hill and Wang.
Wollstonecraft, Mary. 1999. *A Vindication of the Rigths of Women*. New York: Bartleby.com.

SECTION III

Seeking Justice

6

Sustaining Democracy within the Family through Family Courts
An Exploratory Analysis

———•◆•———

Sita Vanka and M. Nirmala Kumari

The *family* is an institution much discussed and much worried over. The press, television, religious institutions, doctors, lawyers, politicians and the general public often engage in debate and discussion around issues related to the family. Although it is considered to be a personal and private institution, it has clearly emerged as an institution with a high public profile and one in which everyone is presumed to participate (Leonard and Williams 1988) to the extent of society getting 'familialised'.

FAMILY—VARIOUS VIEWS

Theoretical perspectives view the family from a variety of angles and have added different dimensions to it. It is often said that the family, in some form, was the first society. Family is a primary social group consisting of parents and their offspring, the principal functions of which is provision for its members (Hankspatrick Collins Dictionary 1988), more so in the nature of a 'unity of interacting personalities' (Burgess cited in Goode 1989). The term 'family' is used in a variety of connotations. While botany and zoology use 'family' for categorising organisms, in common usage it includes ancestors (as in a 'family tree'). Colloquially, it is used to denote a common household, though consisting of related people. Whatever ambiguity the term carries, the general consensus sees the 'family as an institution pertaining to marriage, birth and raising of children and household of related persons' (Encyclopedia Americana 1976). Studies have highlighted the family as a process (MacIver and Page 1985), as representing an active principle (Morgan cited in Goode 1989), as a dynamic changing phenomenon (Engels 1978) and as a continuing and basic primary group (Hunt 1972) to bring out its sociological significance. The family is where we learn to be human and to be citizens (Cott 2005). This claim underpins Cott's (ibid.) argument that gender disparities in the family must be eliminated, if society is to be characterised by democratic justice. This idea that democratic citizenship is rooted in family characteristics—that as the family is, so the citizens and, therefore, the sovereign will be—often crops up in the commentary on American society and government. This conviction that the most reasonable and humane qualities of mankind arose in social interaction rather than in isolation, set the stage for American republicans to see the family, and particularly the marital relation between a man and a woman, as training grounds for citizenly virtue.

Indian views on the family vary from viewing it as an 'extended family of relatives' (Panikkar 1984) to regarding the whole humanity as one family and a 'god ordained institution' (Gandhi 1978). These views can be traced to the earliest moral and ethical writings of many cultures, including the ancient Indian cultures, which assert the significance of family. Confucius thought, the Old Testament, the codified literature in India—for instance, the Rig Veda and the Laws of Manu—bring out the cultural importance of the family (Tuvuchis and Goode 1973). Social analysts and philosophers offered new familial roles for traditional social problems. Plato's *Republic* was one such attempt. Anthropological evidence, too, offers evidence of the family forming a major part of the social structure (Goode 1989). These sources reveal relations among family members and also relations between family and the society at large. Thus the significance of the family is evident from the earliest moral and ethical writings to sociological, philosophical and anthropological sources. However, relatively very little empirical research has been conducted (Leonard and Williams 1988) to support the theoretical concerns. The field of the 'family' has attracted the attention of scholars (sociologists in particular) in a systematic way. They have linked the empirical findings related to the family to the complexities of industrialisation, and economic, political and social changes all over the world (Goode 1989). Earlier stray attempts, however, built material in the form of disjointed empirical propositions about the family (Goode, Hopkins and McClure cited in Goode 1989). It was also considered a low-status area of study as the assertions were based more on stereotypes and informal experience than systematic study, and thus remained untouched by the developments in other areas of sociology (Leonard and Williams 1988). It becomes imperative, therefore, to examine and analyse this 'inevitable' institution for theoretical sophistication and methodological soundness.

Contemporary writing on family studies is more prone towards picking up influences from a wide range of writings and shows much less interest in 'grand theory and total systems' (Gittins 1985). Evidence of stability and continuance no more hit the headlines. Indications of instability, neglect of family responsibilities and climbing divorce rates (Allan 1985), all leading to a 'medicalisation' of the family, have become common (Morgan cited in Goode 1989). Moreover, the emphasis on family privacy is encouraging men and women to advance individual liberty claims, which may neglect differential power among family members, thus, creating conflicts between the goals of freedom and equality (Cott 2005). Therefore, the 'problem family' has not only influenced the current writings but also brought together a number of state agencies to rethink on the issue and initiate policy measures to check the disturbing trends and apply correctives at the appropriate time. The declaration of 1994 as the International Year of the Family by the United Nations has been a step in this direction.

India is no exception to this worldwide trend. The post-liberalised era with its accompanying effects has disturbed the otherwise peaceful family system. A host of factors have contributed to the present situation in India, which not only led to a number of legislations to safeguard the family but also the provision of legal remedies for the same. The 'family courts', established 1984, are one such channel for men and women to seek speedy justice in the event of disharmony and discord in their familial lives. The decision of the Government of India in 2002 to set up 85 family courts all over the country evidences the rise of family related problems. This also encourages empirical studies in the direction to inquire into the new notions of family life and the effectiveness of the agencies in their reconciliatory efforts to guide both policy and practice. As elsewhere in the country, the state of Andhra Pradesh, which is on a growth trajectory in information technology, biotechnology and other sectors because of the favourable economic climate, is facing the problem of family disputes, in view of the opportunities of employment for both men and women and the accompanied tensions of growth and development as well. Moreover, Andhra Pradesh is one of the proactive states to implement the Family Courts Act by setting up the family courts in selected cities taking, clues from the central government legislation.

FAMILY COURTS IN ANDHRA PRADESH

Administration of justice is one of the functions of the state. Though it appears as a single activity, it is embedded with various types of functions—the most important being protection of the rights of the people, enforcement of their fundamental rights, resolving conflicts over several aspects, and so on. The judicial process is lengthy and causes delays. Hence, special courts have been established to try cases of a specific nature in order to tide over the inconvenience caused by the existing judicial system. The 'family courts' are one example of such courts of special nature and aim at providing solutions to the family disputes, with a view to promote conciliation (Family Courts Act 1984). As a first step, family courts were established in four states—Tamil Nadu, Uttar Pradesh, Madhya Pradesh and Maharashtra—and the union territory of Delhi. Subsequently, Rajasthan, Sikkim, Karnataka and Pondicherry got the benefit of family courts. By 1992, family courts started functioning in Goa, Assam, Bihar, West Bengal, Haryana and Manipur. The number of courts is increasing year after year. The announcement of the Government of India in 2002 to establish 85 courts in different parts of the country evidences both the rise of disputes and the significance of the family courts. As per the provisions of the Act, family courts were established in the twin cities of Hyderabad and Secunderabad, Warangal, Kurnool, Tirupathi, Visakhapatnam and Vijayawada. In view of the large number of cases pending in the twin cities (3408), another family court was established at Secunderabad in 1996 (Government of Andhra Pradesh 1996).

The Procedure in Family Courts

According to the Family Courts Act (1984) the family courts should try in the first instance to effect conciliation or a settlement between the parties to a family dispute. During this stage, the proceedings will be informal and rigid rules of procedure shall not apply. They can take the help of social welfare agencies, counsellors, and so on, during the conciliation stage and also the help of medical experts if needed. The parties to a dispute before a family court shall not be entitled, as of right, to be represented by legal practitioners. However, the court may, in the interest of justice, seek the assistance of a legal expert.

Studies on the functioning of the family courts focused on the jurisdiction (Grover 1995); procedures and powers (Dutta 1992); personnel and staff of family courts; functioning of the family courts (Kanetkar 1995); reasons for approaching family courts (Suvarchala 1996); content of the family law (Rao 1996), and so on, in the different parts of the country. Studies that focus on the functioning and the usefulness of the family courts in the administration of justice are, however, limited. The family courts in Andhra Pradesh are also relatively in their infancy. However, the number of cases being registered and the pendencies reveal a more active role for the family courts in Andhra Pradesh. This chapter seeks to assess the effectiveness and usefulness of the family courts in Andhra Pradesh in restoring democracy within the family and the larger social system in the process.

Methodology of the Study

The study is in the nature of an exploratory analysis at the micro level. The family courts established in Hyderabad and Secunderabad in southern India form the research area for the study. Men and women who approach the courts on a variety of familial issues form the sample of the study. Empirical data—both factual and opinions—was collected from men and women who approached the family courts. Responses on the reasons for approaching the court and the problems encountered in the process, along with, personal data, were collected through a structured questionnaire from a randomly selected sample of 30 respondents. The opinion and the role of the judiciary regarding the institution of family and the trends that emerge would be known through the opinion of the advocates—15 advocates were interviewed to throw light on their role in restoring the family system, the working of the family courts, the implementation of the Family Courts Act, and their opinions on their usefulness and the legal battles taking place in the modern social system. A content analysis was done for the data collected and this was presented in a descriptive way, using simple statistics to arrive at inferences and conclusions.

Analysis

The analysis focused on the clients—their personal-social data and their opinions on the usefulness of the family courts, followed by the opinions of the advocates. The results are based on a simple statistical analysis restricted to percentages.

Personal-Social Data and Opinions of Clients

The personal-social data in terms of religion, sex, education, employment and income of the clients was collected to examine how their personal background contributed to the family disharmony. A majority of them were Hindus (66.66 per cent); the rest of were either Muslims or Christians. Male domination still continues in legal matters as 60 per cent of them who approached the family courts were males. The female initiative was to the tune of 40 per cent, indicating the continued subjugation and hesitancy of women to come out openly to seek justice. This may partly be attributed to the low educational level of the clients—both men and women. A majority of them (86 per cent) had education only up to the higher secondary level, which may be a deterrent in a variety of ways right from their comprehension of the external world to their crude and rigid mental outlook because of the lack of exposure. It is in a way puzzling to know that the educated men (14 per cent) were also unable to solve their marital and familial problems on their own. The employment record shows that some of the problems might be due to economic factors—30 per cent either did not have any job or were engaged in semi-skilled labour. A good majority of them (56 per cent) were in petty businesses and private employment, thus experiencing anxieties on a day-to-day basis, and the rest were government employees. It automatically follows that the income levels were low, with 30 per cent of them earning less than Rs 4,000 a month. About 30 per cent of them did not reveal their incomes and the rest were equally divided in the income ranges of Rs 5,000 and more and Rs 10,000 and more. The nature of the family was equally divided between nuclear and joint family systems (53 per cent and 57 per cent, respectively). The personal-social data thus shows that the clients seeking justice in family matters did not differ much in their personal-social backgrounds compared to the clients of the other legal agencies.

The opinions of the clients were related to their knowledge of the family courts, the problems that they encountered in the process, the reasons for approaching the family courts and their overall opinion on the functioning of the system. It was interesting to know that in a majority of cases the elders (33 per cent), relatives (27 per cent) or parents/parents-in-law (25 per cent) of the clients (and in the remaining cases the clients themselves) did initiate some advice and counselling before approaching the family courts. Their knowledge about the legal remedies through the family courts was their own in some cases (28 per cent), through friends, relatives and parents (33 per cent) or other sources like newspapers, leaders, and so on (40 per cent). The data thus evidences a rise in the general awareness levels.

Speedy justice and disposal of cases related to certain specific issues were the aims of the family courts when they were set up. However, the responses of the clients reveal otherwise—a majority of them had to wait for justice for three years (60 per cent) or six years (33 per cent) and a few for more than six years. The recent announcement of the Government of India that the cases should be disposed within a six month period goes a long way in recognising the adage 'justice delayed is justice denied', but the functioning of family courts over a period of more than seven years in Andhra Pradesh and 18 years in India is to be seen to be believed.

The problems that the clients cited also confirmed this fact. Apart from delays (55 per cent), spending the whole day when the case comes up for discussion (27 per cent), problems from the advocates, change of judges, corruption, and so on, were the other problems that were experienced by the clients. These problems point to the casual way in which the family courts function. The callousness of the government too can be seen in the transfer of judges at regular intervals and the appointment of judges in the family courts as a punishment posting (rather than appointing senior judges who take their job as a societal mission to reduce social tensions). These problems underline the need for advocates and judges, as the custodians of justice, to work with commitment for societal cause.

Men and women approach the courts for a number of reasons. The purpose behind the family courts appears to have been defeated, given the reasons cited by the clients. Reconciliation was nowhere reported a reason. It is sad to note that India is fast catching up with the US, which has the highest divorce rate (Corcoran 1998), as 40 per cent of clients approached the family courts seeking divorce. A good number of them had approached for maintenance (27 per cent) and the rest for the custody of their children and restoration of conjugal rights. They were highly critical, therefore, of the overall functioning (66 per cent) of the family courts. The rest expressed that there existed no other choice for them to seek justice.

Various suggestions were offered by the clients, ranging from a quick disposal of cases (66 per cent), employing more staff (14 per cent), appointment of committed judges (24 per cent) to making it compulsory for the parties in the dispute to appear in the court, more maintenance, implementation of the verdict, and so on. Men and women appear at the family courts to seek justice on account of various problems in their family life and hence are already depressed and disheartened. The state's responsibility does not end merely by offering some remedies and structures for the citizens in the name of welfare. Monitoring and evaluating the effectiveness of agencies from time to time would help in facilitating conflict resolution and mediation at the right time for a healthy and happy family reunion—the very reason for the establishment and existence of family courts.

The acid test of the usefulness and the effectiveness of the family courts could be seen from the result of the cases. The objective of the family courts is to promote reconciliation and secure speedy settlement of disputes relating to marriage and family affairs, and matters connected therewith (Family Courts Act 1984). The family courts could succeed in only about 14 per cent of the cases as far as their objective of reconciliation was concerned. More than 33 per cent of the cases were still pending and the rest were either granted divorce (21 per cent) or maintenance (21 per cent) or not accepted by the parties concerned and were in the consideration of appeal to higher courts. Research evidences the lack of appreciation or empirical studies in the area of family behaviour and hence is not able to deal with the theory of social change (Goode 1989) and is unable to prescribe any possible correctives for the situation which is spreading very fast. It is time the scholars examine the fast changing landscape of family sociology. The policy makers did, in principle, focus on the role of the family and its contribution to the society and economy at large. The family as the centre stage of electoral agenda in the US in 1990s, followed by the UN declaration of 1994 as the International Year of the Family are some evidences of the political initiative. The worldwide changes in economic policy and its effects on the family system are yet to be explored. The immediate future, thus, lacks the needed direction, both in theory and practice.

Personal-Social Data and Opinions of Advocates

The role of advocates is immense in the judicial system. Though the advocates do not directly deal with the family courts procedure, the help and assistance of the advocates could be granted by the judges in some cases. To elicit opinions on the working of the family courts, the implementation of the provisions of the Family Courts Act, and their relevance and usefulness to the public, about 15 senior advocates were interviewed.

As for their background, they equally represented the Hindu and the Muslim communities. It is heartening to note that about

40 per cent of the advocates were women, which shows that there would be empathy and sympathy for women in legal matters in due course of time. The educational background showed not only their legal qualifications but also their knowledge in other areas, as seen in their post graduate qualification in other streams—science, commerce and humanities. A majority of them (60 per cent) have been practising law for more than six years and the rest for about two to five years. Almost all of them were married and were in a position to understand marital and family problems. A good number of them (50 per cent) were young, that is, below 35 years and the rest were middle-aged. They unequivocally supported the family courts system for dealing with family related cases. The personal-social background thus showed that the advocates were young and energetic to deal with the depressed clients, and possessed the knowledge and the requisite background to deal with cases of familial nature.

They observed that the family courts would benefit the clients in a number of ways. While quick justice topped the list (85 per cent), the other reasons included privacy for women (40 per cent) because of the women advocates, the service of experienced judges (30 per cent); reconciliation (30 per cent), medical and other fees granted to the parties concerned, and justice at a relatively low cost (20 per cent).

The advocates' views on the procedural issues were found to be interesting. While a majority of them (60 per cent) felt that it was almost the same, some opined that the in-camera proceedings would bind the parties to their confessions as the person appearing in the family courts is the same as the person involved in the case, unlike other courts where it is possible for the advocate to represent the aggrieved. Simple procedures and advocates needing a petition to appear also show the uniqueness of the family courts.

The advocates also cited a number of problems which limited the functioning of the family courts and made them just 'another' court, both in procedure and the results. The adamant nature of the men and women (80 per cent), procedural delays (50 per cent), insufficient staff and heavy workload (30 per cent), ego clashes (60 per cent), and so on, made the judiciary helpless and ultimately fail in its mission of reconciliation. They suggested quick justice, more courts, sufficient support staff, education—both academic and moral—for the men and women to comprehend the world in a broader perspective, and so on, for the family courts to realise their goal of reconciliation. It is not surprising that a majority of them (60 per cent) reportedly accepted that the family courts were useful only to the tune of 25 per cent; the rest opined that they could achieve results up to 50 per cent, thus questioning the very basis of the family courts.

Findings

Family courts are specialised courts which were established with the objective of maintaining the welfare of the family by utilising a multidisciplinary approach to resolve family problems within the framework of law. The basic premise of the family courts emerged from the conviction that family being a social institution, the disputes connected with it, like divorce, custody of children, maintenance, and so on, need to be viewed from the social rather than the legal perspective. Women in the Indian context are the weaker party in family disputes and, hence, require special attention, protection and judicial arrangements. The UN sponsorship of 1975 as the Women's Year, and the ensuing national level support, along with the women's movement of the 1980, added the necessary impetus to the setting up of family courts in 1984. Although the Act makes it compulsory for the states to establish family courts, only a few states have established them (Andhra Pradesh established family courts in 1995) and even there the inbuilt flexibility of doing away with the tedious procedures was not taken advantage of. Some of them do not have rules and regulations laid down for their proper functioning (Verma 1997). The novel features of the Act—both in perspective and envisaged implementation—are to be lauded but its success depends on a variety of supportive services, the absence of which hampers its functioning. As could be seen in the study, the women belonging to the lower strata of society did not comprehend the procedures and were forced to rely on the staff of the family courts. In the process, they neither got justice nor any special benefit from the courts.

The existing family courts are also expected to handle cases in the nature of family disputes transferred from the other courts, thus, leading to an overload of cases. The large number of pending cases defeats the very purpose of speedy settlement. The study clearly brought this fact to light. The recent decision of the Government of India to set up 85 courts in the country is a welcome step in the right direction but the pending cases can be disposed off only if courts are set up at the block level too (Verma 1997).

The judges play an important role in conciliation. Rightly, the law has built-in flexibility and provides discretionary powers in the hands of judges. One of the issues haunting the family courts is the appointment of judges, which appears to be more in the nature of promotion of judges from the subordinate judiciary or those who are in waiting rather than committed judges interested in reconciliation. The result of the cases, as per the study, confirms this trend. Seniority, training the judges in the new roles and reasonable tenure are aspects that need to be immediately addressed to make the courts effective.

Reconciliation is no doubt important, specifically in the context of Indian and also Asian culture and heritage. Till recently, family disputes leading to legal divorce were low. Asian family law and policy is in contrast to western law. Korea, for example, is one place that is hardly touched by the divorce culture despite its modernisation. Family is still an overriding value and the 'family law' deals with inheritance, perils of marrying someone with the same surname, and so on (Lee 2002). The concept of 'no-fault' divorce takes care of separation with mutual 'consent' in 90 per cent of the cases and hardly any go for trial. India has a family law for members of different religions. Both the Hindu and the Muslim laws are oppressive to women and unilateral (Dutta 2002), but very few men go for legal divorce. While dowry deaths and child marriages are causing problems among the Hindus, the unilateral 'talaq' from the husband (and not the wives) is a problem among the Muslims. This phenomenon still continues, though concern is being voiced, of late, without much change either in the law or the custom. The family courts' 'conciliatory' approach, in the name of preserving the marriage, should not violate the basic assumption of equality of men and women. The family courts, as custodians of law, should not allow oppression to continue. Instead they should try to restore equal power relationships and sustain democracy within the family. The western countries, especially the US, with the highest number of 'broken homes' are advocating reduction in the number of divorces by all means because of its effects on the family and society (Croach 2002), and are even taking this up as an electoral issue.

The help of advocates, counsellors, medical and other service organisations is provided for in the Act. The courts should entrust the conciliation to these agencies after ascertaining their authenticity and experience in the field. This would enable a speedy disposal of the cases and also ensure service from trained, efficient agencies. The success of family courts depends to a large extent on its conciliation function. Coordinating all family disputes, including the criminal cases and collaboration with these agencies, would provide a minimum standard of administration of justice within the framework of law.

The involvement of women as judges in the family courts would help deliver gender justice and family justice. Training the personnel of the family courts also assumes significance in so far as the knowledge required for dealing with the cases is inter-disciplinary in nature.

CONCLUSION

Family is the basic unit of society. India has witnessed far-reaching changes in family relationships. Rapid industrialisation, education of women, legislation allowing divorce, changing perceptions about the role of women, and so on, have given rise to new stresses and tensions, thus leading to newer agencies and forums for the administration of justice. Attempts have been made to introduce family courts only recently in India. The existing experience of the family courts is too meagre to condemn them without a fair chance. The social fabric of India is undergoing a major metamorphosis. The family courts, thus, should aim at resolving the family disputes from the 'social' rather than the 'legal' angle and in a way which sustains justice and restores democracy within the family.

The institutions of marriage and family have been traditionally researched by social anthropologists and sociologists (Chanana 1988). Yet, research on the changing social realities on account of various factors—education, employment, and so on—relating to women and its impact on the family and marriage has been scanty (Leonard and Williams 1988; Chanana 2002). While historians have focused on the history of family and women, it is the sociologists who have been more critical in their approach, touching the hours of unrecognised housework, caring in families, its impact on employment and family, and so on (Hartman and Banner 1974). The global changes in family patterns in different societies thus need closer examination. Moreover, inter-disciplinary research linking different aspects is the need of the hour as the family court concept relies more on the social rather than legal concerns; it would also help ascertain facts more accurately and develop adequate theories to account for them. Research in the nature of empirical studies is needed for theoretical sophistication and better understanding of the changing phenomena. Cross-cultural studies across nations would also help in defining models for replication in similar settings.

REFERENCES AND SELECTED BIBLIOGRAPHY

Allan, Graham. 1985. *Family Life*. London: Blackwell.
Chanana, Karuna. 2002. 'View from the Margins', *Economic and Political Weekly*, 37(36): 3717–20.
———. 1988. *Socialisation, Education and Women: Explorations in Gender Identity*. New Delhi: Orient Longman.
Corcoran, Kathleen. 1998. 'Psychological and Emotional Aspects of Divorce'. Available online at www.mediate.com, accessed in May 2001.
Cott, Nancy F. 2005. 'Democracy and the Family'. Available online at www.yale.edu/tercentennial/democracy/media, accessed in June 2001.
Croach, John. 2002. 'New Reforms Abound', *Family Law News*. UK: Jordan Publishing.
Dutta, Nilima. 2002. Unpublished Article in the International Family Courts Conference, Washington D. C.
———. 1992. *Family Courts*. The Lawyers Volume-5.
Encyclopedia Americana Corporation. 1976. *Encyclopedia Americana*. USA: Kingsport Press, Inc.
Engels, Fredrick. 1978. *The Origin of Family, Private Property and the State*. Peking: Foreign Language Press.
Family Courts Act. 1984. Hyderabad: Suryajyothi Publishers.
Gandhi, M. K. 1978. *Hindu Dharma*. Ahmedabad: Navjeevan.
Gittins, Diana. 1985. *The Family in Question: Changing Households and Familiar Ideologies*. London: MacMillan.
Goode, William J. 1989. *The Family*. New Delhi: Prentice-Hall.

Government of Andhra Pradesh. 1996. *Official Records*. Hyderabad: Government of Andhra Pradesh.

Grover, Anand. 1995. *Jurisdiction of Family Courts—Need for an Amendment*. The Lawyers Volume-10.

Hankspatrick D. (ed.). 1988. *Collins Dictionary of English Language*. London: William Collins Sons Co.

Hartman, M. and L. W. Banner. 1974. *New Perspectives in the History of Women*. London: Harper Torchbooks.

Hunt, Elgin F. 1972. *Social Science—An Introduction to the Study of Society*. London: MacMillan.

Kanetkar, Neelima. 1995. 'Family Courts Act, 1984 and its Analysis', *The Bombay Law Reporter*, July.

Laing, R. D. 1965. *The Divided Self*. Germany: Pelican.

Leach, E. R. 1966. *Rethinking Anthropology*. Berlin: The Athlone Press.

Lee, Kyung-Hui. 2002. Unpublished Article in the International Family Courts Conference, Washington D C.

Leonard, Diana and John Hood Williams. 1988. *Families*. London: MacMillan.

MacIver, M. and H. Page. 1985. *Society—An Introductory Analysis*. London: Kogan.

Marx, K. 1975. *Grundrisse*. Germany: Pelican.

Meclure, Helen. 1971. *Social Systems and Family Patterns*. Indianapolis: Bobbs-Mersull.

Morgan, D. H. J. 1986. *The Family, Politics and Social Theory*. New York: Routledge and Kegan.

———. 1979. *Ancient Society*. London: Roultedge and Kegan.

———. 1975. *Social Theory and Family*. New York: Routledge and Kegan.

Panikkar, K. M. 1984. *Hindu Society at Cross Roads*. Lucknow: Prakashan Kendra.

Rao, K. V. R. 1996. *The Family Courts Act, 1984*. Hyderabad: Andhra Legal Decisions.

Suvarchala. 1996. 'Family Court: Its Dynamic Role—Some New Approaches', *Andhra Law Times*, February.

The Federal Research Division. 2005. *Country Studies—India*. The Federal Research Division, The Library of Congress, USA.

Tuvuchis, Nicholas and William J. Goode (eds). 1973. *The Family Through Literature*. New York: Oxford University Press.

Verma, Ratna. 1997. *Family Courts in India*. New Delhi: Inter-India Publications.

7

Private Concerns in Public Discourse
Women-initiated Community Responses to Domestic Violence

—•◆•—

Nandita Bhatla and Anuradha Rajan

INTRODUCTION

In India, and probably the world over, domestic violence perpetrated against women by partners and close family members continues to remain a matter of silent suffering within the four walls of the home. Despite the awareness others may have of a woman's ongoing experience of abuse, the phenomenon of intimate violence against women is typically identified as a private matter, made invisible by society and kept under wraps because of concerns of guilt, shame and secrecy. The norms that perpetuate silence and the stigma around domestic violence in family and community settings permeate the formal institutional response as well.

Available evidence indicates that this silent crime reigns rampant within Indian homes. Not only has the overall number of cases of crimes against women (CAW) gone up in the past five years, there has been a dramatic increase in violence against women within the household. Torture (cruelty by husband and relatives) forms the largest category of reported CAW, constituting 32.3 per cent of the total recorded CAW in 1999, showing a 5.9 per cent increase over the previous year (NCRB 1999). A series of research studies—that examined prevalence rates, and analysed government and non-government records and responses to the issue—provide further evidence and a comprehensive understanding on domestic violence in India. Results from a multi-site household survey—the IndiaSafe study (INCLEN 2000)[1]—reveal the pervasiveness of violence perpetrated against women by intimate partners across class, caste, education and employment status. Of a sample of 10,000 women across urban slum, non-slum and rural populations in seven sites across India, about 50 per cent women reported experiencing at least one form of domestic violence[2] in their married life, and nearly 50 per cent of the women reporting physical abuse experienced it during pregnancy.

Of a sample of 10,000 women across urban slum, non-slum and rural populations in seven sites across India:

1. About 50 per cent women reported experiencing at least one form of domestic violence in their married life.
2. 43.5 per cent reported experiencing at least one form of psychological abuse in their married life.
3. 40.3 per cent reported experiencing one form of physical abuse in their married life.

These figures are disturbing as they highlight the extreme vulnerability that women experience, not only in society, but within the home as well, questioning the fundamental belief that the family is the safest place for women. However, equally disturbing are the findings that point to the wide acceptance of and the normalcy accorded to domestic violence being an integral part of marriage. This notion forms one of the primary barriers preventing women from seeking any kind of help for their situation. A household-level study in Gujarat (Visaria 1999) reveals that 40 per cent of the women reporting abuse did not share this with any outsider. In the IndiaSafe study mentioned earlier, 58 per cent of women reporting partner violence said that they continued staying with the abuser because of the perception that violence within marriage is normal. Examination of records of NGOs (Rao et al. 2000) and the Special Cell for Women and Children (Dave and Solanki 2000) shows that most women tend to seek external help only after the violence has been ongoing for many years and/or when faced with situations that threaten their immediate survival such as loss of shelter, income, threat to life of self/children and threat of loss of custody of children. Even then, domestic violence may not be the reason for which help is sought. These results make it obvious that violence is seen to be a matter of individual responsibility, and the woman is perceived to be the one responsible for either adjusting more adequately to the situation as dictated by cultural norms or developing an acceptable method of suffering silently.

Even when women gather the courage to approach external institutions, they are met with insensitive attitudes and inadequate redressal mechanisms. A study on judicial records (Elisabeth 2000) has shown that conviction rates in cases of domestic violence are very low. Lengthy court proceedings, inordinate delays in investigation and irrational procedures such as requirement of sufficient evidence to prove intimate partner abuse are serious deterrents for women to approach courts, let alone see the entire case through. Content analysis of police recordings reveals that women's experiences are often filtered through an institutional lens of what is legally acceptable as violent behaviour, usually undermining the history of violence within marriage.

This lack of a sensitive and effective response to domestic violence and the social pressures to keep it silent and private have their roots in the deeply embedded cultural and social norms and values. Domestic violence is not seen as an aberration, let alone a crime. There is an obvious bias evident in the lopsided emphasis of the state responses towards reconciliation. Feelings of shame, guilt, backlash and lack of support from family and society often leave women entrapped within violent abusive situations. It is critical, therefore, that any attempt to transform the situation must enable fundamental normative changes to occur in institutions across society.

As a result of feminist advocacy within the arenas of international human rights and development, social responsibility for domestic violence is slowly being acknowledged in many parts of the world. In India, for example, families and community leaders are beginning to organise together at the local level to reshape community norms and attitudes regarding violence against women within marriage. This chapter is based on a participatory research study that sought to explore the dynamics of such community-based responses to domestic violence across five sites in India.[3] The research study was intended to provide better documentation of how these women-led innovative responses have emerged, how they operate, and how successful they are in addressing the needs of women facing violence and the communities they live in. The study shows that, indeed, one of the primary features of these innovative programmes is their ability to transform one woman's private complaint into a communitywide concern. It also demonstrates the ways in which this transformation is operationalised, and how family dynamics become topics for democratic discussion such that progressive decisions for the woman are sanctioned and validated by the larger community. For this reason alone, these methods of addressing domestic violence offer significant insights for similar efforts.

STUDYING DOMESTIC VIOLENCE

The prime objective of studying domestic violence was to document the process of identified women-initiated community responses and to assess the impact of these responses, thereby deriving indicators for evaluating such responses. The study also sought to build the institutional capacities of organisations in the areas of research, process documentation and evaluation. The initiatives studied were:

1. The 'shalishi' which is a traditional system of arbitration utilised extensively by the group Shramajibee Mahila Samity (SMS) in West Bengal.
2. The 'nari adalat/mahila panch' initiatives evolved and run by the Mahila Samakhya programme in Baroda and Rajkot districts, respectively, in Gujarat.
3. The 'nari adalat/sahara sangh' initiatives, evolved and run by the Mahila Samakhya programme in Saharanpur and Tehri Garhwal districts, respectively, in Uttar Pradesh.[4]

The research was designed and implemented through an innovative process that utilised participation through all steps of the study as its key principle. Intensive interactive workshops became the sites for designing the study, training the research teams in methods of data collection, and discussing issues emerging during data collection, debriefing and analysis, thus ensuring that all the partner organisations collectively participated in each stage of the research study. In addition to being an important data source, the experiences of the women who implemented the response formed the basis for conceptualisation and analysis of the study. A critical outcome envisaged by participants in the project was an impact on the intervention itself.

Central to all the responses studied was the presence of a structured community-based arbitration forum and dispute resolution process dealing with cases of domestic violence.[5] Here the term community is not necessarily used to describe an idealised homogeneous setting, but to distinguish these efforts from state and national initiatives. It is also a way to characterise and focus upon the smaller scale social mobilisation that is occurring at the village and cross-village levels. The fact that women-oriented dispute resolution mechanisms have emerged independently from any wider national strategy or government directive is worthy of close attention. Thus, identifying features that distinguish a community-based response from a more formal state-initiated or institutionalised response was the first task. The discussion eventually generated certain key elements of an informal community-level response to domestic violence. It had to be situated within the community setting and implemented by members of the community. Further, it had to derive its authority and acceptance from the community in contrast to a more formal codified system of law. The ownership of the process and the decision had to lie with the community, and it is their sanction and responsibility that validated the decision and its enforcement. Most importantly, the process had to be one which sought to shape and change existing community norms. The unusual role that women and women's collectives have played in the initiation, conceptualisation and implementation of these processes was another significant element characterising these responses.

STUDY DESIGN

The study design consisted of a mix of qualitative and quantitative tools, aimed at exploring the depth and extent of change experienced by different actors associated with the interventions. In Gujarat and Uttar Pradesh, only qualitative techniques (case studies, process documentation, organisational analysis workshops, focus group discussions and in-depth interviews) were employed. In West Bengal, in addition to these tools, analysis of institutional records as well as a survey with 151 women were undertaken to assess changes in various facets of their lives. Table 7.1 details the sample size covered and the tools utilised at each of the sites.

RESPONDING TO VIOLENCE

The sahara sangh, mahila panch and the nari adalats are structured centralised forums that have evolved out of village-level processes initiated by the village women's collectives or sanghas.[6] The sanghas, in turn, were established through the Mahila Samakhya (MS) programme. The core activity of the MS programme, a women's education programme of the Government of India launched in 1989, is the formation of village-level women's collectives for reflection, learning and collective action. The work of 10 villages is overseen by a sahyogini.[7] In the identified communities, it was found that sanghas initially mobilised around issues of concern to the entire village, such as water, health facilities and education. Success with these issues enhanced the social status of the collectives and paved the way for more controversial and complex issues such as violence.

In all the four districts, violence emerged as a significant community issue taken up by the sanghas. However, addressing violence at the sangha level had certain limitations, and the formal legal system was found too distant and unresponsive. To create a more structured paralegal forum for dispute hearings or for advising and supporting local sanghas, inter-sangha linkages were formed. In this process, village-level sanghas gradually created a separate forum specifically designed to deal with cases of violence. Thus the nari adalat, or women's courts, in Baroda, Gujarat, were the first of their kind to be formed within the MS programme. Rajkot district implemented a similar institution, the mahila panch, or women's council. In Uttar Pradesh, villages in Saharanpur district also began to run nari adalat forums. In Tehri Garhwal, the sahara sangh evolved as the support mechanism for arbitration by village-level sanghas.

Table 7.1
Study design to assess change

Tool	Site	Number	Domains of information covered
Case studies	West Bengal	25	History of the case; the intervention process; present situation of women; change in women's situation; changes among the various actors associated with the case
	Uttar Pradesh	24	
	Gujarat	27	
Focus group discussions	West Bengal	35	Perceptions about the organisation and intervention; change in the attitude of the broader community
	Uttar Pradesh	39	
	Gujarat	41	
Process documentation of cases	West Bengal	7	Detailed process of mediation in a case; role of the activists; strategies employed in dealing with the survivor and the perpetrator; forms of community pressure
	Uttar Pradesh	7	
	Gujarat	6	
Survey of influential people	West Bengal	40	Perceptions about the intervention and the organisation; change in attitudes and beliefs, if any; perceptions around the role of women as mediators
	Uttar Pradesh	10	
	Gujarat	10	
Workshops to analyse organisational processes	West Bengal	2	Growth and evolution of the intervention; stories of personal and collective struggle; core non-negotiable principles in working on violence against women; challenges and successes; organisational values and ideology on the issue
	Uttar Pradesh	4	
	Gujarat	2	
Profiles of activists	West Bengal	–	Stories and narratives of personal growth and struggle in working against violence against women
	Uttar Pradesh	–	
	Gujarat	116	
Survey	West Bengal	151	Socio-economic profile of women accessing the shalishis; cause and consequences of violence faced; experience of the intervention and changes in the woman's condition as well as self-esteem
	Uttar Pradesh	–	
	Gujarat	–	
Analysis of institutional records	West Bengal	1,671	Nature of cases; geographical spread; reasons for seeking help; socio-economic and religious profile of women seeking intervention
	Uttar Pradesh	–	
	Gujarat	–	

Both the nari adalat and the mahila panch meet at a centralised place on fixed days in a month. Women from the local sanghas as well as a few sahyoginis conduct the meeting where people with complaints come to get their case heard. In that sense, the nari adalat and mahila panch follow certain procedures that are quasi-legal and are similar to existing formal forums. What distinguishes these from other methods of addressing violence is the perspective that informs them and the processes which follow. In a typical case brought to either the nari adalat (NA) or mahila panch (MP), one 'side' files an application stating the complaint, and then activists of the NA or MP write letters summoning the other 'side'. Only when both sides are present is the process of arbitration initiated. While a lot of the dispute resolution and arbitration processes take place at the meetings of the NA and MP, important village-level processes remain at the core of the process of arbitration. The local village sangha plays the role of collecting all basic facts, generating opinion in favour of the woman at the village level and monitoring the decision. Occasionally, if necessary, a special meeting at the village or inquiry visits might be constituted as part of the case resolution process. Usually a number of sessions of the NA/MP are required before a mutually agreeable solution is arrived upon. The resolution is formalised through a written and signed agreement.

The sahara sangh (SS) initiatives are federations of village-level collectives in the hill district of Tehri. Sahara sanghs were conceptualised differently from the NA, in that they aim to function as a centralised pressure group or think-tank, which aids the resolution process of the village-level collectives. Cases that the village-level sangha feels unable to handle, or on which they need advice, are referred to the sahara sangh, wherein certain representatives from the sanghas discuss strategies, suggest particular courses of action and coordinate inter-sangha links. Thus, the actual cases are very rarely heard at the SS. Rather, the discussions and strategising of cases occurs at a centralised place, and the action and follow-up are localised at the village level. By meeting in a centrally located place away from the village, the sahara sanghs can also raise public awareness of each case outside of the village and increase pressure on district police and administrators. Geographic and social isolation of each mountain village has contributed, in part, to the significance of this particular function.

Shalishi is a word of Persian origin meaning mediation or arbitration, and has long been practised as a traditional method of dispute settlement in the villages of West Bengal. Consisting primarily of a sitting where a few respected community members arbitrate on any dispute between two parties, the form is unusually resilient and adaptive, and is seen to be partially responsible for helping to maintain the self-sufficiency of these villages through multiple regimes and political epochs. Community sanctions and the fear of community ostracism continue to be one of the main forces that make people listen to the decisions of the shalishi. Adapted and utilised by a regional women's collective called the Shramajibee Mahila Samity (SMS), shalishis are now being used to address cases of violence against women. The shalishidars, facilitators, are women who have been trained and sensitised to adopt a women-centred approach. The shalishi process encompasses all that occurs in resolving a case—from receiving an application, to an enquiry at the village level, to talking to the families and neighbours after the application is filed, to the actual shalishi meeting for the arbitration of the case involving the two sides and other community members, to an extensive follow-up after the decision is taken. An important additional feature of the shalishi approach to domestic violence is that the women's collective (SMS) is part of a larger peasant's activist organisation with the explicit aim of building a mass movement. Within the uniquely politicised atmosphere of West Bengal, the women's shalishis are thus carefully crafted to both; they contribute to the spread of the organisation's membership as well as avoid partisanship and bias by distinguishing it from other shalishi processes associated with party politics.

COMPARING RESPONSES

All these community-based initiatives across multiple sites have evolved spontaneously and independently, yet they have several similar features and follow similar steps/procedures in the process of case resolution around domestic violence. They have evolved public and community-based responses to domestic violence because of the limitations experienced of the earlier methods and the interactions with formal justice systems. Each form of mobilisation requires community support to effectively undertake face-to-face arbitration. This is a significant event in the process of dealing with a case, as it seeks the involvement of the larger community through participation in an open and public forum in dispute resolution around the private and personal issue of domestic violence.

However, there is also distinctiveness in the conception and operationalisation of community involvement and dispute resolution in different ways. The enquiry, for example, that is conducted as part of the shalishi process, is non-negotiable in each case taken up by SMS, but this is not so with the MS initiatives as they expect the sangha to fulfil this complementary role as a norm in each case. The presence of the sangha women is therefore a critical feature in the meetings of the MS initiatives. Similarly, the follow-up is a responsibility of the sangha as well, and thus does not require a formalised procedure. In the shalishi process, this is prescribed as the specific responsibility of certain individuals, who may constitute a follow-up committee in villages where the presence of the organisation may not be strong. Another distinction is the constitution of the community at the arbitration forum. The MS initiatives are characterised by a very strong presence of the women from NA/MP and village sanghas. The shalishi, on the other hand, has a broader participation including participants from the general public and, more often than not, locally important people like panchayat and local political leaders, or members of youth clubs. The political and cultural specificities of the region and of the community play an important role in shaping the unique character and strategy of each programme.

The evolution of a response to domestic violence that is largely community-based has its roots in the ideological pinning of the organisations and an ever-sharpening perspective arising from reflections on the ongoing work on violence. Initial work on violence saw more interactions with the formal legal system for redressal of violence cases. However, the inadequacies and limitations of the system and a strong feminist perspective enabled organisations to articulate their position as an alternative to the formal structures. For example, a lot of violence cases in Gujarat stem from the existence of suspicion in the husband's mind about the character of his wife. The arbitrators say:

> There is no way such a case can be fought in court. It is purely based on what the man says and feels is right versus what the woman says. How can any 'proof' solve this problem, when it has actually got its roots in the attitude and perspectives around relationships? All the while that the case is pending in the court, who will take responsibility and care of her shelter and other needs? Moreover, the voice and experience of women are hardly given any recognition and respect in courts. It is money that plays a larger role than concern for finding solution to the problem. We need a justice system that gives respect to women.

Apart from these practical concerns, the arbitration process is based on a fundamental perspective that decisions can be more effectively enforced if the people of the community are involved—that they own, control and validate the decisions. This is based on the realisation that the community forms an important reference point for the individual that is not just geographic but emotional as well, and that disapproval by the community can have more power than the judgments pronounced by a much more removed institutional system. The woman, the perpetrator and their families all form part of the community; and if that very community can be convinced of a decision that is progressive for the woman, it not only pushes the boundaries of existing social norms to create spaces available for women, but also contributes to the larger organisational agenda of transformation and social change. Since the community is part of a democratic and open participatory process of resolving the case, the implicit ownership creates a sense of responsibility among local citizens towards a problem that they have played a part in solving. Moreover, the conviction that true change in the situation of the woman necessitates change in the unequal gender dynamics within the family and community, ensures discussions on issues of gender and relationships in the process of case solving. As the women say:

> If the man is given a six-month sentence by the court, this does not mean that he has changed, or that the woman has got justice

or that their situation is any different from before. He, his family and community need to feel that what happened was wrong, such behaviour is not right. Taking the family and the community along, their thinking must be changed, only then can the woman live with respect, in peace and with her rights intact.

It is evident that punishment for the perpetrators does not equal justice for the woman. Each organisation is guided by a belief that reinstating the woman's rights within the family is more important than simply punishing the perpetrator and that these two ends are not the same. The processes thus seek the twin tasks of social accountability towards violence and the reinforcement of values that would democratise gender relations within the family, using the democratic arbitration processes at the forums as a means of public education and debate on norms and family dynamics. While links with the formal legal system and administration remain an inevitable key feature, the role for which they are approached has changed. The knowledge of law remains a critical framework within which they operate; the threat and pressure helps negotiating with the perpetrators; and their presence remains a system which can be resorted to if all else fails.

DEMOCRATIC PROCESSES

The objective of ensuring community participation and ownership is governed by the principle of democracy. This is evident not only from the processes followed at the forums, but also from the logistics of organising the sittings. For example, the shalishi is held at a place that is central and accessible as 'community' space—either beside a major road junction or next to the marketplace. Often passers-by come and watch, and even actively participate in the proceedings. Since the idea is to make the event as public as possible and encourage as many people to be part of it, even the meetings that are held at the village level are done as in the most open space available. Similarly, the NA/MP is held in formal community places like the panchayat bhavan, the premises of the block office, where several government offices are located, or in front of the district court. Besides these being the most accessible places, this also accords a semi-official status and gives visibility to the NA/MP. It is also making a statement about the rights of women over public and mostly male-dominated spaces. As the arbitrators say, 'It is an open meeting, we want everyone to see and know what is happening. What is wrong has to be hidden, not what is right!' Additionally, the proceedings start with a brief, but formal opening, stating certain rules followed by the forum and emphasising that everyone in the community is welcome to participate in the proceedings, though in a disciplined and neutral fashion, and this sets the tone of the meeting.

This public place also fulfils two other critical functions. One is the subtle psychological pressure that is exerted on the perpetrators. The very fact that the perpetrators have to be publicly present, 'serves as social punishment'.

> Everyone at their village and neighbouring ones obviously get to know that they are going to attend the meeting. They lose face in the community as it becomes an open fact that they have done something wrong. If they have to go repeatedly (as is when a decision is not reached quickly), then it usually adds to the community feeling against them—first they have treated the woman badly, on top of that they are not agreeing to the suggestions given by the women.

The second function is that this forum is perceived as a safe middle ground for negotiations by both the organisations as well as the community members who access it. One of the limitations faced by the women of the collectives in dealing with issues of violence at the village sangha level was that kinship ties placed restrictions on the extent to which they could take objective or radical stands on the issue of violence within their own villages. This joint community forum provides a space that is objective by virtue of the fact that it belongs neither to the accused nor the complainant, either geographically or through personal kinship ties. Cases can thus be brought to this space irrespective of kinship ties, heard by women who participate in the forum as women with the aim of arbitration and not because they are associated with either party, or belong to a particular village or caste group. It is emphasised that the people present there, including influential leaders, stand for truth and justice and not for any personal reasons. There is collective representation, giving a collective show of strength. It also gives a neutral place for the activists to share their views and hold discussions without the pressures of kin relations.

The feature of being a public and open forum goes hand in hand with the non-negotiable aim of providing a safe environment for the woman, where she feels physically and psychologically supported and safe to share her personal experiences. This is governed by the feminist principle of making the process woman-centred, such that it validates the women's experience of going public. There is a strong presence of the woman from the organisation at the meetings. While the shalishi sitting has both men and women from the organisations, the NA and MP are public spaces that are uniquely woman-centred, with a large presence of women who are part of the NA/MP and from other sanghas as well.

The democratic process is also evident in the sequence of events followed in the arbitration process. It illustrates how the community is taken along in the entire process of negotiation and reaching a decision, a process that is, of course, carefully balanced and skilfully manoeuvred by the activists. Typically, the procedure followed is that the applicant (usually the woman, but may also be the man) is asked to speak first and narrate whatever she/he wants to say about the problem and the situation, followed by the other person's narration. Activists ensure that these detailed narrations are patiently heard out by everyone present. The narration of the problem amongst the larger community presence means that the facts of the case are known to all, everyone can participate, various versions can be corroborated and the areas of differences thrashed out. After this, the people present also share what they know, give opinions about what has been said, and clarifications, counter-clarifications and discussions flow. This not only takes the responsibility of reacting from one or two women, but also helps in giving direction to the arbitration process towards a mutually agreeable decision, making it a process that is 'owned' and 'validated' by the community involved in the discussions.

CHANGING SOCIAL NORMS

In the arbitration process, the fabric of relationships is often laid threadbare on what is right and wrong in relationships, and what are its boundaries, responsibilities and duties. In deciding which aspects of the problem to focus upon, arbitrators also give meaning to what is held to be important and what is not. As perpetrators express their own reasons for violence within this public forum, and facilitators do not reinforce them, the participants gradually see that violence is never justified or acceptable. Another critical feature is that it becomes difficult to justify 'wrong' or 'violent' behaviour publicly. The women are highly skilled in the way they deliberately allow some discussions to proceed and nip others in the bud, depending on what is useful to the case. In similar ways, certain gender stereotypes, such as it is masculine to beat, feminine to tolerate, are challenged. Thus, private matters become issues for public discourse. The following is an excerpt showing how perspectives on violence and discussion on gender relations are tackled.

> The girl is asked to speak first about what kind of a solution she wants. She says, 'Before that my father-in-law must make a public promise that he will not raise his hand or touch me.' Immediately one sahyogini explains to the girl, 'The father-in-law has taken a vow that he has not done any kind of harassment. You said that he has harassed you wrongly, you must apologise.' Another sahyogini does not agree and says that the girl has not done anything wrong by objecting to this behaviour by the father-in-law.
>
> If the girl did not like any particular behaviour, she should and can say so in this forum. Everyone should know what she is upset about. Let's clarify everything here. That's why we are together and all can speak without fear. Let the girl say what happened. The girl says, 'He caught hold of my arm and my shoulders and was trying to say something to me. Why should he touch me in the first place? Only my husband can do that. Is it not obvious that I got scared.' The father-in-law meanwhile murmurs that he did not touch her. However, there seem to be no voices supporting him. A sangha woman says, 'There is a thin line between touching

and touching with a wrong intention. We believe you, but why give anyone the chance to talk? The sahyogini adds, 'Hitting, touching, using force, none of that is needed. If there is a problem you talk it out, you can always ask us for help.' Another says,

'Any issue that is bothering you can be shared, talked and sorted out. Here we like to sort out everything face to face and don't like to leave any resentment uncleared. If something remains in your mind, then the problem will be back to the start. Aise kaccha faisla nahin karte hum' (we do not take a decision which is not sound) (From a case documentation at Mahila Panch, Gujarat study).

In this region of Gujarat, it is apparently unusual for the father-in-law to be involved in any physical confrontation. It is not seen as a behaviour that lies within his purview and the activists wished to highlight this, as well as use it as a subtle warning. Culturally prevalent beliefs, customs and sayings are often used as acceptable ways to emphasise certain points, but are also openly challenged when they represent patriarchal values. Thus, the notion that the husband has the physical rights is not equated to mean that he has control over her and can beat her. In such a situation, discussion on spousal relationships, reinforcing values of mutual trust and respect and non-use of violence are stressed upon.

REDEFINING JUSTICE

The community responses to violence use an open, democratic form of dispute resolution and model an unusual degree of flexibility and accessibility in the decision-making process and its enforcement. Apart from being an inexpensive, accessible forum, the fact that the decision-making involves giving time to think of the best solution, rather than focusing on polarised positions of absolute wrong and right, and includes the possibility of renegotiating if the decision does not work out, add to the acceptance of these forums. During the study, it was found that the common perception of these fora among community members is that they are transparent, non-partisan, objective and sites where 'justice' is done. The findings showed that the responses manage to operationalise an objective process through a feminist perspective. Their neutrality is maintained by giving equal space to the woman and the perpetrators to share their experiences and express their points of view, by presenting 'facts' about the case collected through interactions with neighbours and villagers, and by facilitating a mutually agreeable consensus decision with members of the community. A feminist perspective was seen in the placing of the woman's interests as the starting point for negotiations. The explicit effort to change situations and create improved spaces for women by pushing the cultural and normative boundaries of the community, whose sanctions they seek, are additional expressions of a feminist perspective. The feminist agenda was also evident in the processes that determined which voices, issues and concerns were articulated during arbitration, which individual voices were deliberately highlighted and which were suppressed or viewed to be debatable. Nevertheless, the dependence on community consensus may also place limitations upon the extent to which the arbitrators are able to challenge community norms to obtain progressive decisions in favour of the woman. Thus, decisions may be a blend of forward movement and necessary compromise.

BEING AN ARBITRATOR

A prerequisite of implementing a community response is the critical role and perspective of the women who arbitrate. Across sites, it appears that developing a community response to violence is constantly plagued by the incessant conflicts of operationalising an ideal feminist ideology on the ground. Skilful diplomacy and facilitation are required to: (a) balance and negotiate contradictions between the ideal solution and the pragmatic circumstances, (b) push and redefine boundaries for increased rights to the woman while appealing to existing cultural norms, and (c) gain acceptance from the community while simultaneously holding it accountable and changing it. Arbitrators have to carefully monitor and direct this process of seeking opinions from all, without compromising the interests and the voice of the woman. Unlike the formal legal system that codifies such principles on the basis of which judgments are given, the mediation here is based on the articulation of the two disputing parties and what is perceived to be the truth. Formal codification attempts to minimise the chance of the subjective interpretation of a case. While intensive training on law and feminist analysis form part of the inputs to the women arbitrators, particular decisions are also based on the understanding, perspective and interpretations of certain individuals within the collective. The women who arbitrate at the forum are from the local socio-cultural milieu. Along with sensitivity to women's issues and an understanding of violence, they also draw upon an intuitive cultural sense of the beliefs, value and normative codes of that area. This contributes to the effectiveness of their judgment, which is based on an intrinsic understanding of the cultural value system and the extrinsic information gathered from the immediate community about the family and the situation. It is the innate knowledge and awareness of local idioms, beliefs and particular values that are held dear and thus invite community approval and that are used creatively during the process of negotiation. In the analysis of these responses, it is apparent that the family and the immediate community or neighbourhood form the moral base for an individual and it is this notional sense of a community that is utilised by these dispute resolution methods.

It also needs to be pointed out that the understanding and perspectives have evolved over time. For example, the decision not to use violent methods during arbitration has been the topic of many discussions. It has meant dealing with one's own anger and frustration at points. Similarly, the arbitrators describe certain key understandings as non-negotiables that guide the trade-offs between the perpetrator's interests, the community will and a woman's rights. Opportunities for continual reflection and analysis by facilitators are the only means of maintaining a radical edge in the arbitration process and emerge as the pivot for a successful response.

The conflicts and responsibility that the process of negotiating and balancing required to operationalise a community response can take several forms. Since the woman's narrative forms a central pivot for negotiations around the case, complete knowledge of all the facts is essential and yet may not actually happen in reality. This can sometimes be due to the woman not sharing everything with them, which can happen when there is no village collective. There are cases where what the woman wants and what the family is willing to negotiate for, cannot come to any kind of compromise. Pressing for a decision in cases of sexual violence within the family is particularly difficult. Sometimes the woman wants to go back, come what may, but the husband is not willing to accept her at any cost. The role of the natal family in influencing the case is another factor that also has to be examined carefully by the activists.

Though concerns plague activists, there is also the knowledge of sure change that the forums have been able to achieve, especially in addressing the norms around violence. The most obvious and critical community norm being challenged and reshaped is that of violence being a private personal issue. Women believe violence is wrong and that it is their right to protest publicly. The forums have also promoted a heightened sense of responsibility among community members regarding violence, as indicated by findings at each site. The survey of women who approached the shalishi clearly shows that women facing violence see their neighbourhoods and local communities as the first form of critical support that enables them to protest and seek help. In villages where organisational presence is strong, the neighbourhood and community responses are more proactive and helpful to women. Most women describe the collectives formed under the MS programme as the source of support and, thus, approach them for help.

The recognition of the work done by these forums by several community members underscores their acceptability. Recognition of the right of women to publicly arbitrate and dispense on matters of justice is a fundamental reshaping of norms about women's public roles. These forums have expanded the definition of maintenance to include the time the woman spends away from the matrimonial family without formal divorce. This is an important community norm being reshaped. Other examples include the reinterpretation of local idioms pertaining to women's gender roles, the increasing number of cases of suspicion and other more subtle forms of violence being reported. All these point to the expanding definition of violence within the community and the ability of these forums to mobilise community support around them.

INDIVIDUAL TRANSFORMATIONS

The condition of most of the women who sought help appeared to have improved. Across sites, there were a substantial number of cases (more than half in each) in which women reported that violence had stopped completely. Although violence continued to occur in other cases, it had reduced or transformed into other forms of abuse, reported as more subtle psychological forms of violence in Bengal. However, a very significant finding was that complete resolution of the problem was not a necessary precursor for a positive change in the woman's self-image. Almost all the women in all sites reported an increase in confidence that can be attributed to the process of case resolution. This provides a dramatic and non-negotiable impact indicator that shows the value of the process and the innovative forum environment. This is especially important as the vision with which these forums were initiated was not that violence should end, but that the women should recognise and exercise their agency and rights as individuals. This also points to the ability of these community-based forums to publicly validate the woman's personal experience with honour and respect. Women are thus able to break the barriers of shame and guilt, probably the two biggest hurdles that they face in seeking help. Transformations in several other key beliefs responsible for perpetuating violence also occurred. A majority of the women in both processes report that they now believe that the violence was not their fault, that it was not acceptable or inevitable and that they did nothing wrong by bringing it out into the open. Many of these women also frequent the forums now.

However, it must be borne in mind that though the violence has stopped, this reflects a change in behaviour but not necessarily a change in attitude, which is more difficult to measure. Though actually measuring change in the attitudes of perpetrators poses difficulties, the change in the woman's situation, her behaviour and of others towards her seem to be more accurate indicators of change.

For all the activists, changes in their personal lives, their families and their relationships have been inevitable. There has also been a definite increase in social and familial status as they are perceived with increasing respect and sought for their opinions in resolving crucial family situations. The families of activists are primarily supportive of their work and there has been a noted redefinition of gender roles around household tasks as husbands and families adjust to her long hours away from home. Women activists also reported an increase in self-worth, confidence and competence that they often translate into redefining social customs and rituals for themselves and their children. Increasingly, radical stands on dowry, education and widowhood have been taken up by many of the activists. However, these kind of changes do not occur without conflict and tension, and the process of negotiation within families and communities is ongoing. Women's roles and identities constantly cross the fluid boundaries of the public and private, creating continual conflicts and upheavals in the family. A significant contribution to the increased status has been the redefining of the domain of justice. Women from lower castes and classes, and marginalised communities now hold centre stage and arbitrate publicly, thus, gaining acceptance for this role within certain sections of society. This new status in the village and community adds to the negotiations they can hold with the families as well.

CONCLUSION

In conclusion, it can be said that these responses incorporate a strong element of preventive justice. They differ from the traditional justice forums by incorporating a perspective that is feminist and a process that is truly democratic. They do not reflect the interests of any dominant group. In order to resolve domestic disputes effectively, they create a forum where large numbers of stakeholders gather to air private grievances and engage in spirited arguments. The process relies on the community's right to enter the sphere of private family matters in order to restore collective peace and accept its responsibility in a public shaming of the guilty party. The forums operate under the assumption that community pressure can indeed act as an effective deterrent to further violence if the process strives not only to restore peace, but also to oppose values and customs that harm women. The potential of such forums is demonstrated not only by increasing community participation in an issue such as violence but also in pushing the ideology of human rights, and improving the accountability of existing structures like the police and the panchayats. It is in the creation of such safe and accessible spaces for dialogue between men, women and other members of the community that the potential of availing of justice lies.

ACKNOWLEDGEMENTS

This paper is based on a research study conducted by research teams of Mahila Samakhya, Baroda, Rajkot, Saharanpur and Tehri Garhwal, and Shramajibee Mahila Samity, West Bengal, and International Center for Research on Women (ICRW). This study was made possible through support from US Agency for International Development (USAID). The guidance of the project director, Nata Duvuury, and the involvement of the state programme directors of Mahila Samakhya, Uttar Pradesh and Gujarat, were critical for the research study. We also wish to acknowledge Barbara Burton for her valuable inputs in the summary report.

NOTES

1. The IndiaSafe and other studies quoted were part of the first phase of research programme initiated by International Center for Research on Women (ICRW) to gain a comprehensive understanding of domestic violence in India by examining prevalence rates, and analysing government and non-government records and responses to the issue.
2. All the ICRW studies specifically focus on violence in the inter-spousal relationship.
3. The research study was a collaborative effort born of a mutually felt need between the ICRW, Mahila Samakhya (MS), a national education programme for women and Shramajibee Mahila Samity (SMS), a rural working women's organisation in West Bengal. Through the course of their work, both SMS and MS were faced with numerous questions regarding the effectiveness of interventions for violence against women and the need to undertake intensive documentation. ICRW initiated the process of building capacities of the implementing organisations to undertake participatory research for this purpose, resulting in an enriching partnership among ICRW and MS/SMS organisations with different but mutually beneficial strengths and skills.
4. Tehri Garhwal was a part of Uttar Pradesh when the study was conducted; it now comes under the state of Uttarakhand. However, the district still functions as a part of MS, Uttar Pradesh, and will be referred to as such in the document.

5. Cases of domestic violence (as defined by the study and in this chapter) formed a majority of those handled by these forums. However, other issues of violence as well of social concern were also discussed by them; however, these were not the focus of this study.
6. Sangha is the term for a collective of women from a village, formed under the Mahila Samakhya programme, who meet regularly to discuss and then take up action on relevant issues.
7. Sahyogini is the term used to refer to the paid woman worker of the Mahila Samakhya programme who coordinates the work of 10 villages.

REFERENCES

Dave, Anjali and Gopika Solanki. 2000. 'Special Cell for Women and Children: A Research Study on Domestic Violence', in *Domestic Violence in India 2: A Summary Report of Four Record Studies*, pp. 25–33. Washington, D.C.: International Center for Research on Women (ICRW) and The Centre for Development and Population Activities (CEDPA).

Elisabeth, V. S. 2000. 'Patterns and Trends of Domestic Violence in India: An Examination of Court Records', in *Domestic Violence in India 2: A Summary Report of Four Record Studies*, pp. 34–38. Washington, D.C.: International Center for Research on Women (ICRW) and The Centre for Development and Population Activities (CEDPA).

International Clinical Epidemiology Network (INCLEN). 2000. *Domestic Violence in India 3: A Summary of a Multi-site Household Survey*. Washington, D.C.: International Center for Research on Women (ICRW) and The Centre for Development and Population Activities (CEDPA).

Leela Visaria. 1999. 'Violence against Women in India: Evidence from Rural Gujarat', in *Domestic Violence in India 1: A Summary Report of Three Studies*. Washington, D.C.: International Center for Research on Women (ICRW) and The Centre for Development and Population Activities (CEDPA).

NCRB. 1999. *Crime in India*. New Delhi: Ministry of Home Affairs, Government of India.

Rao, Sandhya, Indhua S., Ashima Chopra, Ngamani S.N. and Rupande Padaki. Hengasara Hakkina Sangha (HHS). 2000. 'Domestic Violence: A Study of Organisational Data', in *Domestic Violence in India 2: A Summary Report of Four Record Studies*, pp. 15–24. Washington, D.C.: International Center for Research on Women (ICRW) and The Centre for Development and Population Activities (CEDPA).

8

The Shalishi in West Bengal
A Community-based Response to Domestic Violence

———•◆•———

Shramajibee Mahila Samity*

INTRODUCTION

'Shalishi' is a word of Persian origin that means mediation or arbitration. It implies a method of dispute settlement that has existed traditionally in the villages of West Bengal. Traditionally, during a shalishi, the parties between whom a dispute exists tell a set of people (known as 'shalishidaars') whom they consider unbiased but powerful, about their dispute. They also bring along witnesses and proof of events as they occurred. In the end, the shalishidaars give their verdict, which could involve a punishment or a fine or an understanding between the two parties. The little material that is available on the shalishi and local mechanisms of dispute resolution point to their resilience and their adaptability to changes in society through the ages. Local methods of dispute resolution seem to have been an integral part of the self-sufficient village that existed in pre-Mughal India. P. Saran (1973) speaks of their persistence through the Mughal period and their use by British administrators. The British introduced the system of the private proprietorship of land owned by a few

---

* The team members include Bela Adak, Swapna Tripathi, Alpana Das, Suchitra Mondal, Tahamina Begum, Asthabala Maity and Anuradha Talwar.

landlords. While this led to the virtual extinction of India's ancient village communities in the formal sense, they continued to linger in the speech and minds of the people. Saran (1973) shows how an able collector during the British period found 'in village after village, a distinctly effective, if somewhat shadowy local organisation in one or other form of panchayat, which was in fact giving decisions on matters of communal concern, adjudicating civil disputes and even condemning offenders to reparation and fine.' In today's West Bengal, Jayati Gupta (2000), in her study on gram or village shalishis, estimates that almost 95 per cent of all disputes in rural areas, and even in urban areas, are settled through shalishis.

The shalishi seems to have certain advantages over the formal legal system as far as dealing with issues of domestic violence is concerned. According to Jayati Gupta (2000), 'there is a greater understanding of the exact nature of the compulsions that both parties in the dispute have and a closer view of the complexities through which relationships are established and broken.' Several hearings are possible in which it is possible for the parties to make their representations to the community; the parties feel free in expressing themselves amongst familiar faces and surroundings; and it is possible to get a balanced mix between provisions of formal law and the social reality.

A second advantage seems to have been the tendency to arrive at a consensus decision rather than deliver 'justice' or a judgment. According to P. Saran (1973),

> Sir Herbert Risley once expressed this point with great clearness as follows (speech, Bengal Legislative Council, July 23, 1892): 'The method by which the Panchayat is elected cannot be expressed in terms of European political phraseology. The people get together and they talk, and eventually an opinion emerges which is the opinion of all of them. There is no majority for they are unanimous; there is no minority, for the minority has been talked over and casts its lot with the majority.'

In cases of domestic violence where the woman herself often wants her family life to be restored and wants a reconciliation with her husband, the tendency to arrive at an understanding based on consensus between the husband and the wife tends to have an advantage over a system which speaks of only punishment and justice. Community sanctions and fear of community ostracism continues to be one of the main forces that compels people to listen to the decisions of the shalishi, and the sentiment that one should speak the truth in a shalishi persists. The community, especially for poor people, is an important source of support and help in the absence of other social support systems or any kind of welfare state, so people are not very willing to disobey decisions reached in the community.

While a shalishi or a village-level dispute resolution system may have inherent advantages in the processes that it adopts over a formal justice system, two very vital problems remain in the course of dealing with domestic violence. The first problem concerns the concept of 'justice' or fairness. It is clear that those who dispense justice within such a system would be governed by community norms and values predominant in society. Also, as the sanction or the legitimacy for this system is drawn from the community itself, its decisions would have to take community sentiments into account. Where community sentiments are generally in favour of keeping the family intact at all costs and where feminist notions are foreign to tradition-bound villagers, what kind of justice can such a system deliver to survivors and to perpetrators of violence against women? How much does it lend itself to use by an organisation like the Shramajibee Mahila Samity (SMS) that claims to work for women's freedom?

The second problem is related to the first and is regarding who controls the shalishi. Community mechanisms seem to have traditionally excluded the weaker in society. According to Irfan Habib (2001):

> In the early centuries of the Christian memory ... when the headman summoned the villagers through the crier for consultation, only the notables responded, not the ordinary peasants and labourers and women: they do not count. Some fifteen hundred years later (during the Mughal period)...commodity production having intensified internal differentiation, the oligarchs (those who controlled the panchayat) were probably more powerful in respect of their weaker brethren.

In today's reality, the village structure continues to exclude women and lower caste/class people. Does this, therefore, mean that women and the poor cannot get justice from such a system?

In West Bengal, where many of the old hierarchies of caste and the zamindari system have broken down, the shalishi is no longer controlled by caste leaders or by large landlords. However, new power-brokers have emerged who often exercise their power through political parties. These power-brokers are from the middle and rich peasant classes or are a part of a new and upcoming salaried middle class, who have managed to grab positions of power in various political parties. Public space is now completely or almost completely dominated by party politics in West Bengal. Thus, party politics influences the shalishi and ensures that the more powerful wins or that the disputants are sharply divided along party lines; justice and principles often being the most expendable items in these settlements. The words used by people for what happens in these meetings are derogatorily partisan.

What is, however, interesting about the shalishi is that it does not seem to have been a highly structured system, or a system that is difficult to penetrate by an upcoming power group in the village. For example, in a *para* or neighbourhood, one of the first public spaces to be captured by upcoming youth groups and *mastans* (anti-socials) is the *parar bichar* (local dispute resolution). On the other hand, the control of panchayats or school committees or hospital committees is more strongly institutionalised and, therefore, harder to capture by an upcoming political group. The shalishi is also an arena in which there is very little at stake, as compared to, for example, the control of the panchayat, so the resistance that a new power group in a village or *para* or neighbourhood encounters is not so heavy. When it comes to women's issues, the stakes are perhaps even less for the community, as compared to, say, a dispute over land rights.

The SMS, a non-party mass organisation of working women in rural West Bengal, has adopted the shalishi as a means of dealing with cases of domestic violence. Has the SMS, which now undertakes 70–80 shalishis every month, been able to deliver justice to survivors of domestic violence? Has it managed to occupy this public space and has it used this to the advantage of the women it claims to help? Or, has it compromised with the community in order to gain legitimacy? These were questions that the SMS faced both internally and from other people with whom it interacted, after it had been carrying out shalishis for over a decade. These questions led to a collaborative study with the International Center for Research on Women (ICRW) from May 2000 to November 2001.[1] This chapter provides the major findings of the study and is based on the longer report of the study.

One of the objectives of the study was to document the SMS's use of the shalishi as a model of intervention that has involved key actors within the community to provide meaningful solutions to women suffering abuse within marriage. A second major objective was to assess the impact of the intervention and to identify issues for campaigning and advocacy that the SMS could use to strengthen the impact of shalishi's intervention in the future.[2] For the purpose of this study, domestic violence was defined as spousal violence in particular and included violence (mental, physical and sexual) by the husband and/or his family on the wife.

The following terms have been used in the report to describe the nature of violence:

- 'Deprivation of basic needs' means depriving the woman and her children of food, clothes, medicine, hair oil, soap and other things which the woman feels are of daily necessity. It also includes turning the woman out of the house, as this implies deprivation of shelter.
- 'Physical violence' means physical assaults on the woman, causing mild or severe injury, and attempts to kill her. 'Mental violence' has included taunts, abuses, scolding, restrictions on mobility, threats of violence or killing, threats to throw her out of the house, abuse of alcohol, gambling, extra-marital affairs, bigamy, threats of divorce and also complaints of neglect by the woman.
- 'Sexual violence' has included, in the case of the husband, deprivation of sex, marital rape and excessive sexual demand; and in the case of in-laws, unwanted sexual advances.

THE ECONOMIC CONTEXT

Most of the areas covered by the SMS are rural in character. The majority of the people who take help through the shalishi process are agricultural labourers, marginal and small peasants and other rural workers. According to the study data, only 3.8 per cent of the family members of the women surveyed were in regular jobs. The largest numbers worked as casual labour (31.4 per cent) or were self-employed (23.2 per cent), while women worked mainly as unpaid household workers (41.2 per cent). Overall, West Bengal also shows one of the lowest female work participation rates in India as shown by the census reports. These figures, in our experience, do not reflect the non-working character of adult women in West Bengal, but the non-recognition of their work. Their work often contributes in irreplaceable ways to the survival of poor families, but, as it has no 'economic' value in the parlance of Indian planners and statisticians, it is not counted as 'work' in the census. This also indicates that women do not have access to paid work (this aspect has also been recognised by the census). Amongst the women who were surveyed during the study, 78.1 per cent, that is, the largest group of women, were involved in unpaid labour. Very few women, therefore, have wages or income on which they can rely on if they leave their husbands. As most of the husbands are self-employed or work as casual labour, it also becomes very difficult to obtain maintenance through courts, as there are no regular incomes from which this money can be deducted.

Women also face shrinking work opportunities in agricultural development. For example, a single power tiller in one eight-hour shift displaces 15–20 workers. In North 24 Parganas, huge areas of paddy are being converted into brackish water prawn fisheries for export, a low employment activity. As far as other kinds of employment are concerned, very few new jobs have been created in West Bengal and the number of the unemployed has risen hugely. In government programmes designed to create employment, the number of person days created per agricultural labourer has more than halved from 10.22 to 4.79 from 1990–91 to 1999–2000. Also the number of people benefiting from the government's income generating schemes like the Integrated Rural Development Programme (IRDP) and, in its newest form, the Swarnajayanti Grameen Swarozgar Yojana (SGSY) has declined by 38 per cent from 1990–91 to 1999–2000 (Government of West Bengal 2001).

Women's share in poverty alleviation programmes has been low. The 2000–2001 economic review of the government of West Bengal shows that in 1999–2000, 21 per cent of the employment generated under the Jawahar Grameen Samriddhi Yojana (JGSY) and 29 per cent of the employment generated under the Employment Guarantee Scheme (EGS) were provided to women, while 32 per cent of the beneficiaries under SGSY were women. This is in spite of the fact that there is a government order which says that 33 per cent of the work under Jawahar Rozgar Yojana (JRY), now known as JGSY, should be provided to women and 50 per cent of the funds under SGSY are to be allocated to women only. SMS has also over the years tried to mobilise government funds for survivors of violence. Its experience has not been very positive. Factors such as low levels of education, and lack of land-ownership and skills have all worked against these women benefiting from government programmes.

Women have also not benefited from the much vaunted land reform programme of the Left Front. According to Jayati Gupta (2000), by 1988, land redistribution was almost complete and *patta*s (titles) had been issued. This was done according to provisions of orders passed in 1979. These orders, however, had no provision for women to be included in the general category of either the landless or the *bargadar*s (sharecroppers). If it is assumed that the government's claims of distributing land to some women at least are true, still the figures are not very impressive. According to one of their women ministers, Chhaya Bera, in an article dated 20 June 1997 in *Desh Hitaishee*, 9.7 lakh acres of land had been distributed to 23.48 lakh beneficiaries, with 0.44 lakh being distributed to women. This forms only 5 per cent of the total number of beneficiaries.

CASTE, COMMUNITY AND RELIGION

Caste and differences between tribals and non-tribals have not been treated as important factors in this study because they are not burning issues in areas where the SMS works. A long history of the Left movement and Hindu reform movements have broken down caste barriers in West Bengal to a large extent. On the other hand, Muslims tend to be a comparatively socio-economically deprived group in these areas. The laws and community norms that exist amongst Muslims are also somewhat different from those of Hindus. This makes religion an important factor. According to the study data, 39.5 per cent of the women surveyed were Muslims.

Many of the women surveyed (43.7 per cent) lived in joint or extended families. Relations of the woman with other female relatives in the matrimonial family are often tense. The status of women within the family is low. Studies show that women get married when they are minors. Dowry is a very big problem and there are a large number of bigamy cases. There is also a tendency for society to feel that the payment of dowry at marriage means the end of a woman's claims on her natal home. The *para* or the neighbourhood is a very important factor in the lives of the rural poor. It is often an extension of the family, with people from an extended family and members of the same caste group forming a neighbourhood. The neighbourhood also constitutes a social force that controls women's behaviour and perpetuates values and customs that create violent situations. At the same time, it can also be helpful in stopping domestic violence by becoming a social force that creates pressure on the perpetrators and controls their violent behaviour.

An extremely important force that has become an integral part of community life in West Bengal is party politics. A long history of grassroots party activity has sharply divided villages into groups with a mixed class character, which owe allegiance to various political parties. These groups have acrimonious relationships with each other and the concept of the village, as a whole, is more or less absent. Party affiliations play an especially important role in all local disputes—people from one political party take shelter with their leaders, while their opponents in the dispute most often go to the party that opposes the first political party. Needless to say, the leadership for most political parties is generally from amongst the rural elite. Disputes between groups that owe allegiance to different political parties could sometimes turn violent and the use of arms in such disputes in parts of rural Bengal is quite common. Another distressing feature is the tendency of local-level party leaders to keep such disputes alive instead of resolving them, as they seem to think that more the number of people involved in such disputes, the more will be the dependence on the leaders. Incidents of violence against women have unfortunately become areas for such narrow partisan behaviour. SMS sometimes finds itself in the midst of such disputes and has to sometimes face threats of violence from one of the disputants and the party that supports him/her.

INTERVENTIONS IN VIOLENCE AGAINST WOMEN

The women's movement in West Bengal has also centred around Left party politics. It is only in the last two decades that an autonomous women's movement has emerged. Along with this, there has been the emergence of a number of non-governmental organisations (NGOs) which consider violence against women their main concern. A positive consequence of the long and, at times, militant history of the women's movement in West Bengal (and the upheaval of partition) has been that people are used to seeing women in non-traditional roles. The taboos against their participation in public life are perhaps much more easily broken. Along with this, barriers of caste and religion, which are much stronger in other parts of India, do not hinder the formation of women's collectives at the village level.

One of the gains in post-Independence India has also been the various laws in favour of women. The credit for this must definitely go to the Left women's organisations that were active in the earlier decades. The membership of the Paschim Banga Ganatantrik Mahila Samity, the CPI(M)'s women's wing, was 3.2 million in April 2000, an impressive figure. Other Left Front affiliated women's organisations also have large memberships. However, their work amongst members, as far as the building of class and feminist consciousness is concerned, seems to have been minimal. There is, however, a large mass of rural women who have been totally untouched by the women's movement. To quote Soma Marik (2001),

> Today we can get two different pictures of the women's movement: on the one hand, we have women's organisations like the Ganatantrik Mahila Samity which support the Left Front, and who are able to gather huge numbers of women, but where the

thinking and the organisational control is largely in the hands of the party. They do not look specifically at how class has been divided by patriarchy. On the other hand, many feminists analyse patriarchy very deeply and see its connections with caste, class and community. However, it is not possible for them to reach out to large numbers of women.

The SMS thus finds that its talk of gender and violence and the exploitation inherent in society is often totally new to the rural women it works with. Also, organisations like SMS, which raise issues favouring poor rural women and are critical of government policy, are treated very guardedly by the larger party affiliated women organisations, though at the ground level there is often cooperation between the activists of the two organisations on specific incidents of violence against women. There is always a latent tension between these organisations. The emergence of Maitree, a network of NGOs, women's organisations and individual activists, in the last five to six years has meant that issues of violence against women have been brought up outside the party framework in a fairly regular manner. This in itself is a positive development—though still very city based—as it has brought the issue of violence against women to the forefront.

THE FORMAL LEGAL SYSTEM

Figures at both the national level and in West Bengal show the increasing reportage of crimes against women. It should also be noted that cruelty by the husband and relatives formed the largest part of crimes against women at 31.5 per cent of the total crimes against women all over India in 1998. A report placed by the home minister in the West Bengal Bidhan Sabha (legislative assembly) showed that though there has been a decline in crimes on the whole, crimes against women have increased from 3,947 in 1990 to 7,489 in 1998. In 1999–2000, the Bidhan Sabha's estimates committee for police matters reported that in the preceding eight years, reports of dowry deaths and cruelty by husband and relatives had increased a great deal, especially in village areas. The committee felt this was a result of greater awareness of rights amongst women. The districts in which the SMS does almost 80 per cent of its work against domestic violence are South and North 24 Parganas. These two districts, according to the National Crimes Record Bureau Report of 1998, had the dubious distinction of being the districts with the second and third highest number of cases of cruelty by husbands and relatives all over India.

In direct contrast to this increasing reportage of domestic violence is the dismal record of the way in which the legal system disposes off these cases. In West Bengal, according to the National Crime Records Bureau, convictions were given in only 8.5 per cent of the cases of cruelty by husbands and relatives in 1998. This was well below the figures for the rest of India and was also less than the conviction rate for other Indian Penal Code cases. Records from the public prosecutor's office in South 24 Parganas for the years 1995 to 1999 showed that the number of cases of crimes against women pending investigation had been increasing every year (except in 1999), as had the number of cases pending trial. Conviction rates have been as low as 16 per cent for dowry deaths.

Reports from NGOs like Swayam and Jana Sanghati Kendra and Jayati Gupta's (2000) study show that women litigants complain of expensive and confusing procedures, exploitation by lawyers and a general feeling of helplessness when dealing with the legal system. The increasing reportage of crimes against women, combined with the inefficiency and the problems of the legal system, has two consequences for the SMS's work. On the one hand, people have become much more aware about women's legal rights. On the other hand, the long delays in the courts and the problems of using the formal system imply that women and their families also look for other systems and institutions that can deal with their problems. This makes them turn to processes like the SMS's shalishi in increasing numbers.

PANCHAYATS AND WOMEN

The state of West Bengal has taken certain pioneering steps in the establishment of panchayati raj institutions. It was one of the first states to reserve one-third of the seats in all panchayati raj institutions for women. It has also ensured regular elections in the panchayats, and has ensured devolution of some power to the panchayat bodies. All this has meant that the power of the bureaucrat has been replaced by that of the elected representative. Parties have also occupied the public space almost totally. Power within these political parties is exercised by a section of the traditional elite (who have managed somehow to fit themselves into the new order) and the newly rich in rural areas. The latter include school teachers and government employees who have benefited tremendously from repeated pay revisions by the government; contractors; land owners who have shifted to investments like rice husking machines, and so on. This has definitely not meant an inclusion of the men from the landless and poor working classes in rural areas in the new power structures, let alone the empowerment of women from within these classes.

As far as the women are concerned, Bisakha Datta (1998) quotes studies which show that women entering the political system are in a stronger position when there is a critical mass of 25–30 per cent women in a political body. Unfortunately, in West Bengal, divisions along party lines ensure that the women who form 33 per cent of the elected representatives do not work together. According to the ISST Seminar Report (1995),

> In Kerala and West Bengal, dominated by the left parties, little space is available for women. In these states the party is omnipresent, its diktat being transmitted down a fairly rigid framework to the village level. This framework constricts the freedom of the panchayats, which are then more likely to be implementers of government schemes than viable institutions of self-governance. However, if gender is adopted as a party plank it is likely that it will permeate most levels of policy and action.

There has, however, been no sign of any of the parties in West Bengal adopting gender as a party plank. Nor is the link with the women's movement or with their own party women's organisations live enough to ensure that women members work on gender issues.

On the other hand, there has been a change in the way people look at women in public life due to reservations. Participation in public affairs is a much more legitimate activity for women. There is an increasing consciousness and rising expectations within the public and amongst women about the redress that they can get for their problems from society. There is dynamism in rural life, which has been brought about by the establishment of the panchayat system. However, due to the continued control by people and parties, who are not sensitive to the needs of women or the poor, the benefit for women who are victims of violence, or for the poor, is minimal. These people, therefore, still seek the help of organisations like SMS, instead of going to the panchayat.

SMS ORGANISATION

The SMS started formally in 1990. However, its launch was preceded by the work of Jana Sanghati Kendra (JSK), an NGO that took the position that the formation and promotion of mass organisations of the poor was the only way to bring about change in society. Work with women and gender issues thus began in 1987. This period of work laid the basis for SMS's later work amongst rural women and with violence. In 1987, a wage struggle by agricultural workers led to the formation of the Paschim Banga Khet Majoor Samity (PBKMS), a union of agricultural labourers. However, very few women were also agricultural workers in the areas where the PBKMS and JSK operated. Hence, it became very difficult to involve women in the struggles of the PBKMS. Women also found it difficult to speak out in the meetings of the PBKMS in the presence of so many men. A debate began within JSK and PBKMS on the need for a separate organisation for women and culminated in the formation of the SMS on 10–11 June 1990, at a convention at Dum Dum.

Today, the three organisations, JSK, SMS and PBKMS, work together. JSK plays the role of a support NGO, while SMS and PBKMS are mass organisations of the rural poor. Both the organisations have regular fee-paying members and elected committees from the village to the state level. The two organisations generally work together. Insights into the relationship that existed and continues to exist between the PBKMS and SMS show that male activists of the PBKMS dealt with women and with survivors of violence even before the SMS became active on such issues. Many of the women have a dual membership in both organisations. There also exists a relationship at the personal level between the two organisations. Many of the activists have married each other.

In addition, many of the full-timers of both the organisations live in communes or collectives. They pool all their income in a common fund and their kitchen, medical expenses, education of their children, and so on, are all run from this common fund. This collective life has many important implications for their work in general and for the work on violence. For example, there is a day-to-day discussion between the full-timers about their work, making for good coordination and fast decision-making; women have backup services of child care and cooking, which enables them to devote all their time to the building up of the organisation; full-timers actually practise in the communes the kind of lifestyle, with sharing of child care, household work, and so on, and non-stereotyped gender roles which they 'preach' through the shalishis or their awareness building work. As far as the villagers are concerned, the study showed that they do not differentiate between the two mass organisations. They see them as one entity very often and call them 'the Samity'.[3]

Three very important ideological issues form the basis of the SMS. These are: (*a*) a belief that exploitation of women in society is based both on class and gender, therefore believing that men and women must work together on class issues, but without losing sight of issues of gender exploitation; (*b*) a strong critique of the way in which political parties have subordinated the functioning of the women's organisations affiliated to them to their political goals, and therefore declaring itself to be an autonomous non-party mass organisation of working women; and (*c*) a belief in democracy, which manifests itself in the emphasis on participation and lack of hierarchy within the organisation; in the promotion of a dialogue at all levels in society; and in the need for women to become more and more visible in society.

The SMS's activities focus around making its members aware of the rights that they have and of the various ways in which they are being exploited. The shalishi and the work on violence is therefore only one part of its work. It works towards organising its members to fight for better wages, more employment, proper implementation of government programmes, and so on. It also focuses on organising women to break liquor dens and to stop gambling. Its work on violence against women focuses around the shalishi, taking up campaigns to pressurise the police to function properly and organising legal aid for women who cannot be helped through the shalishi. It has also, from time to time, taken up wider-level campaigns on the issue of violence by itself and as a member of Maitree, a network of women's organisations.

PROCESSES PRECEDING A SHALISHI

An examination of the processes that precede a shalishi revealed that the Samity activists were deeply rooted in village life. Hence, often before even the receipt of a formal application, activists of the Samity had begun to intervene in a woman's problem as neighbours or family members. They also played an even more proactive role of encouraging women to protest and sometimes (in the case of Shefali Bera, a woman who was locked up by her perpetrators) to run away from home. The Samity's organisation acts as a network to reach out to women in distress. Thus, 45.7 per cent of the women who were surveyed have said the Samity's (PBKMS or SMS) committee members and ordinary members have referred them to the Samity. Its mere presence, in some case studies, had also encouraged survivors of violence to protest.

In this task of reaching out to women in distress, women in the neighbourhood also played an active role; 65.1 per cent of the women surveyed were referred to the Samity by other women. Men and perpetrators, however, also have been taking recourse to the Samity's shalishi. Of the 1,499 records in which the applicant was traceable, 360 or 24 per cent were men or members of the matrimonial family; 82.1 per cent of the women surveyed said they came to the Samity expecting their family life to be restored. This has important implications for the processes that the Samity adopts. It means that the Samity has to ensure that its actions do not antagonise the man and do not lead to a break up of the family, as the woman is not ready for it. It also means that the Samity's intervention has to be long term, so that if peace is not restored in the family, it can help the woman through repeated shalishis and other supportive action to build up the courage to leave a violent home. The Samity's initial action when a woman comes to it is to provide the woman with, first, mental support. Other practical help is also organised such as filing a General Diary Entry (GDE) at the local police station in case legal action needs to be taken in the future; arranging for medical treatment at the government health centre; arranging for basic needs like food, clothes and bedding; and arranging for a temporary shelter.

After receipt of a written application, the Samity begins its enquiry into the case. It visits the two families concerned and has discussions with the neighbours and important people in the neighbourhood. Through this process, the activists gather information about the problem and the points of contention between the two disputants. The visits also help the activists gauge the mood of the neighbourhood and the kind of support or opposition they are likely to get from the villagers.

The enquiry is also an occasion for making public what was earlier private. As the central aim of the Samity is to create organisations of the rural poor, reaching out to villages through the visits becomes very important, as they become steps towards mass involvement and mass organisation. It becomes the first attempt by the Samity to get the public to participate and cooperate in dealing with this particular problem of domestic violence. It becomes an occasion when the process of getting the public to take responsibility for this problem starts.

A major problem in every enquiry visit to perpetrators is to convince them that they should come for the shalishi being arranged by the Samity. The activists use a number of strategies to persuade the perpetrators to come for the shalishi. They listen patiently to what the perpetrators have to say against the woman, and even express sympathy when the perpetrators blame the woman and her family for the problems. The policy is one of not antagonising the perpetrator at this point. The perpetrators are given the assurance that the Samity will play a non-partisan role. They also put pressure, explaining the legal implications of neglecting the problem and ignoring the woman's complaint. They give examples of other shalishis or cases of legal action in the area to make the consequences of neglecting the Samity's call for a shalishi clear to the perpetrators. Written notices about the date and place of the shalishi are given as an added pressure. Activists also mobilise the Samity members in the area to continue to pressurise the family even after the visit is over in order to ensure that they come for the shalishi. The perpetrators could also take the protection of other political leaders and influential people in the area, after the Samity visits them. So, one of the tasks of the Samity activists is also to convince these leaders of the need for a shalishi and the justification of the woman's complaint, and to seek their cooperation and involvement in the shalishi.

THE SHALISHI ITSELF

The Samity generally conducts shalishis at its own centre, as it is considered a neutral place by the disputants, or in the village itself, when it wants to involve the local people in large numbers. The shalishi is attended by the woman, the perpetrator(s), and the natal and matrimonial families, along with their witnesses and well-wishers. The Samity also invites locally important people like panchayat members, the secretary of the local youth club, and so on. Besides them, at least two to three Samity activists and some ordinary members of the Samity are present. The Samity activists have to be on their alert to see that a fight does not break out between the two families and their supporters. To set the tone for the shalishi, after a brief introduction on the Samity's work, the main activist, who is going to facilitate the shalishi, lays down rules for the shalishi to ensure that the discussion takes place peacefully.

The Samity organises the shalishi like a public hearing where everyone, starting with the complainant, is first asked to give a narration of events. This has several advantages.

1. It boosts the woman's self-confidence, as this is in contrast to the usual practice where women are not allowed to say much in public.
2. Speaking out acts as catharsis for everyone present and helps to clear the air between the disputants to some extent.
3. It is very difficult for anyone to justify physical violence in a meeting where Mahila Samity activists are present. There is, therefore, condemnation of the perpetrator's behaviour.

4. Everyone acts as a mirror, with the disputants facing the others' reflections on what they have been doing.
5. All the facts are collected and verified, versions of events are corroborated and areas of difference identified.
6. Everyone knows the same thing so it becomes simpler for the entire forum to take a common decision, also making the activist's task easier.

It emerged from the process documentation of the shalishis that the main activist plays the role of a facilitator during the shalishi. With the help of other activists, she ensures that each person gets a chance to speak, that the same points are not being repeated and that the discussion is moving ahead. In the more sophisticated sense, the main activist acts like an orchestra conductor. She makes space for ideas and speeches that are supportive of the woman, and she tries to avoid people and norms who could speak against her. Part of the facilitating role is to also talk to the husband and wife in private because the main activist and those helping her get the feeling that problems are not being revealed in public. For instance, in Noorie's case, a young newly married couple was having problems in living together. The wife had left her husband and the husband had applied to the Samity for help. In the shalishi, no clear reason was emerging for their problem. Swapna, the main activist, after listening to what each person at the shalishi had to say, decided to talk to the husband and wife separately. Swapna later came and gave a summary of what had been discussed to the others present at the shalishi.

As facilitator, the main activist also ensures that after a heated discussion (which is usual in all shalishis) that follows the problem, decisions are reached. If they feel that things have reached a stalemate, facilitators sometimes also ask the forum to break up into smaller groups and discuss things. The main activist also tries to ensure that people do not get entangled in non-issues and that they concentrate on the main problems. For example, the two families may get into an argument about each other's behaviour and the actual problem of the violence the woman faces might fade into the background. During the latter part of the shalishi, as it emerged from process of documentation, an important aspect of its role is dealing with community beliefs and norms. The narratives and statements made by perpetrators and the villagers who support them, and even by the victim and her family, are full of traditional ideas about women's roles and violence against women. The activists have to negotiate their way skilfully through these in order to ensure that they are able to change situations for women, without at the same time directly attacking community beliefs. In dealing with the perpetrator, the main activist uses both pressure and sympathy. If the intention is restoration of family life, which is what the women want most often, it becomes necessary to deal sympathetically with the perpetrator. This also springs from the philosophical underpinnings of the Samity that it is not a man versus a woman situation and that even the perpetrator can be changed sometimes.

During the shalishi, the pressure by the activists on the perpetrator is generally towards the latter half. By then, the narration of the events and cross examination by the main activist has made it clear to the others present that the perpetrator is at fault. The pressure could be in the form of other Samity members and activists taunting the man and passing sarcastic comments. Scolding him in public is also a tactic that is used. Asking questions repeatedly and giving examples of other cases, especially where there has been recourse to legal action, are other methods used. The last role that the main activist has to play during the shalishi is to help everyone present come to a decision. Decisions are, however, made as participatory as possible, with the woman's wishes being the most important factor. At this stage, it is especially important for the activists to include the opinions and proposals of locally influential people and important family members in the discussion, so that they do not feel left out and do not create problems later. The last part of the shalishi consists of writing down the decisions that have been taken and getting the signatures of the two disputants and of other witnesses. A committee is also formed from the people who are present to follow up the case and to see that the decisions are followed. The entire shalishi would take about an hour or two if the problem is fairly simple, but could last for four to five hours if the problem is complicated.

After the shalishi, the task of the activist does not end. She keeps in touch with the couple, or the couple and their families keep in touch with the Samity. Generally, matters do not end with a single shalishi. Follow-up shalishis are arranged whenever things get out of hand and when the committee reports or the woman reports that the violence or problems have not got sorted out. The committee was formed in the case of 62 per cent of the women surveyed. Its role is to keep in touch with the couple and to also keep the Samity informed if any problem takes place. Members are chosen by the disputants for their accessibility and because they are likely to play an unbiased role. The Samity keeps in touch with the committee informally.

The Samity involves the SMS and PBKMS members in the shalishi process as and when possible. The PBKMS male activists also play many of the roles that the women activists of SMS do, even to the extent of conducting the shalishi. The only difference is that dealing with violence is considered the main responsibility of the women, and male activists respond with support as and when they are asked to do so. In certain situations, SMS finds the services of the PBKMS male activists very useful.

These involve, for instance, discussion of sexual matters with male perpetrators. From experience, SMS has found that discussions on male chauvinistic ways of thinking (for example, sharing housework with a woman or not being violent) are often better received by men if other men tell them about it. Also, when it comes to deciding on the strategy to be adopted in a particular case, which involves dealing with local political and social dynamics, the SMS activists consult their male comrades and decide on such strategy together.

The Samity tries to involve the panchayat in some of its shalishis, if it feels that its involvement will be beneficial to the woman or in finding a solution. In other cases, it avoids the panchayat. In cases where the Samity fails to resolve the case through its own shalishi, it also uses the panchayat as 'a higher court of appeal', as the panchayat has more of an official status than the Samity. It would appeal to the panchayat and ask them to call for a shalishi.

The police are the last resort taken, at an even later stage, and only when both the Samity and the panchayat have failed. The police also used to call for a shalishi, which is not part of their official function (as they are always telling the Samity). They, however, take this extra legal step in order to avoid the filing of a case and all the extra work involved in that for them. They also do it out of consideration for the Samity and in order to help the woman in distress.

The final resort is always the court of law, as the Samity is well aware of the pitfalls, expenses and the huge time gap before a legal solution can be reached. However, the threat of legal action is always there in the background when the Samity deals with the perpetrator of violence and is used when, for example, the perpetrator refuses to come for a shalishi or when he refuses to obey shalishi decisions. In addition, even where legal action is taken, often the perpetrator comes back to the Samity requesting an out of court settlement. The Samity then organises a shalishi again to clear up matters.

The Samity ensures that the documentation at the shalishi, the shalishinama, has proper signatures, witness details, and so on. It also ensures that the conditions laid down there or the recording on the behaviour of the perpetrators and the woman before the shalishi is such that the document can later be used as evidence in a court case. There have been problems in this regard in the past because not all activists are well conversant with legal matters and also because the ground reality sometimes means that the disputants do not want everything put down in writing.

FIVE DETERMINANTS OF THE SHALISHI PROCESS

During the study, the activists of PBKMS and SMS identified five factors that they feel influence the shalishi process and determine its course.

1. The feminist ideology of the organisation: The Samity has a particular understanding of gender and women's rights. For example, it believes that men and women should have equal rights over property; that polygamous relationships by the men are unfair and exploitative of women; that dowry is unfair and the reason for a great deal of neglect of women; that a woman's relationship with her in-laws, and that of her husband with his in-laws, must be one of mutual respect, care and love; that women must have control over their bodies and their sex lives; that women's work is undervalued; that sex role stereotyping must be broken; that child marriage and deprivation of the girl child is wrong, and so on. The Samity activists try to see that

these beliefs are actually put into practice when decisions are made in the shalishi.
2. Community beliefs and norms: The Samity may believe in a number of things but it has to work within the reality of the villages that it works in. The Samity cannot ignore the village people because it is ultimately they who enforce the decisions of the shalishi—they are the source of the Samity's power. In addition, the woman has to ultimately live with the village people—the Samity cannot keep protecting her, so the community must accept what is decided for her. In the long term, the Samity also wants to organise the villagers and to change the attitudes of people towards violence, so it would be counter-productive to antagonise them. The activists, therefore, have to be tactful with community members. On the other hand, the Samity also knows that it is the conservative beliefs of the people that are responsible for the woman's problems. Therefore, during the shalishi process, the activist has to forever balance between tact and the push for change, for an expansion of the space that is allowed to the woman. The Samity also has to constantly do a self-evaluation to see that it is not compromising on principles or the safety of the woman in order to get mass support. The building up of the organisation in itself is a way of increasing space for the woman. As the organisation has grown and its reputation has spread, people's trust in the Samity and its decisions has also increased. With the expansion of the support base for the Samity, activists feel that they are able to take decisions and stands about community beliefs that are much more radical, as far as the woman is concerned, compared to the decisions it could take earlier.
3. The organisation's belief in democracy: The Samity believes that in all fora people should have an equal right to participate in the discussions and decisions. To create space for those who are silent traditionally, the Samity shalishi tries to ensure that the woman who is the victim of violence is given support to speak and that she is given a patient and sympathetic hearing. If the activists feel that the public space of the shalishi is proving to be a barrier for the man or woman to express their problems, the activist makes space for private discussions with them. It

also tries to ensure that women in general can speak out and, that besides the leaders, ordinary people too can express their views, by giving each person a chance in an orderly manner to speak. Also, decisions are taken after the opinions of all concerned on possible solutions have been debated threadbare. Consent from both the disputants and definitely the woman and her family is sought. The activist is, therefore, a person who facilitates a process in a particular direction; she/he is not a person who gives a decision or a judgement, as was done by the shalishidaars who traditionally did the shalishis. The Samity's belief in democratic functioning also manifests itself in other ways—money power displayed by any one of the disputants and party politics are not allowed to influence the decisions and processes adopted.

4. The legal and administrative framework: In the background of the shalishi process is the legal and administrative framework within which the Samity functions. Laws such as Section 498A of the IPC against physical and mental torture of the woman by her husband and matrimonial family, the section on maintenance for the woman (125 CrPC), the Hindu Marriage Act, and so on, are always kept in mind while pushing for the rights of the woman in the shalishi process. The Samity may often take decisions that are beyond the rights accorded by law, but they also know these have to be implemented through people's pressure. They are also aware that if people's pressure fails, these rights will not be legally enforceable. The activists in the shalishi also know what their relationship at that point with the panchayat and the police is like. They keep this in mind when they think of what they can enforce in case the shalishi fails. The increasing responsiveness of the police to the Samity's demands on behalf of survivors of violence in many areas has meant that the activist feels more secure in creating more pressure on the perpetrator, whereas in a new area, where the police and panchayat are unknown, the activist would also be more cautious in the shalishi.

5. The organisational goal of the Samity: The long-term goal of both the PBKMS and SMS is to become strong, non-party, independent organisations of the rural poor. They also want

their work on violence against women to become a movement instead of being responses to individual cases. The intention is, therefore, to use the shalishi as a tool to educate the people present about women's rights. The activists also often ask people who attend the shalishi to help them start a Samity in new villages and areas. It also encourages the woman and members of the two families to get involved in the other work of the Samity.

IMPACT ON WOMEN

The general premise with which this study started was that the Samity's intervention in matters of domestic violence has been effective in terms of leading to an improvement in the status of women in the family and in the society. The study found this to be true in certain ways. Thus, in its most crude form, the growth of the intervention in numbers, in geographical spread and in the ability of the Samity to reach out to Muslims—an economically and socially backward community in the areas where the Samity works—shows that it is an effective and popular intervention.

The study also found that there had been a distinct change in the woman's condition. A majority of the women were definitely better off in all aspects of their problem or in some ways. A small minority reported being in unchanged or worse situations. Almost all, however, had gained in self-confidence. The change in self-confidence was in the form of the ability to protest and express themselves, increased mobility, courage and mental strength. All these changes would help them combat any further violence that they might be subjected to in the future.

Women had also gained positively in their ability to seek help. As far as change in involvement in the movement against violence is concerned, the study found that the Samity had not been able to involve a substantial number of the women in its long-term movement against violence. The intervention has not been efficient against all aspects of violence. The most positive developments have been in dealing with the issues of physical violence and provision of basic needs by the husband. The aspects that were least effective were that of mental violence by the husband and sexual violence by in-laws and husband. It seemed that the aspects where laws existed (IPC's Section 498A for physical violence and Section 125 of the CrPC for maintenance) were those which had shown the most improvement. It was also comparatively easier to mobilise community opinion against the more severe forms of physical violence and around the belief that once she is married, it is the husband who must feed the woman. It was also found from case studies that the difference between a successful case and a failure often lay in the ability of the Samity to follow up cases consistently. Another important factor was the Samity's ability to change its intervention and the kinds of solutions being decided on in the shalishis with the changing situation of the woman.

In addition, younger women showed greater improvement in condition, just as Muslim women fared better. Women in joint families were also comparatively better off as compared to women in nuclear families. Women who had separated reported better conditions than those who were still with their husbands. Women residing in a place which was neither that of the natal family nor of the matrimonial family also reported being better off. Moreover, women from families with small amounts of land were better off than the totally landless and better off than those with plenty of land.

Women seemed to prefer to follow the strategy of tolerating the problem first and then trying to solve it while staying at home. Only when this failed did they turn to their families, the Samity and the neighbours for help with their problem. The patterns of help-seeking behaviour show the limited options that are available to women who face violence. The presence of the Samity seems to be an important factor prompting women to seek help. On the other hand, it is also apparent that other measures by the state like arrangements for income and temporary shelter would make it much easier for women to protest the violence in their lives. This has been confirmed by the views of women and those of locally influential people on the policy measures necessary to make women protest sooner.

IMPACT ON FAMILY AND SOCIETY

The family is, needless to say, the most important institution as far as domestic violence is concerned, both as the cause of the problem and the arena in which solutions are found. From the study, it emerged that both the husband and other members of the matrimonial family were important as perpetrators. It seems that the Samity has caused most change in the husband's behaviour and the least in the natal family's behaviour. In addition, wherever there has been change, it has resulted in more improved behaviour towards the woman and less deterioration in behaviour. This can also be taken as a positive indication of the impact of the Samity's intervention, which has resulted in making the natal family more supportive and made perpetrators less violent.

Amongst the factors that aid change in the perpetrator's behaviour and which have been identified from case studies, it was noted that fear of legal action and its threat help to change the behaviour of the perpetrator. Consequently, the study found that change is more in areas where legal remedies are available (such as providing basic minimum needs and putting a stop to physical violence). The Samity's follow-up and repeated intervention built up pressure to make the perpetrator change. The Samity's intervention, through discussions and feedback in public forums, makes the perpetrator reflect on his own behaviour and this could be seen as the first step towards change. The public exposure of a private affair makes it a matter of prestige for the perpetrator and helps to change his behaviour. The discussion of problems and the airing of differences in the shalishi between the husband and the wife and between the wife and her in-laws help clear the air and make for better relationships. There is internal and real change in the perpetrator(s) due to his/their involvement in the Samity's work and due to the long-term work with him/them by Samity activists, in terms of making the perpetrator(s) member(s) of the PBKMS and SMS and participant(s) in its various programmes. When attempts to change the perpetrator fail, the Samity helps the woman separate so that she is no longer endangered by the perpetrator's behaviour.

Just as the family is the arena where incidents of domestic violence take place, the role played by the neighbourhood in all affairs in West Bengal is very important. The *para* or the immediate neighbourhood is a very important reference point for all kinds of matters—it is a resource to help in the resolution of disputes, it provides a social support system of sorts for the poor in times of trouble and it is also the force that keeps women in subjection, through the upholding of community taboos and norms. For the Samity's intervention, which relies on a mass-based approach to deal with violence against women, its impact on the neighbourhood is also of vital importance. The Samity believes very strongly that violence can only be ended by the intervention of a neighbourhood that believes in women's rights. Hence, it is essential that opinions be changed at the very local level. Its attempt through the shalishi process is to create public opinion against the perpetrators of violence against women (VAW), and to make the village and immediate neighbourhood more responsible for the woman.

Other important institutions in rural Bengal that deal with or are supposed to deal with cases of domestic violence are the panchayat and the police. People belonging to a political party, generally the CPI(M), also play a significant role. Besides these, there are often people who are locally influential, but who may not necessarily belong to any party. The study has attempted to look at the functioning of all these people and institutions and the impact that the Samity's intervention has had on them as well as the change in their behaviour towards the woman.

The study results show that the men and women in the neighbourhood seem to play a much more active role than the police, panchayat and political leaders in solving a particular woman's immediate problem. The neighbourhood's role also seems to have an impact on the woman's condition. The study found that there was a positive association between the condition of the woman and the role played by the neighbourhood. A large percentage of the women who reported an unchanged or deteriorating condition were also those who said their neighbourhood women played no role. Similarly, women who were better off have the largest percentage of those who say their neighbourhood women helped them.

The Samity, through various strategies, seems to have influenced the neighbourhood in favour of the woman, more so within its organisational area. It has especially made neighbourhood women active in helping the woman. The Samity's strategy of forming committees of concerned people seems to have worked well, both to prevent further violence on the woman and as a means of getting society involved in the problem of VAW. The committee's role seemed most positive in areas where the Samity had its organisational base, where it played the role of making organisational members active, and for women in far away areas, where it played the role of filling in the gap caused by lack of organisational backup.

There has also been some change in the values of ordinary people, for example, with regard to the ability of women to live alone and against physical violence. However, another value, that men and women should have equal rights to property, does not have wide acceptance. The Samity's shalishi process seems responsible to some extent for the change in values and beliefs—in at least 10 focus group discussions, a definite answer was given that being in the Samity's shalishi had changed people's values. In addition, some political leaders sometimes seem to see the Samity as a threat and tend to wash their hands off or oppose women who come to the Samity for help. After the neighbourhood, the panchayat seems to be the institution most involved by the Samity in its intervention. The Samity is able to influence the panchayat and police in favour of the woman, perhaps because it is able to pressurise them into fulfilling their legal or statutory duty towards such women.

The study brings out quite clearly that the shalishi process has been used fairly successfully to deal with cases of domestic violence; it also brings out the kind of caution that must be exercised in its use. The intervention seems to be a kind of balancing act between opposing tendencies. The Samity adopts dual strategies of pressure and persuasion with perpetrators. It is working within the community to change it, and with conservative community norms to find support for progressive decisions for the woman. It is also organising women along with men and ensuring that both gender and class get first priority on their agendas. The need for constant evaluation of such local dispute resolution mechanisms is, therefore, of great importance, as is the need to exercise caution when drawing conclusions about whether such interventions are the preferred way of dealing with domestic violence or not. The conclusion, therefore, is not to give a clean chit to community processes per se but to say that in this balancing act, one must understand community processes along with their ideology. The shalishi process thus emerges as a traditional system which has the potential for adaptation by women and men for resolving their own disputes, and for increasing their ability to take decisions about their own lives. It is, therefore, a possible means of empowerment, but must be used with caution.

NOTES

1. The International Center for Research on Women (ICRW) is a Washington based research group focused on women. In India, ICRW has been engaged in initiating studies on the issue of violence since 1997. ICRW has been working in partnership with local institutions on gender and development issues with the objective of building capacities and advocating for effective policies. It provided SMS with both technical and financial support for this study.
2. As SMS had few skills in research, the research design was, therefore, arrived at through a process of workshops in which two members of ICRW and the entire research team of 10 to 13 women from SMS participated.
3. The study also uses the same terminology and refers to the intervening force as the Samity rather than only SMS, as we found that the intervention, even though it was into cases of domestic violence, was not by women from the SMS alone. The male members of PBKMS were also often equally important partners.

REFERENCES

Datta, Bishakha (ed.). 1998. *And Who Will Make the Chappatis', A Study of All Women Panchayats in Maharashtra*. Kolkata: Stree.

Desh Hitaishee. 1997. 'Paschim Bange Nareer Agragateer Beesh Barchar' (Twenty Years of Women's Progress in West Bengal), *Desh Hitaishee*, 20 June.

Government of West Bengal. 2001. *Statistical Appendix to Economic Review, 2000–01*. Kolkata: Government of West Bengal State Planning Board.

Gupta, Jayati. 2000. *Women, Land and Law: Dispute Resolution at the Village Level*. Kolkata: Sachetna Information Centre.

Habib, Irfan. 2001. *Agrarian System of Mughal India*. New Delhi: Oxford University Press.

Institute of Social Studies Trust (ISST). 1995. 'Women in Panchayati Raj: Perspectives from Different States', Report of a National Seminar on Women in Panchayati Raj, 27–29, Bangalore.

Marik, Soma. 2001. 'Introduction', in Maitrayee Chattopadhyay (ed.), *Esho Mukta Karo: Nareer Adhikar O Adhikar Andolan Bishayak Prabandha Sankalan*. Kolkata: People's Book Society.

Saran, P. 1973. *Provincial Government of the Mughal Empire*. Mumbai: Asia Publishing House.

SECTION IV

Including the Excluded

9

Family, Gender and Masculinities

Radhika Chopra

INTRODUCTION

Gender studies, gender theory and gendered interventions have always been arenas inhabited by women. It is the lives and the contexts of women's material and social conditions that provide key issues for research and interventions. One of the critical concerns of gender studies is the issue of women's agency and autonomy. While feminist writing and research has established the fact that women are not passive subjects, but agents and subjects in their own lives, their agency and subjectivities are not fixed or absolute. Neither is women's agency wholly recognised. A great deal of attention has been paid to the unacknowledged nature and 'subterranean' existence of women's subjective agency, as well as to the way in which these subjectivities need to 'surface' through a discourse of rights, claims and entitlements. Some feminist theorists have insisted that agency cannot only be understood as an exercise of volition in the abstract; Martha (Nussbaum 2000), for example, has argued that the exercise of agency is a human right. Further, it has been asserted that both agency and human rights have a location in material conditions of everyday life such as access to health, adequate nutrition, education, income, safety and other indices of human development. Thus, agency as an issue has to address the horizons within which it is articulated and realised as a political and substantive position.

None of these material conditions of autonomy or agency are produced outside of the social relations that give shape to human existence. Social relations create conditions of survival and relations of deprivations or entitlements. The politics of gender and feminist research have outlined the deprivations and unequal entitlements in the lives of women. It is precisely this frame—of women's agentic positions located within material conditions of existence—that has also produced the view that understanding women's lives is incomplete without looking at their everyday locations within families that must, of necessity, include relations with men.

It is the conceptualisation of the material world producing conditions for the exercise of volition that gives us a way of entering the debates around entitlement and deprivation, which can be thought of as absolute concepts. There is no denying the absolute deprivation of nutrition during food scarcity conditions, for example. At the same time, it is important to recognise that entitlement or deprivation are not only about absolute access or loss of some object, like money, medicine or safe streets, but also vis-à-vis someone else, in relation to some other person or sets of people. Within households, not every member has equal rights and entitlements to food or health. There is enough evidence to demonstrate the unequal gendered distribution of critical resources, an inequality that is weighted against women. When gender is combined with age, or with caste, then the question of entitlements and deprivation becomes part of a politics of distribution, a relational politics shaped and sustained by cultures of deprivation.

It is clear that entitlement and deprivation are related to each other. Thus, the next question is whether all conditions of entitlement, and therefore all entitlements, translate equally and exactly across all cultural and political locations. If we take the social and cultural unit of the household as an object of analysis, it has been adequately demonstrated that men have greater entitlements to household resources, like food. Does this entitlement and access remain true for men across all household contexts? If an individual man works as a domestic labourer in households and with families other than his own, does the fact of his gender and the entitlements associated with his gender 'move' with him, from his own home into the homes of others? Are both families and households identical in terms of the way in which he can translate his entitlements, define his power and articulate his subject positions? How does a person negotiate and experience entitlements within different households? How do culture and power become critical sites that define deprivation and animate agency when located within contexts of unequal distributions?

Aspects of class divide a household and family along lines of entitlement and deprivation. The household is an arena of political divisions along fractured lines of deprivation. However, the fact that households are part of different social, cultural and class locations impels us to reopen the issue of how men's entitlements are to be understood and evaluated. The experience of being male needs to be placed within these questions and masculinity as an identity has to be understood as a complex negotiation between gender, class and power.

Outlining deprivation has produced another dynamic: the need to redress unequal distribution. This redressal is part of a politics that seeks to 'enter' households and rework inequality and gender imbalances through what have been termed gender intervention and gender sensitisation. The interesting point about this politics of entry is that it moves along a terrain of materiality—in effect, it seeks to address the issues of power and deprivation by looking at health availability, food access, educational assistance, safe work spaces, equal pay, and so on. Thus, for example, the provision of micro-credit has sought to provide women with the means to secure livelihoods for themselves and their families. Micro-credit enters the house through a material path—loans and skill formation—but its translation into household dynamics and household micro-politics expands the loan beyond the monetary. Micro-credit provisions gender relations by expanding the role and attributes of the breadwinner, displacing the role away from the male household head to include women (and sometimes, younger men and children).

In part, the politics of entry seeks to change material conditions within households. Simultaneously, it seeks to encourage the emergence of a form of domestic democracy. The efforts of this entry, via programmes of intervention, are geared towards persuading the 'entitled' members—mainly the men—to play a more supportive role in the lives of their more deprived partners—mainly the women, but also children. Men-as-supportive-partners campaigns undertaken after the 1994 International Conference on Population and Development, Cairo, and the 1995 United Nations Fourth World Conference on Women, Beijing, or the Men-in-Maternity programmes of the Population Council (Caleb et al. 2002) focus primarily on involving men in reproductive healthcare.[1] However, both the conference agendas and the population council programmes focus primarily on a single category of men in households—husbands. The campaigns also focus primarily on one category of women—wives in the reproductive phase of their lives. Within the focused terms of these campaigns, husbands are being encouraged to play an active role in the lives of women in specific areas like women's reproductive health. The rationale for this encouragement is to animate the view that babies and their pre- and post-natal care is not the work of women alone, but must include men. Such intervention, in fact, seeks to expand the role of men beyond the sexual and to actively demystify the view that the only part men need to play is to make babies, not tend them. The attempt at involving men in the healthcare of their wives and children is to encourage men to think of reproductive health as 'their' work as well. Equally, encouraging men to participate in the reproductive health of women seeks to rework men's subject positions within the home by expanding and elaborating the role of men beyond the sexual, into the intimacies and the 'work' of care. Such interventions shift the 'target' from women to men. Unlike micro-credit schemes that focus on provisioning women with the means to sustain themselves and their families, and in the process expand the number of breadwinners within a family or a household, newer policies of reproductive health strategise ways and means of getting men involved in the work of pre- and post-natal care. The outcome of including men in reproductive health reworks the division of labour within the household, and locates men directly in the domestic work of care and reproduction.

    The dimensions of gender violence and violence in the family are another point of entry into households through gender interventions that address issues of gender inequality. Studies like the International Center for Research on Women (ICRW) research on masculinity and domestic violence (ICRW 2002), or the National Health and Family Survey, rounds I and II (Government of India 1999, 2001; Chopra 2002) have been important in outlining the range and categories of violence within the household. These studies have analysed the dimensions and forms of violence against women. Domestic violence is categorised variously as abuse, molestation, battery, rape, and so on, or occurring within more than one set of relations and across different contexts. Further, the data in these and other studies (Visaria 2000; Menon-Sen and Kumar 2001) demonstrates that violence is also framed and formed by cultures of power and deprivation.

Violence within a household does not remain untouched by political ideologies of violence and valour or cultural dimensions of caste. Histories of Rajput celebrations of violence against the self, for example, enter the household not only through men's violence against women, but also women's violence against themselves, for example, through their understandings of sati (self immolation), which is not a historical issue alone, but a contemporary 'real choice' for women (Sangari and Vaid 1981; Sunder Rajan 1993). Equally, caste is critical in the way it generates violence between women and men as well as within men (Anandi and Jeyaranjan 2002). Social and cultural contexts make the question of men's role in violence a problematic issue, and one that needs closer attention and explorations. Men need to be located through a series of subjective, agentic positions—as perpetrators, victims, witnesses and narrators of violence. The question of violence and men demands that we rethink the ways in which men inhabit particular subject positions in relation to violence.

More critically, no analysis that seeks to understand men can confine itself to understanding them only in relation to violence. Any analysis of cultural contexts reveals the multiplicity of subject positions that men inhabit. Investigation that is one-dimensional is incomplete because it mutes a range of aspects that define human relations. Feminist analysis of women's resistance has enabled us to pay attention to everyday speech and 'hear' what lies within and behind a statement. The question this raises is that when men give accounts of themselves, do they always use the language and idioms of violence to talk about themselves and their subjective perceptions? An analysis of men's everyday speech will allow us to tease out another dimension of gender relations that has remained muted, the support that men extend towards their families.

The concept of supportive partners is a relational question because support can really only be understood in its relational context. If support is relational, it is also context-specific. Just as the question of men across different households (as heads of households and as domestic workers) gives a sense of their different locations as subjects of power, equally, the idea of supportive relations must open us towards the question of a multiplicity of support relations and supportive positions. Like violence, support is not homogeneous and can be both material and ideological. In the way that dimensions and forms of violence against women have been analysed in their various categories as abuse, molestation, battery, rape and so on, or as occurring within more than one set of relations or for more than one reason (Visaria 2000), it is important to look at the opposite scenario. We need to address ourselves to the forms and dimensions of support as a substantive set of practices. In South Asia, for example, there is a cultural expectation that sons need to extend support to older parents, particularly widowed mothers, an aspect that the men-as-supportive-partners programmes overlook. In these campaigns, the position and role of men is restricted to a single dimension of their subject positions within households—as husbands, but not as fathers or sons. There is no denying that the conjugal partnership is critical within the family. Young pregnant women are often the most vulnerable in the household, and need vital health and nutritional care. But it is equally important to be self-conscious that 'gendered interventions' that focus only on men as husbands mute whole sets of practices that define the roles and subject positions of men as sons, fathers and brothers. Taking these other roles into account enables an expansion of the idea of men-as-partners and is conducive to working with men in households.

One of the ways to think through the question of the multiplicity of support relations is to think of support as social practice and, therefore, part of everyday contexts. Locating support within the frame of the ordinary and the everyday alerts us to the fact that supportive practices need to be culled from existing gender relations and not just from those that come into being through interventions like gender sensitisation programmes. Those who seek to enter the household through interventions need to ask whether supportive practices already exist at the level of the everyday. It is presumptuous to assume an absolute absence of male supportive practices within families and households of South Asia. At the very least, existing practices of support may be an ideology that might be drawn upon and elaborated when the whole question of domestic democracy and gender equality is sought to be addressed.

Further, the concept of the everyday highlights the fact that everyday practice and patriarchal social structure are not necessarily the same. Structures of power do not necessarily translate wholly or exactly, nor are they identically replicated, in everyday practice. Supportive practices need to be located in relational contexts between men and women, as well as between men and men. In other words, we need to address a dimension of relationships that patriarchal structure often hides or mutes and look more closely at the everyday practices of men.

There is a need to explore men's perceptions of supportive practices. Perhaps we need to ask whether men already have notions of supportive practice 'for' the family. To reiterate a point made earlier: when men give accounts of themselves, do they always use the language and idioms of violence to talk about themselves and their subjective perceptions? More pertinently, do they use 'talk' of supportive practices as a disguise to veil violent practices? Do supportive practices have no existence per se in the life histories of individual men in their relationships with women or with other men? Is there no substantive material existence to the support that men say they give to their families?

RESEARCHING SUPPORTIVE PRACTICES OF MEN

The research undertaken for the project 'From Violence to Supportive Practice: Family, Gender and Masculinities in India' (Department of Sociology, University of Delhi, and UNIFEM, South Asia Regional Office) sought to raise and address some of these issues. The research offered a view of support in its substantive material manifestations as well as at the level of ideology. However, in the way that women's work remained invisible in its doing until feminist research and analysis uncovered its histories, the doing of support by men may also have remained unaddressed, if not invisible. Through this research, an endeavour was made to make visible the 'doing of support' by men.

It is important to outline the choices that were made before the fieldwork was undertaken. The first was the choice of the family as the single most definite institution within which to explore the lives and everyday relational practices of men. It is more accepted to outline public expressions of masculinity. Nevertheless, masculinity is equally expressive within the contexts of domesticity and family. It is important to understand that male subjectivities are differentiated within the home by age, work, space and class. Understanding masculinities is an exercise that must address itself to key institutional locations like the family and not confine itself to 'public' spaces like streets or factories. In South Asia, family plays a comprehensive role in defining relations of gender as the arena where the ideologies of difference are expressed and learnt, where everyday forms of power and resistance are articulated. Thus the site of the family was an important starting point for the exploration of masculinity and maleness.

The second choice was to demarcate the kind of contexts within which to explore masculinities and male supportive practices within families. In the literature on South Asia, one of the missing or muted areas is relations between men. Men's relations within the family and their relations with one another was therefore a critical focus. Four field sites were demarcated for this exploration.

Since the father–son relationship is a significant one and defines the parameters of male–male relationships within the family, it was important to select a field site where the father–son relation would be at the forefront and most articulate. Family businesses were chosen to begin an exploration of this relationship. The research enabled a view of the father–son relationship within the domestic domain as well as the expansion of the family ideology beyond the immediate boundaries of the home.

To explore the manner in which the question of hegemony and dependence work in male relations within the domestic and family domains, the second field site was the lives and histories of male domestic workers. Since work has been posited as the crucible of male identity, this field site allowed us to probe further the issue of men and work. However, by choosing to look at unconventional work performed by men, we were able to analyse both existing paradigms of divisions of labour and how these are contravened in everyday choices that very ordinary men make.

It was important to push the understanding of the relation between men and work. A critical examination of the assumptions in the literature on men-as-breadwinners highlighted the fact that this literature has based itself primarily on an examination of men in conventionally male arenas of work or in the domestic division of labour within their own homes. It became important, therefore, to outline the substantive and material choices that confront men when they enter the world of work. There is no guarantee that 'male work' is always readily available to men. Any analysis of men and work must, therefore, focus on work that is 'unconventional' in the way it lies outside the accepted division of labour. For example, when men worked as domestic labourers, work that they talked of as 'effeminate' or 'not male' within the division of labour, they said they did domestic work despite this feminine orientation 'for the sake of the family'. The doing of effeminate work and the doing of support were telescoped in workers' narratives; one was offered as the reason for the other. The primary methodological focus of the research was not to 'change' the way people think. Rather, it was to track the way people think differently with the horizons and limits of their cultural and social positions. The fact of doing work that flew in the face of their entitlements made the entire research team recognise and acknowledge the extraordinary choices that ordinary men make to support key people in their lives.

Such a frame enabled us to look at the modes and styles of male–male relations within workspaces, as well as examine the way that these relations subvert hegemonic convention. The third field site was, therefore, also one that looked at men in work situations that were unusual and 'normally' associated with women. Male beauty parlour workers were the focus of the third piece of research. The deliberate choice of a non-family field enabled an exploration of the ideology of the family as an institution of care and learning and the way that care is articulated in non-family contexts. Thus, the deliberate choice of a non-family field like the beauty parlour enabled an exploration of the ideology of the family and the ways it is elaborated and given substance. How do the idioms of care, usually associated with the women in the family, translate into 'beauty care'? How does the fact of creating a 'beautiful' body rework concepts of femininity and effeminacy? Most of all, does the socialisation of men into beauty work replicate or mime socialisation and learning practices undertaken by women in families? Does the ideology of protection that contours parent–child relations translate into relations between employers and workers? Does kinship as an idiom transcend its own boundaries and inform practices outside the family?

On the other hand, a site like the boys' club in Kolkata, the fourth field work site, provided an opportunity to explore formations of masculinity in the public, or non-domestic, domain. At the same time, it let us analyse the extent to which boys' clubs were actually 'free' of familial ideologies. For example, boys' clubs made visible the process of 'passing on maleness' from adult men to adolescent boys, through the process of 'learning', replicating modes of inheritance within the family. Structures of familial authority between father and son were imitated in the relations between adults and adolescents. The passing on of vital knowledge between older club members and new or potential members imitated, in some part, the idea of passing down inherited knowledge that was more overt in the family businesses.

Two field sites therefore directly addressed 'the family' in customary, recognisable and institutional ways. The non-family field sites, on the other hand, enabled the exploration of the ideology of the family and the supportive practices that exist between men who work or forge relationships 'for the sake of the family'. While each research was distinctive in the issues and questions it raised, all four research sites also cross-cut and interlinked with each other in terms of the way in which family, masculinity and gender identity are framed in South Asia.

'DOING' SUPPORT

In the first research area of the family business, small, urban-based family businesses, with a minimum life span of 40 years and with at least a three-generational family structure, were chosen for analysis. This delimitation enabled an exploration of the way the family is reproduced, not just as a biological unit but also as a social, cultural and economic entity through inter-gender and inter-generational support relations. The analysis of family businesses highlighted the material substance of supportive practices and the affirmation of the ideology and ethos of the family when extended towards the economic institution of the shop or business. The ethos of the family shapes the outlines of the business and, in turn, is forged and changed by the support structures that develop over the lifecycle of the business. The father–son relation, the paradigmatic relation between men, explored within this expanded familial domain of the three-generational business, enabled us to track the variety of supportive practices across time and through various male–male relationships (for example between fathers and sons, uncles and nephews, employers and *karigars* [artisans]).

The second location was of male domestic workers in families other than their own. The exploration of this 'expanded' family location indicated the ways in which male domestic workers form a bridge between two families—their own and the family of their employers. Living between two families in two startlingly contradictory positions—as a fully entitled male member in one family context and as a partial member in the other—the subjective position of the man is 'split' between the two contexts in which power dynamics play out very differently. The domestic worker is 'party' to the creation and establishment of both power dynamics— as a man of entitlement and as a man deprived of that entitlement. The point at issue is that the family needs to be viewed as an arena within which not just women, but particular categories of men occupy positions of deprivation as subalterns. Domestic workers may exemplify this position, but their situation and experiences draw attention to the aspect of gender and deprivation translated within the micro-politics of the family and in relations between men of the family.

The methodological imperative of doing fieldwork has also raised a number of other questions and highlighted some issues that do not relate directly to support. But they do point our attention towards the subject positions of men, the cultures of male existence and the formations of masculinity. For example, the question of hierarchies between men is one critical issue. At the same time, this hierarchy is counterpoised with the 'spirit of egalitarianism' that also seems to be crucial in forming relations between men. There is some literature on the peer group that has outlined egalitarian relations between boys belonging to the same age-set. Forms of egalitarianism have been specifically explored in the context of urban street gangs in cities and metropolises in the West (Brake 1980; Jankowski 1991; Willis 1975). But in such cultural locations, egalitarianism as a value or a principle of group dynamics is tied in with adolescent rebellion and a deliberate forging of an anti-hierarchic, anti-structure and anti-adult stance (Osella and Osella 1998) by the gang members. Much of the analysis of street gangs is in fact placed within a discourse that produces adolescents as social problems needing to be 'solved' through impositions of control and regulation. The gang and the street are one formation within which all-male egalitarian relations are explored. Urban institutions and spaces like pubs or beer halls have also been analysed as arenas of friendship and equality between men.

The choice of the boys' clubs of Kolkata was made to explore some of the assumptions of this literature. The masculinist spaces of the boys' clubs that are part of every city neighbourhood and small locality give the city of Kolkata a distinctive character. The club as male space, outside of home and work, is a distinctive space like the pub or the street. One of the issues that emerged from the field-based study was the fact that these clubs are not hidden or marginalised spaces. They are part of every urban neighbourhood of the city of Kolkata. The clubs are supported by donations of land and money by the people of the neighbourhood for whom the club is an intrinsic, albeit entirely male, institutional space within the locality. These all-male institutions are accorded an authorised existence; in turn, their young members contribute to the collective life of the neighbourhood. The point that this study highlighted was the value placed on friendship by men, who nurtured, enabled and supported the bonds. Why was friendship given such value at all? What place does friendship have in the lives of men? These questions emerged through the research and were sought to be addressed in the analysis of the field material.

Most interestingly, it was the men who worked in beauty parlours who provided an insight into the value of friendship as social and cultural capital. Many parlour workers were migrants into cities and led precarious footpath lives. In almost every case it was their friends, or informal networks of friendship, that enabled them to get work in beauty parlours, in jobs that sustained them and their families. It was friends who 'taught' them the skills necessary for beauty work and passed on valuable knowledge and skills in a spirit of friendship. It is this 'spirit' that translates substantively into supportive practices between men, and if extended and elaborated, by men 'for the sake of their friends' families'. Thus men's supportive practices may not only orient themselves towards their own families, but to other families as well.

The doing of support for other families was also clear in the context of family businesses. Help was extended to families other than a man's 'own' or nuclear family. This support could come by way of loans, labour, exchange of goods, sitting at shops to 'help out' or advice. Support towards the extended family had an additional material and substantive existence in inheritance patterns where uncles and nephews, rather than fathers and sons, were placed in relations of inheritance and support. Uncles were key players in business families in creating the circumstances for young men who often began their careers in their uncles' shops and businesses. This expansion of the role of fathering undertaken by a variety of men is not unusual in South Asian contexts. The expansion allows us to view the whole context of the authority of the father as both reinforced and simultaneously dissolving as it expands beyond the single person of the genitor. Further, it questions the focus on one person as fulfilling prescribed roles. In fact, the dispersal of fathering over many men demonstrated the need to think about supportive partners in a more elaborate and a far more nuanced way.

The two field sites 'outside' the family provided a contrast for the research within the family. In addition, these two sites simultaneously enabled the possibility of understanding how work and non-work were key issues in the formation of masculine identities and in the lives of men. The first point to note here is that as researchers we were not attempting to dismiss or nullify the fact of work as a 'crucible' of male identity. Rather, our objective was to take the statement and then begin to explore the issue of the relationship between men and work. Therefore, it was more important for us to explore what the men were saying (and in the process explore the formations of masculine identity) by questioning ourselves as well as the statements that men made. Thus, if men said they work for the sake of the family, and offer themselves and their bodies as 'sacrifices' to ensure the survival of their families, then what kinds of work are they willing to undertake for the sake of their families? How does the need and necessity to work for the sake of the family translate into substantive choices that men make in the course of their working lives? Male domestic workers always cite this reason (*majboori*—need, necessity or compulsion to support their families) when explaining why they made the choice to enter servitude and compromise their autonomy and their maleness in this effeminised position.

As researchers seeking to excavate supportive practices of men, the lives of exemplar men like Gandhi, Nehru or Rammohan Roy are readily available and provide insights into extraordinary, but clearly upper class lives. We think of these men as extraordinary in many different respects, but most crucially, as models for other men. Unfortunately, biographies of ordinary men often disappear from the pages of histories, even though they are a rich source for understanding changing social contexts within which lives are lived and choices made. In the course of recording the working histories and narratives of ordinary men doing domestic work or working in beauty parlours, all of us were struck by the nature of the choices these men made. They transgressed divisions of labour, made a break with 'masculinist' work ethics and without self-consciously professing a politics of the personal, 'passed on' these transgressive choices to their friends as a form of help and support. We thought of these men as extraordinary because in their own small way their lives are 'models' for others to rework how gender identity is made, fixed and remade, within the limits and horizons of social and economic conditions.

It is their statements that led us to explore the questions of effeminacy, work and identity further. It is the link between work and effeminacy that enabled us to question the single stranded way in which effeminacy has been framed solely in relation to sexuality. The research highlighted the way that the concept of effeminacy needs to be expanded to be able to address sexual identity through work and labour. Labouring bodies confront the issues of male identity and effeminacy in extremely complex ways that complicate the relationship between sexual identity and effeminate bodies.

To explore the link between work and effeminacy, it was therefore important to look at a profession that, like domestic work, has been associated primarily with women. The work in beauty parlours yielded important insights and allowed us to explore both the subversions of masculinities and the reassertions of the male self through the performance of work.

There is interesting literature on male 'body work'. But most of this has focused on sports like wrestling, football, polo (Alter 1992; Archetti 1999; Hargreaves 1987), and so on, through which the physical body is produced as 'powerful' and virile. While the emphasis is on the anatomical, this literature also demonstrates the way the male body becomes a sign for the display of power and virility. The second set of literature that draws attention to the male body is the work on initiation rituals (Bloch 1986; Herdt 1981, 1984) through which the male body is adorned and marked as a transformed body. The point that is important for this research is the way that initiation rituals produce masculinity through transactions between men.

An aspect that emerged from the research and analysis in the context of beauty parlours was the nature of care that men extend to other men. Beauty work entails a physical exchange between the bodies of men who 'care' for the appearance of the male self. New formations of masculinity and the male self are produced through cultures of body care. Caring for the body and the production of a beautiful masculinity are a joint endeavour of clients and workers who share a particular view of the male body and the presentation of the masculine self. In a broader sense, caring through hands may be said to be a way in which support is extended between men, when one man places himself, literally and metaphorically, in the hands of another.

One of the critical arenas of support between men was through friendship. Friends were responsible for enabling migrants to get jobs as domestic workers or in beauty parlour. Friends created the context for an entry into the work and also taught them the techniques of how to work. Jobs and skills were key modes through which men 'passed on' something of value to their friends. Like inheritance patterns within family businesses, which moved along kinship and family networks, male friends worked 'like family' to enable their friends to work and earn 'for the sake of the family'.

Friendship networks were critical at significant junctures of men's lives. On the one hand, they enabled entry into working lives and the reproduction of necessary skills. On the other, friendship networks were the context for men to rearticulate autonomy, a sense of male self 'lost' through the performance of 'women's work'. Hanging around with their friends at the milk-booth or playing volleyball with friends in neighbourhood parks made it possible for male domestic workers to capture a part of the sense of autonomy and masculinity, away from the families of their employers. Friends and friendship groups provided the context for this reassertion. Friendship groups enabled the emergence and the rearticulation of agency and autonomous subjectivities.

If friends are a key group within which male selves are articulated and supported, then clearly this is a significant group for exploration. Here, the boys' clubs provided insights. One of the puzzling questions was why young boys are permitted to be away from the direct control of their fathers and families, and spend so much time hanging out and seemingly doing nothing at the club. No work happens in the club. Sometimes no games take place either. In fact, nothing of significant 'social' value seems to happen. The real question was why such licence was permitted to the boys, given the structures of patriarchal obedience and dependence that mark the lives of adolescent males vis-à-vis powerful fathers and adult men.

Clearly, there was something else that lay within the 'hanging out' that was not immediately apparent. Our attention was drawn to the hidden social value of hanging out by the substantial contributions made to the club by the entire neighbourhood. Despite the seeming waste of time, the club—the space and context of this hanging out—was supported in myriad ways (via donations, money, land and permissions) by the adults of the neighbourhood. It seemed clear, therefore, that the entire community recognised the club as a significant institution and was willing to donate valuable resources, like land and money, to establish the club and keep it going.

It is these substantive support practices extended by the neighbourhood to the club that impelled a different understanding of what the hanging out represented in the eyes of the community. It made us recognise that hanging out in the club is a way in which something of value—time—is given or spent freely to create something of value—the all-male friendship group. A second aspect was the way these clubs are spaces and sites for the articulation of formations of masculinities 'outside' the home. The clubs are collective bodies that initiate and introduce boys into worlds outside the family. Unlike schools, however, they are non-formal sites of socialisation of boys into the world of power and support. Boys and men of various ages go to these clubs, within which each age-set forms its own group, forming friendships through an exchange of ideas, views and feelings.

The non-family location of the club draws attention to the friendship group and its independent logic. The spirit of egalitarianism is a fundamental principle of the friendship group that counters relations of hierarchy in which boys, as adolescent 'incomplete men', are placed within the family. In constituting support and supportive practices, it was interesting to track how support was extended between men along egalitarian lines of friendship and community. The egalitarian mode or the idiom of fraternity was most apparent in the boys' clubs, but emerged in nascent and overt ways in narratives of male domestic workers and beauty parlour workers as well.

The spirit of egalitarianism can be posed against the structures of hierarchy in understanding relations between men. In terms of relations of support, this opposition has a particular significance. Within the hierarchic mode (and in relation to the field research), the father–son relation might be said to be the paradigmatic representation of the hierarchies that operate between men. The figure of the father represents the epitome of the authoritarian patriarch. Feminist literature has drawn attention to the figure of the patriarchal father, a figure that has represented and been the focus for articulating a series of oppressions experienced by women within patriarchal structures of power. Given the relative positioning of senior and junior, adult and adolescent, father and son, it is possible to assume that the latter positions (junior/adolescent/son) are the natural places to look for supportive practices. The former positions in the oppositional dyad (senior/adult/father) would be the sites of autocratic, repressive practices. One of the issues raised by this research, most importantly in the field of family businesses, but also in the other field sites, is the ways in which practices that constitute fathering might also be placed within the context of supportive relations and support practices.

In fact, what is importantly demonstrated is that fathering is a role centred on more than one man. Fathering as an ideology extends beyond the single man, the father, and is taken on, as it were, by men other than the genitor or the 'biological' father. Business families, for example, adopt strategies of deflecting conflict that might be inherent in the father–son relation. Within the family business (the expectation is that the son step directly into the father's shoes), it is often nephews who inherit businesses from their uncles, resolving, through deflection, the conflict inherent in the direct line between the father and son. By looping inheritance outwards on to tangential lines of affinal and collateral kin, a key relationship within the family, the father–son relation, is protected from disruptions. The family business is continued not necessarily in a direct lineal or agnatic line, but along affinal or collateral lines. This looping out has a bearing on the issue of fathering and fathering practice because it brings forward the idea that the fathering as a supportive practice is not done by the genitor alone, but by a whole group of men who stand in place of the father. It draws attention to the fact that just as there might be a proliferation of businesses that make up 'the family business', there is the equal possibility of a proliferation of fathers who play a critical role in the lives of younger men, not necessarily their sons.

Therefore, it cannot, and should not, be assumed that relations of hierarchy are divested of all forms of support. Support was offered along lines of hierarchy like father–son/uncle–nephew in family businesses as well as between higher and lower castes among barbers and their higher caste clients. Adult or older members of clubs offered advice to newer members, passing on skills of organising locality affairs, account keeping, and so on.

Thinking about the substance of support and its locations, the question of fathering as a wider set of practices done by a group of people highlights the material and the ideological existence of support. Support in business is substantive and actualised in loans, labour, space in shops and business networks. It also has a social and cultural existence through advice, business and craft skills, ways of the family and, most importantly, social networks inherited from elders. The social networks of support are those that are drawn upon during times of need and times when a family affirms and celebrates itself (for example, at ritual moments or family occasions).

Certain individuals exemplify this aspect of institutionalised support networks. In the life histories of such individual men, support might be extended along lines of hierarchy in the beginning, but may translate into friendship or egalitarian forms of support in subsequent periods of time. Deepchand, a man belonging to the caste of barbers, was supported in the initial stages of his working life by a high caste village fellow, who was also a professor at the University of Delhi, and, then later, by the university's vice chancellor. Both men helped him establish his barber's shop in the university campus. Like the young men in the club, Deepchand cultivated his networks of support that constituted his social capital. In his latter years, the caste distances and hierarchies gave way to more egalitarian relations. Now, Deepchand is formally invited to his clients' homes and they send their cars for him in gestures of friendship, acknowledging his 'worth' as a friend and not just as a barber of a low caste.

REFLECTIONS ON RESEARCH AND METHOD

Research such as the kind described in this chapter engages with the social worlds and the narratives of individual people in their different locations or contexts and begins from a stance that is critically different from the stance adopted by intervention research. For the sake of clarity, I will term the two kinds of research practices as 'anthropological' research and 'intervention' research. The two forms of research methodologies differ in their stances, strategies and methodological practices. Anthropological research begins with the assumption that its project is to discover what people say both obviously and subtly. The assumption is that people have their own conceptual capital and this must form part of the research 'findings', as much as the researchers' own conceptual frame. The point, of course, is that by choosing a particular paradigm or a set of questions (like the shift from violence to supportive practice when talking about men in families), anthropological research displays a prior point of view through which an anthropologist frames the issues at hand. Such framing will necessarily enter the process of interpretation as well.

Intervention research is far more self-conscious in performing this exercise. There is a choice already made—for example, involving men in women's health—and the agenda is to work out how best this objective may be achieved through strategies that involve rather than alienate the target group. So in some senses we might acknowledge the more up-front nature of intervention research, which anthropological research may not so readily display.

The problem with intervention research is that it is not always self-conscious of its own power position in relation to the target groups. 'Intervention' is a political word in that it expresses a relationship that positions the person who intervenes as 'active' and the people towards whom this intervention is directed as 'passive'. In its action, intervention does in fact seek to penetrate a target audience with a set of agendas and, in doing so, it comes accompanied by the politics and practices of power. In essence, intervention echoes the same problems that lie in words like penetration. Feminist writings have alerted us to the power of penetration, which blanks out agency and subjectivities of those who are positioned as penetrated. Both penetration and intervention involve notions of active bodies, influential points of view and powerful subject positions directed towards those who need to be altered, changed and transformed, as passive recipients of new knowledge, different roles and good practices.

This is not to claim that transformation is not a valid agenda. But I think it is important to recognise that people confront and engage with change and transformation continuously in their everyday lives. Daily lives are altered through movements of migrants, through doing effeminate work, by expanding the role of fathers towards other adult men. As researchers of all hues, we need to collectively understand the dynamics of these transformations, acknowledge their existence and then draw on them to think through ways of engaging with people's lives and their own conceptual capital as a source for our own supportive practices. It is an exercise in engagement that we need to strive towards, not the politics that underlies intervention.

CONCLUSION

A few issues emerge when thinking about practices of support. First, it is quite clear from the field research and analysis that support has a material and a non-material aspect. Second, support practices are diverse in terms of the cultural contexts within which they are articulated. Thus, family businesses and boys' clubs are both contexts in which supportive practices can be configured, but each context has its own set of distinctive practices.

Third, supportive practices are distinguished between those that already exist and those that come into existence or are created when people find themselves in situations of deprivation and a perceived loss of autonomy. In the latter instance, supportive practices have a transformative potential—as, for example, among male domestic workers who reaffirm their 'loss' of maleness by asserting friendship networks. Friendship is a form of capital that 'grows' into social networks of support. Great value is, therefore, placed upon creating friendship bonds, not just by those who are engaged in its immediate creation (like the boys of the neighbourhood clubs), but even by adults who enable the formations of friendship gangs. Friendship is an investment in the future and may, in fact, be viewed 'as if' it had a material existence.

Support—at least among men—is not taken for granted. It is cultivated with care and time (a thing of value) is freely spent in the cultivation of support networks. Strategies are developed to enhance support and deflect conflict within the family, especially where the reproduction of family fortunes depends on the continuance of the family. Conflict between the father and son standing in a direct lineal relation may be 'diverted' by overemphasising the support from 'other' fathers (maternal uncles, for example). The future reproduction of the family is assured by the strategic displacement of support and the consequent deflection of conflict.

How do these conclusions engage with the larger issue of gender equality and domestic democracy? First, this research has tried to bring into focus the way men's support can be outlined and reflected upon. Men's friendship groups may become an enabling site within which issues of domestic democracy can be parleyed into a discursive context. This potential of the friendship group is already present and was demonstrated by the example of the boys' club group in the role it played in the resolution of a marital dispute within a neighbourhood family. Second, older men in the family play very different roles and offer different kinds of support to younger men. Apart from uncles in business families, hierarchically placed upper caste men do assist low caste men to get work and support their families, indirectly entering as 'supportive partners' of lower caste men. Often the most direct kin relative may not be the most critical player in the life of a younger man.

Drawing from these instances, it may be possible to argue that in the case of women's reproductive health, the husband (the most direct partner) may not necessarily be the most supportive partner. A woman's genitor—her father in her natal home—may, in fact, be a more supportive partner in the context of her reproductive health than her husband or her father-in-law. Such support is already in place within the kinship networks, at least, of north India and might be drawn upon and expanded. The elaboration of fathering through the practices of group fathering helps us think through the idea of 'deflection of conflict' and in locating the key supportive partner in deflected rather than direct relations.

Asserting support as a frame enables us to engage with a particular language and practice of masculinity. In talking about themselves and their lives, men did not have a very articulate vocabulary to speak about themselves, except when they were narrating the support they received or had given. Supportive practices are, therefore, more than an 'alternative' frame within which to place men. They enable us to hear an aspect of men's lives and expressions of their subjective positions in ways that have not so far been addressed. Supportive practices are an idiom, which explicate agentic subjectivities and provide a language of engagement with the lives and cultural locations of men.

NOTE

1. As part of the 'Frontiers Programme in Reproductive Health', the Population Council's Men-in-Maternity Study was designed to help men '...redefine their roles in reproductive health... [and] to assess the impact of male partnership in improving pregnancy outcomes and reproductive health... [because] studies suggest that the lack of men's participation in reproductive health actually undermines women's health...'(Caleb et al. 2002: 1–2).

REFERENCES

Alter, J. 1992. *The Wrestler's Body: Identity and Ideology in North India*. Berkeley: University of California Press.
Anandi, S. and J. Jeyaranjan. 2002. 'Masculinity and Domestic Violence in a Tamil Nadu Village', Research Report, International Center for Research on Women, Washington, D.C.
Archetti, E. P. 1999. *Masculinities: Football, Polo and Tango in Argentina*, Oxford: Berg.
Bloch, M. 1986. *From Blessing to Violence: History and Ideology in the Circumcision Ritual of the Merina of Madagascar*. Cambridge: Cambridge University Press.
Brake, M. 1980. *The Sociology of Youth Culture and Youth Subculture: Sex, Drugs and Rock n' Roll*. London: RKP.
Caleb-Varkey, L., A. Das, A. Mishra, E. Ottalenghi and D. Huntington. 2002. 'Frontiers in Reproductive Health', *Research Update*, No. 2, April. New Delhi: Population Council.
Chopra, R. (ed.). 2002. *From Violence to Supportive Practice: Family, Gender and Masculinity in India*. New Delhi: UNIFEM, South Asia Regional Office.
Government of India. 2001. 'National Family Health Survey (NFHS)', second round conducted in 1998–99.
———. 1999. 'National Family Health Survey (NFHS)', first round conducted in 1992–93.
Hargreaves, J. 1987. 'The Body, Sport and Power Relation', in J. Horne, David Jary and Alan Tomlinson (eds), *Sport, Leisure and Social Relations*. London: RKP.
Herdt, G. (ed.). 1984 *Ritualised Homosexuality in Melanesia*. Berkeley: University of California Press.
———. 1981. *Guardians of the Flutes: Idioms of Masculinity*. New York: McGraw Hill.
ICRW. 2002. *Men Masculinity and Domestic Violence in India: Summary Report of Four Studies*. New Delhi: ICRW.
Jankowski, M. S. 1991. *Islands in the Street: Gangs and American Urban Society*. Berkeley: University of California Press.
Menon-Sen, K. and A. K. Shiva Kumar. 2001. *Women in India: How Free? How Equal?* New Delhi: UNDP.
Nussbaum, C. Martha. 2000. *Women and Human Development: The Capabilities Approach*. New Delhi: Kali for Women.

Osella, C. and F. Osella. 1998. 'Friendship and Flirting: Micropolitics in Kerala, South India', *JRAI*, 4(2): 189–206.
Sangari, K. and S. Vaid. 1981. 'Sati in Modern India', *EPW,* 16(31): 1284–88.
Sunder Rajan, Rajeshwari. 1993. *Real and Imagined Women: Gender, Culture and Post-Colonialism*. London: Routledge.
Visaria, L. 2000. 'Violence against Women', *EPW,* 35(18): 1742–51.
Willis, P. 1975. 'The Expressive Style of a Motor Bike Culture', in J. Benthall and T. Polemus (eds), *Body as a Medium of Expression*. London: Allen Lane.

10

Placing Gender Equity in the Family Centre Stage

The Use of Kala Jatha *Theatre*[1]

◆

Joy Deshmukh-Ranadive

INTRODUCTION

Empowerment is the most frequently used term in development dialogue today. It is also the most nebulous and widely interpreted of concepts, which has simultaneously become a tool for analysis and an umbrella concept to justify development intervention. At the World Summit for Social Development held at Copenhagen in March 1995, empowerment featured prominently as an objective. The Draft Declaration of the Third Preparatory Committee (New York, 16–27 January 1995) adopted by the heads of the states and governments, asserted that 'the most productive policies and investments are those which empower people to maximise their capacities, resources and opportunities.' The same document, in Point 23.0, emphasised that the main objective of development is to empower people, particularly women, to strengthen their capacities. This is to be achieved through the full participation of people in the formulation, implementation and evaluation of decisions determining the functioning and well-being of society. Empowerment is central to the current liberalisation discourse, which transfers considerable responsibility of welfare to civil society. While initially efforts were launched in the name of 'emancipation', today the goal of national and international policies, development programmes and non-governmental organisation (NGO) activity seems to have shifted to achieving 'empowerment'.

Empowerment can be understood as an expansion in spaces.[2] This expansion can take place in physical spaces, economic spaces, socio-cultural spaces and political spaces. Physical spaces consist of two kinds—geographical space and body space. The limited mobility of women over geographical distance restricts their access to opportunities of education, health and employment. Their control over their own bodies is also limited. Economic spaces represent opportunities for livelihoods, employment, property, and so on. It is a known fact that women have always worked. However, their economic contribution has been hidden from view. Unless their work translates into monetary incomes, it is rarely regarded as work. Poverty alleviation programmes often see the generation of livelihoods and incomes as the panacea to pull households out of poverty traps and to empower women. Socio-cultural space is determined by class, caste, race, region, and so on. Poor women from dalit households are thrice discriminated against by virtue of their class, caste and gender. Political space also has two dimensions to it—the public political space and the private political space. The public political space is the access to public office and processes of political activity. It can also be interpreted as the formation of social capital. The expansion of these spaces is one of the most important constituents towards lending voice to the problems of poor marginalised groups. The private political space consists of hierarchies and placements within families and households, which are determined by age, relationship and gender. Kinship, lineage, ideology and socio-cultural norms determine these placements and, consequently, the status of members within households. It is a known fact that the patriarchal, unilateral and patrilineal systems generate the most oppressive circumstances for women and girl children within households.

Interventions such as micro-credit succeed in impacting upon the macro and domestic environments, particularly on the economic dimension, since it enhances opportunities for livelihoods. It also expands the public political dimension when it operates through the formation of Self Help Groups (SHGs). The woman's physical space also expands due to her membership and activity in the SHG. However, the socio-cultural environment is the most stubborn and difficult to alter and, in consequence, the socio-cultural space is difficult to negotiate. The cost of an expansion in this space is often high for an individual woman. That is the reason why collectives and collective action are more effective vehicles to set a process of empowerment into motion. Further, paradoxically, a process of empowerment cannot accelerate unless there is an expansion of socio-cultural space. This is because while an expansion in physical, economic and political spaces can lead to an expansion in mental space, with socio-cultural space the logic has to be turned on its head. For there to be an expansion in socio-cultural space, there has to be first an expansion in mental space.[3] For this to happen, there is need for outside interventions which supplement economic interventions such as micro-credit programmes.

This chapter presents 'Gender Equity in the Family', an experimental intervention conducted during 2002–03, through the use of folk theatre with the intention of altering perceptions of members of households towards more equitable relationships between men and women.[4] The intervention was conducted within the Andhra Pradesh District Poverty Initiatives Project (APDPIP) in the district of Mahbubnagar.[5] The main objective of the APDPIP is to improve opportunities for the rural poor so as to eradicate poverty and eliminate current inequalities that prevent women, scheduled castes (SCs), scheduled tribes (STs) and other backward groups from realising their full potential. In spite of awareness about gender issues within the APDPIP, a vital component is missing due to which the efforts at empowerment of the poor and, particularly, of women do not yield desired results. Perceptions about the role of men and of women are often at the root of conflict in the face of changing identities that come about with interventions such as those of the APDPIP. There was, hence, a need for an attempt to unpack the household, with a commitment towards changing perceptions so as to break the vicious circle of gender destitution and poverty.

Joy Deshmukh-Ranadive

DPIP IN MAHBUBNAGAR[6]

In 1991, the SAARC heads of the states met at Colombo and established the independent South Asian Commission on Poverty Alleviation to study the regional problem of persistent poverty and suggest an action plan. The commission's recommendation led to the 1993 Dhaka Declaration for Eradication of Poverty, which urged for an empowerment approach to poverty alleviation in which the poor are given support to develop and fully utilise their productive capacities. The UNDP assisted the South Asia Poverty Alleviation Programme (SAPAP) pilot project in three districts of Andhra Pradesh, which emerged in 1996 out of this initiative. The project strategy relied on a three-pronged strategy of social mobilisation of the poor, skill development and capital formation.[7]

Encouraged by the impact of SAPAP, the Government of Andhra Pradesh (GOAP) decided to emulate the social mobilisation approach into its major poverty reduction project, namely, the World Bank-supported APDPIP. The APDPIP is a Rs 600 crore World Bank-supported five year (2000–05) project. The GOAP established an independent support organisation by the name of Society for Elimination of Rural Poverty (SERP) to implement poverty elimination projects which aim at social mobilisation to enhance livelihoods and employment generation opportunities of the poor. SERP also oversees the social mobilisation processes of APDPIP. Against this background, GOAP launched a poverty reduction project called DPIP in Mahbubnagar district along with five other districts. The other districts are Adilabad from Telangana, Chittor and Ananthapur from Rayalaseema, and Srikakulam and Vizianagaram from coastal Andhra. In Mahbubnagar district, the project is supposed to cover 1,00,000 poor households in 35 mandals in a period of five years. The GOAP initiated the Rural Poverty Elimination Program under the project Velugu[8] of which the second phase, Andhra Pradesh Rural Poverty Reduction Project (APRPRP), started in June 2002.

The main objective of the project is to enable the rural poor in Andhra Pradesh to improve their livelihoods and quality of life. To achieve this, the project focuses on the following. It helps create self-managed grassroot level institutions of the poor, namely, SHGs,

Village Organisations (VOs) and Mandal Samakhyas (MSs). SHGs have been formed as organisations at the village level. These organisations are then formed into Mandal Mahila Samakhyas at the mandal level. Microfinance is supposed to bind the institutional and human capacity-building components in the project. The formation and operationalisation of women's/youth groups create the entry point for other activities and interventions. The main objective of the microfinance operations is to establish an alternative and sustainable credit system for the poor. These are supposed to empower women to play a dynamic role in social, economic, political and cultural activities in their communities as well as in the larger society.

Mahbubnagar district forms a part of the Telengana region, which is a land-locked region with hot summers, warm winters and sporadic rainfall. The distinctive feature of this region is an undulating topography dotted with monad rocks. Agriculture is the mainstay of the rural economy. Consistent drought is a common phenomenon. Added to it are undulating lands, low fertility of land, seasonal wage employment and consequently large-scale migration. These indicate the economic backwardness of the district. With 25.22 per cent literacy and 13.87 per cent female literacy, and 50 per cent of the population being non-workers, the district presents a poor social development scene. Of the total workers, 82 per cent still depend upon agriculture activity as against 70 per cent in case of the state as a whole. The female literacy rate among SCs and STs is as low as 4.37 per cent and 2.51 per cent, respectively. The female ratio has declined from 983 for 1,000 males to 973 in 10 years from 1981 to 1991. Both covert and overt forms of discriminatory practices, for instance, the practice of the *jogini*[9] system, can still be seen in many parts of the district.

THE PRESENCE AND ABSENCE OF GENDER CONCERNS

In all the endeavours of Velugu, gender equity is stated as an important concern and is being achieved by enhancing the roles of women at the household and community levels. The basic focus is to create social capital for the poor through the creation/promotion of self-managed institutions, developing activists and paraprofessionals from amongst the poor, and enhancing their capacities to manage their resources and also access public services. The project functionaries and community coordinators are regularly trained to develop their capacities to evolve as full-fledged development professionals. The project also supports investments in sub-projects proposed by grassroot institutions of the poor to accelerate their entry and expand their involvement in social and economic activities. The sub-projects enable the poor to increase the productivity of the assets under their control, enable them to enhance their incomes and opportunities, reduce their expenditures and risks, and manage their natural environment. Attempts are made to improve access to education for girls and to reduce the incidence of child labour among the poor.

The SHG women federated at the village and mandal levels have been undergoing various capacity-building programmes for their empowerment. As a result, they have been debating and discussing the issues related to their status in society in all their regular scheduled meetings. Against this background, the DPIP felt that poverty eradication cannot be addressed unless their present status is enhanced. Therefore, the DPIP as a part of its gender strategy facilitated them to form 'Women Rights Protection Committees' in the spirit of self help, with stakeholders addressing their problems on their own. Accordingly, all the five Samakhyas established earlier under SAPAP, formed these committees with the objective of creating a forum for the grievances of women. Subsequently, these committees were not limited to the SAPAP groups and were formed in 15–16 mandals wherever the Mandal Samakhyas came into existence. These committees meet as and when a case of atrocity or injustice is reported to them or brought to their notice. They have organised several legal awareness programmes among the SHG members at the village level. As a result, many cases of injustice against women have been brought to light. During several deliberations of the committee, the necessity for a full-time legal advisor was felt. Accordingly, the services of a full-time lady legal advisor were contracted by the three Mandal Mahila Samakhyas of Kosgi, Bomraspet and Doulatabad. It is her job to attend scheduled meetings of federations of SHGs at the village and mandal levels and take stock of the cases of injustice against women. She takes up the cases, calls for both parties, counsels them

Placing Gender Equity in the Family Centre Stage

and tries for a settlement to the satisfaction of both parties. Her endeavour is to avoid a legal battle in the court and avoid police action.

It was in the course of my attending a workshop, during which SERP had facilitated an exposure visit to the field, that I had the opportunity of visiting the people and women's groups in Mahbubnagar.[10] While it was evident that the women were aware of all the concerns that SERP was addressing through the Velugu project, nothing much had changed fundamentally in the household. Conversations with the activists in the field brought to light how in some areas, the hostility within the household because of the importance that women got in the public space through membership in the groups had been overcome. In some areas, however, the tensions had increased. A case was reported where a husband had violently killed his wife who was extremely active in the mahila sangha. The workshop also mentioned instances of increased workloads for the women in the light of their increased activity outside the house arising out of membership in sanghas.

Conversations with the village people in particular also brought to light the preeminent preference for a son in the family. This was also the case in largely tribal villages where bride price rather than dowry prevailed. An inquiry with the Velugu staff about why this was so, did not meet with any conclusive or convincing answers. Further, there was also repeated mention of the hostile relations between mothers-in-law and daughters-in-law. This was particularly so since it was generally thought that mothers-in-law were supposed to keep their daughters-in-law in line by treating them with unkindness otherwise the latter would ill-treat mothers-in-law. A meeting with a group of young activists revealed their failure to see the difference between working with groups of women and understanding gender discrimination. Somewhere the understanding was that by working with women, gender issues were automatically being addressed and in dealing with specificities like girl child labour, *joginis*, and so on, adequate addressal of gender discrimination was being done. While I could see the tremendous advance in the empowerment of women in the public spaces, there was little attempt to delve into the household in an attempt to change perceptions towards other forms of democracy. They could not comprehend there was gender discrimination in ordinary 'normal' families, for example, in the nature of gendered division of work, in the relationships between women or in son preference. In order to capture the reality of women's lives there has to be a simultaneous focus on two dimensions. One, the specific instances/issues of discrimination (as has been done by the legal advisor). And two, the general structure of exploitative social norms, which guide people's everyday behaviour and are taken as normal, justified and legitimate. APDPIP addressed the first but not the second. Due to the limitations inherent in the perceptions of policy makers, policy interventions most often are tailored to address issues that manifest themselves in public spaces. However, even if conceptually one can divide the two spaces of the public and the private, in reality they intertwine and impact upon one another. Hence, there comes a time when policy has to blur the divide and include the dynamics within households into its scrutiny. Social and political responsibility of familial injustices may be difficult to achieve, but their consideration is necessary.

I was particularly impressed with the performances of the *Kala Jatha* (folk theatre) groups which performed at sangha meetings on the issues of early marriage of girls, child marriage and *jogini*s. The impact of these performances on the women in the audience was phenomenal. I remember a play where the story is told of a girl who is married early and then dies since she was unable to bear the rigours of having a child. I was informed that initially the play had a harsh mother-in-law and the audience consequently related the girls' death to her ill-treatment at the hands of her mother-in-law rather than because her body was too immature to take on marriage and child bearing. The script was subsequently changed to incorporate a kind and loving mother-in-law. Apparently, the problem of harsh mothers-in-law was widespread.

It was after I had expressed my observations at the workshop that there was a suggestion by SERP that I conduct a sub-project to incorporate my suggestions of opening up the household for scrutiny. It was my belief that since SERP had done so much work in social mobilisation and in generating awareness, the ground was fertile for more tricky questions of discriminatory social norms to be brought centre stage. Such an intervention, I believed, was vital for enhancing the effectiveness of programmes like Velugu that sought to empower the poor, in general, and women, in particular.

CONCEPTUALISING 'GENDER EQUITY IN THE FAMILY'

Empowerment does not necessarily take place when incomes are generated or when livelihoods are enhanced or for that matter when groups are formed. Social capital empowers people undoubtedly. However, the scope of that empowerment is limited. This is because within families and households, hierarchies and structures do not alter. Hence, changes in public areas with respect to new formations of social capital or new avenues of income generation, especially when they are directed to and through women, even contribute towards accentuating tensions within households.

An individual woman is placed within a domestic environment and has to negotiate her spaces within it. The domestic unit is placed within a larger macro environment and, as a collective, negotiates for space within that environment. As an individual, the woman too has to negotiate within the larger reality of the macro environment. Both the domestic and the macro environment comprise of the same four components, namely, physical, economic, socio-cultural and political. This macro physical environment is shaped by certain initial physical characteristics depending upon geographical location, soil, climate, landscape, and so on. The macro economic environment is shaped by economic opportunities offered by the economy, institutions, level of industrialisation, state of the rural economy, and so on. The macro socio-cultural environment depends upon the structures of caste, class, race, religion and the inter-group as well as intra-group relations within each category. This environment also depends upon culture, kinship patterns and gender norms. The macro political environment is determined by the level, type, quality and transparency of public office. It also depends on the kind of govern-ance that exists in the state. Citizenship and matters related to public life fall within the ambit of political environment. One finds that macro changes in the nature of state-enforced political and economic interventions alter micro level dynamics, thereby, changing the opportunity patterns of families and individuals.

The policies and interventions made by the state and non-state bodies act upon the macro environment, which in turn alters the domestic environment. This has a consequent effect in altering spaces for the individual.

Interventions succeed in impacting the physical, economic and political components of the macro environment. Hence, it is these three spaces, too, that are expanded by external interventions, be they of micro-credit, education, panchayati raj, and so on. The socio-cultural environment is the most stubborn and difficult to alter and in consequence the socio-cultural space is difficult to negotiate. The cost of an expansion in this space is often high for an individual woman since it isolates her. That is the reason why collectives and collective action are the vehicles to set a process of empowerment into motion. Further, a process of empowerment cannot accelerate unless there is an expansion of socio-cultural space. This is because while an expansion in physical, economic and political space can lead to an expansion in mental space, with socio-cultural space the logic has to be turned on its head. There has to first be an expansion in mental space for there to be an expansion in socio-cultural space.[11]

Through the impact of interventions upon the macro environment, the domestic environment alters. The more immediate impacts are seen in the economic and physical spheres. Political and socio-cultural aspects within a domestic environment are stubborn to alter and this is where many policies fail to make a dent. In that case, only practical gender needs are met and strategic gender needs not addressed.

Policies and state interventions are subject to the usual economic constraints of scarce resources and multiple ends. Hence, when the appeal for women's empowerment has to be made, it is usually found that when it makes economic sense or when the instrumental value (use value) of the intervention matches the goals of the policy makers, only then is the programme implemented faster. Hence, the justification for women's empowerment has to make sense in terms of the broader development goals of the nation.[12] It is difficult for schemes to directly address and focus upon altering power structures within households. However, even while addressing other forms of environment like the economic, there can be modifications or innovations that challenge existing structures of power.

The APDPIP has succeeded in some measure in altering the economic spaces, physical geographical spaces and public political spaces of women. There is a concentrated effort to alter socio-cultural space in the focused treatment of the problems of dalits in the region of Mahbubnagar. However, when the economic and public political spaces of women expand, it often leads to an increase in the burden of work and domestic violence on women, since existing hierarchies within the household are threatened with changes in the role of women in the public sphere. Within policy interventions there is absolutely no direct focus upon addressing the private political space as is vested within families and households. This has an extremely important bearing upon the lives of women and the extent to which they can be empowered. In order for the interventions of DPIP to lead to a more holistic empowerment of women and in order that frictions due to changes in the spaces of women's lives are lessened, such a gender intervention is necessary.

The nexus between poverty and gender equity is also very direct. Gender biases that discriminate against girl-children make them grow into women who are disadvantaged in both health and education. The opportunities, subsequently, available to them are limited. Early marriages, early and frequent child bearing, being subject to violence with the family and sexual harassment both in and outside the home make women the poorer of the poorest class. The life of women without the support of a man— for instance, when they are widowed, divorced or deserted— plummets them into the depths of poverty. Gender biases are the result of conditioning, which is the result of social structures that have been handed down over the years. Perceptions about the role of men and of women are often at the root of conflict in the face of changing identities that come about with interventions such as those of the APDPIP. Hence, the dire need for some attempt to be made to unpack the household with a commitment towards changing perceptions so as to somewhere break the vicious circle of gender destitution and poverty.

GENDER EQUITY IN THE FAMILY

The intervention 'Gender Equity in the Family' was the first of its kind to be attempted and its originality lay in the approach and the non-negotiable aspects that were built into the intervention. It questioned value systems and involved entire households in rethinking traditional knowledge about gender roles and householding. The plays sought to impart information that is contextualised within local realities. Processes, which seek to alter values, can transform understandings of power from the negative to the positive where, at a stage, empowerment becomes synonymous with power. Such attempts seem ambitious but are acutely needed. Even if answers are not arrived at, the exercise of generating and addressing questions produces new forms of knowledge. The intervention was planned in the following manner. It was essentially non-confrontist so as to not pit one member of the family against another. It involved both men and women in the unpacking of the household. The intervention had as a 'non-negotiable' that no single person would be blamed. This was deliberate since the intent was to make even the perpetrator of an injustice realise that the real culprit behind the scene is the larger 'social structure' which causes her/him to behave in an unjust manner. The intervention drew out how both the victim and the perpetrator of injustices are victims of social structures that condition people into behaving in certain ways and patterns. The intervention used the existing understanding of injustice as in the case of dalits[13] to draw parallels within the household. Since the strategy was one of action research, hence, along with sensitisation, consensus and commitment were sought from the sangha[14] members and their husbands who attended the sessions. The attempt was to have this commitment translated into attempts by the community to expand democratisation within their own homes. The communication of ideas was carried out through plays, songs and exposure sessions. *Kala Jatha*[15] (folk theatre) teams and theatre personnel from the villages enacted the plays. The message in all the plays was one of human values and harmony and the necessity of working together for the betterment of individuals, households and communities.

PUTTING ISSUES CENTRE STAGE

A project coordinator specially appointed for this intervention coordinated these plays.[16] The two mandals of Panagal and Koyilakonda, with six villages from the first and five from the second, were selected.[17] The play was performed before entire villages. Performances would start by nine at night and continue till midnight. This time was selected so that the people, after finishing their household chores and having dinner, could come and watch the play. Attention was drawn for almost two hours prior to the play, beginning with the sound of beating drums and songs[18] from the DPIP Project so that the villagers were informed about the imminent performance and the mood was set. The play was then performed and was followed by a discussion conducted by the coordinator. It was observed that entire communities engaged in dialogue with the coordinator in discussing the message of the play. The coordinator also sought a commitment from the community in implementing the lessons in human values.

Initially an orientation workshop was organised for the *Kala Jatha* team that was to perform.[19] Of the intended three plays, the first plot was discussed and the strategy of the intervention was explained. The project director suggested the plot, and the scenes were framed to fit the plot. This plot revolved around the gender division of work in the house. The opening scene is one where the husband is at home with the children and the house is untidy, food is not cooked and everyone is looking fed-up and irritated. The wife had gone to attend an SHG meeting and returns very excited since she has been elected secretary of the group. During the workshop, the team was divided into three groups and these were instructed to write the opening scene. It was astounding to note that all three groups, unknown to each other, had written the same dynamic with almost the same dialogues. The husband while venting out his anger at his wife accuses her of neglecting the home and, in the name of leaving the boundaries of the house for her meetings, of indulging in adultery! Would the findings of any survey on SHGs be as startling?

The first play dealt with the issue of gender-based division of labour within the household and the gendered identities of men and women in ways that lead to violence by men against women. The wife is shown to have become popular in public and also able to generate income through her participation in the micro-credit programme. The man feels threatened, believing that his manhood is at stake. All the while, there are two more characters on stage. One is dressed as a demon and symbolises social norms and is shown to reside in the house. This character has no dialogue. It only whispers into the ears of the perpetrator of injustice. The other character symbolises human values and rights and hovers outside the house.

When things reach a climax, the man beats his wife. At this point, the human-values character engages in a dialogue with the man and draws his attention to the fact that he is actually being made to behave in such manner by the demon. An argument follows between the two, where issues of male and female identities are discussed. The husband is told that the home belongs to all, hence all can contribute and there is no place for a word like 'help' in a home. 'Help' implies that one person is doing the other's work. So, contributing towards income is as much legitimate for the woman as is engaging in household chores for the man. In either case, there is no threat to identities. It is said that this demon resides in all homes and should be thrown out. As the husband starts getting convinced, the demon is shown as collapsing and, in its place, the human-values character comes to reside in the home. The play ends with a song about human values—that a person is first a human being and then a role (wife or a husband). The play is interspersed with songs and situations are explained through them.

After a span of a couple of weeks, this play was followed by the second play on relationships between women, especially between mothers-in-law and daughters-in-law. The thrust of the play was to show that women are not mere victims that suffer but can also be the active perpetrators of violence. However, again the perpetrator is as much a victim of social norms as is the overt victim. The play encourages the audience to see the advantages of camaraderie between women in the household.

Some weeks later, the same villages saw the third play which dealt with the issue of son preference. This play took up the issue of the discrimination of the girl child where both parents were shown as partners in the crime of son preference. The story line in the plot showed that the son is allowed to continue with his schooling while the daughter is pulled out of school. There is discrimination in the serving of food to the two children. The play showed that like there is a caste and class hierarchy outside the home, there is one within the home and the girl child is the dalit and the poorest in the family. The parallel between the outside and inside worlds was understood by the audience immediately. Both the second and third play had the same central character of the demon of social norms and the observatory and advisory character of human rights. All the three plays ended with similar songs with the refrains that the right to be a human being is above the role of being wife/daughter-in-law/daughter.

The experience of participating in this project was empowering for the performing team too. In particular, the coordinator evolved from being a shy unsure woman to an ardent advocate of human rights in the home. The communication skills of the coordinator were put to test since she had to field questions, which raised the standard myths about masculinity and femininity. It is particularly remarkable how the coordinating of this project changed the perceptions and personality of the coordinator herself.[20] While her confidence levels increased, the coordinator reported that where initially she was sceptical whether people would be open to think about such issues, she was proved wrong. Consequently, her skills at arguing, demystifying issues and challenging myths grew stronger.[21] At the beginning, information about alternative value systems was received in a mixed manner. The responses from the audience were extremely dynamic. There were a lot of discussions and arguments. The performance witnessed by the project director saw the younger men more open to suggestion, while the older ones felt threatened and raised their voices. The coordinator, however, reported that in other villages she had seen a positive response from older men too. In fact, one of them asked her why she did not come to their village earlier with such a message. Women initially tended to speak less. As the discussions progressed, they were more eloquent. The rest of the performing team—the actors, song writer, script writer—were also encouraged to move among the audience and answer questions. The entire team reported a feeling of purpose while performing these plays. According to them, the fact that they were trying to change behaviour patterns within the community made them 'activists'.[22] Hence, it can be noticed that the process of transforming information into knowledge and the altering of values has already begun at various levels, one at the level of the audience and the other at the level of the team.

The significance of this intervention was that it was carried out with the support of a state run institution (SERP). Hence, it corroborated the mainstream understanding of the protection of human rights being the responsibility of the state. It is difficult for the state and its machinery to directly enter the domestic unit. Entry is usually indirect through, say, population policies, health policies, education policies, and so on. 'Gender Equity in the Family' is an example of the state's direct attempt to address issues which are otherwise considered 'private' and out of bounds. The reason why the process and progress of the intervention was non-controversial was that the philosophy underlying the exercise was non-confrontist and involved the entire community. The problems addressed also cut across divisions of caste and class. Further, it was located within the larger endeavour of the state to generate livelihoods through micro-credit and SHGs. Hence, it was seen as supportive of the wider development design of the government.

IN CONCLUSION: POWER AND EMPOWERMENT

Power is usually understood in a negative sense where one is a victim and the other an exploiter. It is only recently that feminist writing has begun to see that as much as there is power over, there is also power to, power with and power within (Zoe and Sally 1997). 'Power over' involves a relationship of domination–subordination. It is based ultimately on socially sanctioned threats of violence and intimidation and requires constant vigilance. It also invites active and passive resistance. 'Power to' relates to having decision-making authority and the power to solve problems, and thus can be creative and enabling. The third, 'power with', involves people organising with a common purpose or common understanding to achieve collective goals. The fourth, 'power within', refers to self-confidence, self-awareness and assertiveness. Through this power, individuals can recognise, by analysing their experience, how power operates in their lives, and gain the confidence to act to influence and change this. The first interpretation of power as 'power over' gives the rationale to begin a process of empowerment. The second interpretation of 'power to' talks of the ultimate stage of empowerment when a person has achieved the capacity to take action. Here empowerment and power collapse positively into action. The third interpretation of 'power with' reflects upon the methods by which empowerment processes are initiated and set into motion. Collectives with purpose are the best examples of 'power with'. The fourth interpretation of power as 'power within' can be interpreted as the sustenance of the process whereby empowerment does not remain limited in intermittent actions and can instead be conceived as the building of capacities to carry out future action in a sustained manner.

Interventions at mobilising women around issues of injustice have most often been directed at combating 'power over' with 'power with'. However, it is a mistake to isolate a woman or a collective of women to participate in a process of empowerment. While 'power with' can increase the 'power within' and 'power to', there is a necessity for the other members of the household to be also involved in processes of empowerment. Social change can come about with changes in perceptions about the larger canvas of social behaviour. Major aberrations such as abuse, violation or violence have to be addressed differently. However, the everyday patterns of gender discrimination, which are accepted as justified and socially legitimate, have to be also questioned and placed centre stage. The so-called 'ordinary occurrences' and 'normal' families have to be opened for examination. 'Gender Equity in the Family' was one such attempt.

NOTES

1. An earlier version of this paper was presented at the Xth National Conference of the Indian Association for Women's Studies, Bhubaneswar: 17–20 October 2002 under the Sub-theme 2: 'Promoting Democracy within the Family', conducted by Joy Deshmukh-Ranadive.
2. For a detailed analysis of the concept of 'space' and its use to understand power and empowerment, see Deshmukh-Ranadive (2002).
3. It may seem as if a conceptualisation of power and empowerment in terms of spaces confines empowerment to a static understanding and is in conflict with the actual dynamic nature of its being a process. However, the act of negotiating for more space is the dynamic characteristic of the struggle towards empowerment. Further, in as much as there is action to elbow for more spaces within altered spaces afforded by external stimuli, there cannot be a static understanding of empowerment.
4. The project 'Gender Equity in the Family' was a collaborative venture between the Centre for Women's Development Studies, New Delhi and Society for Elimination of Rural Poverty, Hyderabad.
5. The author wishes to thank Mr K. Raju, IAS, who was then CEO at Society for Elimination of Rural Poverty (SERP), for encouraging and supporting

this experimental venture. If it were not for his commitment to gender concerns, this project would not have seen the light of day. Thank you to the present CEO, Mr T. Vijay Kumar, IAS, for continuing support. Gratitude is also expressed to Mr B. Rajshekhar and Mr Raghunandan Rao, Project Directors of Mahbubnagar district over the period of the project during 2002, for their support. It is difficult to address gender concerns in the field unless officers such as these believe in the necessity of such interventions. The project was implemented by the District Poverty Initiatives Project (DPIP), Mahbubnagar, at the district level and SERP, Hyderabad, at the state level. It was funded by SERP.

6. This section has been drawn from Murthy et al. (2002).
7. This phase lasted from 1996 to December 2002.
8. Velugu means 'light' in Telugu.
9. The *jogini* system is where young girls are dedicated to a temple God or Goddess and then go on to live the lives of socially legitimised prostitutes.
10. Experience Sharing Workshop: Emerging Practices across the DPIPs in India, 25–28 February 2002, Hyderabad.
11. See n. 3.
12. For example, it is always found that those promoting education for women argue that educated girls make better mothers and family care-givers. This justification is better assimilated by policy makers than the counter one of education fostering enlightenment, which itself is a value to be nurtured.
13. The lowest and most discriminated caste in the Indian caste hierarchy.
14. Micro-credit groups.
15. The team received orientation training from the Project Director.
16. The author is extremely grateful for the efforts put in by V. Sunitha, the project coordinator of the Gender-Equity in the Family Project. She has proved to be an effective communicator capable of conducting the plays in the villages and handling the subsequent discussions that follow. It has been her perseverance that has overcome numerous unforeseen difficulties and has kept the flow of performances going. She has also conducted a base line survey to tap perceptions prior to the performances. The framework of spaces was used to formulate the questionnaire of this survey.
17. The villages were selected by DPIP, Mahbubnagar. The criteria were the nearest villages to the district headquarters, deep interior villages, the villages with strong SHGs and Village Organisations, villages with only one community (dalit), villages that are not covered under Velugu so far and villages where social evils are particularly manifest. Since conducting the plays was a logistic problem, the project director left the choice of the villages to DPIP, Mahbubnagar.
18. The songs revolve around various development-related issues. Villagers are already familiar with these songs and some have already achieved the status of anthems.
19. This workshop was held in July 2002. The author is grateful to the cultural team of Mahbubnagar and to Sh. Kurumurthy and Sh. Shreevatsa for their

commitment towards training the team, working out the scripts, penning the songs and writing the music.
20. The author cannot help but mention the role of Sunitha's husband, Satyam, whose gender-sensitivity lent strength to his wife's capacities as coordinator and also increased her credibility to carry the message of democratising the family into the field.
21. Particular mention must be made that Sunitha handled discussions for hours without reacting negatively to the heat generated by the audience. The benign smile on her face took away offence that might otherwise have been felt when she had to be firm. The author found this strategy educative.
22. The plays that the members of this team were used to performing raised awareness about child marriage, child labour and *joginis*. These social issues were identified by SERP as being as critical as the DPIP. The team found 'Gender Equity in the Family' different since it believed that these were more sensitive issues and did not represent overt malpractices as did child labour and the *jogini's* problems. It said that it was not easy to question patterns of households which were age-old and accepted norms of life.

REFERENCES

Deshmukh-Ranadive, Joy. 2002. *Space for Power, Women's Work and Family Strategies in South and South-East Asia.* New Delhi: Centre for Women's Development Studies and Rainbow Publishers.

Murthy, Ranjani K., K. Raju and Amitha Kamath. 2002. 'Towards Women's Empowerment and Poverty Reduction: Lessons from the Participatory Impact Assessment of South Asian Poverty Alleviation Programme in Andhra Pradesh, India'. Report submitted to the UNDP, New Delhi.

Zoe, Oxaal and Baden Sally. 1997. 'Gender and Empowerment: Definitions, Approaches and Implications for Policy', Bridge (development-gender), Report No. 40. Institute of Development Studies, University of Sussex.

About the Editor and Contributors

THE EDITOR

Joy Deshmukh-Ranadive is Director, Indian School of Microfinance for Women, Ahmedabad. She has 20 years of experience in the field of Gender and Development and has worked with premier research organisations like Research Centre for Women's Studies, Mumbai, Centre for Women's Development Studies, New Delhi and International Center for Research on Women, New Delhi. She has several publications to her credit in the areas of structural adjustment; microfinance; women's empowerment; violence against women; women and ageing; and economic, social and cultural human rights. She has particularly focused on conceptualising power and empowerment, linking together the micro, meso and macro into an analytical framework. She has also taught Economics at the postgraduate level at the Department of Economics, University of Mumbai and holds an M.A. and Ph.D. in Economics from the University of Mumbai (formerly Bombay). Prior to joining the Indian School of Microfinance for Women, Joy Deshmukh-Ranadive was Country Director of the India office of the International Center for Research on Women, New Delhi.

About the Editor and Contributors

THE CONTRIBUTORS

Nandita Bhatla, currently with the International Center for Research on Women as a Gender and Development research specialist, is involved with several projects under the GenderViolence and Rights portfolio. She has, in the past, directed multi-site projects to explore links of domestic violence with other issues such as property, and coordinated a uniquely participatory research study to document and evaluate successful community-level interventions on domestic violence across India. She has previously worked extensively with community organisations, focusing on designing and implementing needs based programmes in a constant effort to bridge the gap between the field and policy planning. Apart from conducting extensive training sessions on capacity-building, she has planned and monitored several programmes on health, education and gender. She was part of a pioneering effort to conceptualise and implement a residential continuing education centre for adolescent girls and women. She also serves as a trust member for Sama, a health and women resource group.

Radhika Chopra is a Reader at the University of Delhi, Department of Sociology. Through her research and teaching, she has addressed issues of Gender and Masculinity, with a focus on South Asia. She is currently doing research on militancy and masculinity. She has edited 'Muted Masculinities: Contemporary Indian Ethnographies', a special issue of *Men and Masculinities* (vol. 9, no. 2, 2006), co-edited *Educational Regimes in Contemporary India* (2005) and *South Asian Masculinities: Context of Change, Sites of Continuity* (2004); and contributed to the *International Encyclopedia of Men and Masculinities* (2007). She has been a member and co-chair of the UN Expert Group, appointed by the UN Secretary General, on the 'Role of Men and Boys in Achieving Gender Equality' and a presenter and facilitator at training workshops organised jointly by the UNDP and the Smithsonian Institution for the delegates of the Commission for the Status of Women. She has been the principal investigator and consultant on various projects.

Nandita Gandhi has been active in the contemporary Indian women's movement since the 1980s. She was one of the founder members of the Forum Against the Oppression of Women, a women's rights group and Akshara, a women's resource centre. After a brief stint as a journalist, she turned to research and academic writing and collaborated with the Institute of Social Studies, The Hague, to write two books: *The Anti Price Rise Movement in Mumbai, Maharashtra* and *Contingent Workers: Women in Two Industries in Mumbai*, which was also her doctoral dissertation. She has also written *Issues at Stake: Theory and Practice in the Contemporary Women's Movement in India* with N. Shah. The parallel pursuit of theory and praxis continues with her involvement in political campaigns, research and programmes for women. At present she is the Co-Director of Akshara as an information activist.

Sumi Krishna, currently President of the Indian Association for Women's Studies, is an independent researcher/consultant on environment, development and gender with over 35 years of experience at the field, programme and policy levels. Her interests include the gender dimensions of natural resource-based livelihoods, biodiversity, local knowledge systems and resource rights; participatory governance through community institutions; inter-disciplinary research methodology; and teaching/mentoring young professionals. She has edited *Women's Livelihood Rights: Recasting Citizenship for Development* and *Livelihood and Gender: Equity in Community Resource Management,* and authored *Environmental Politics: People's Lives and Development Choices*, among others. She is the founder-moderator of 'jivika', an e-group for livelihood and gender equity.

M. Nirmala Kumari is a Faculty at the Padmavathi Mahila Kalasala, affiliated to the Osmania University, Hyderabad. She has about two decades of teaching experience in Public Administration. She was awarded a doctorate in the area of women's studies. She has presented papers on public administration and women's studies in national seminars.

Uma Narain is a Fulbright Fellow, a gold medalist in English Literature and has a Ph.D. in contemporary drama. Her post-doctoral work on 'Theatre and the Experience of Vietnam War' at New York University convinced her of the serious intent of purposeful theatre. Since then, she has written on drama, both as literature and theatre, in various Indian and international journals. Theatre and feminist

About the Editor and Contributors

study remain her predilections. Under a Rockefeller grant, she worked with the feminist theatre group Omaha Magic Theatre of Megan Terry and Jo Ann Schmidman at Omaha, Nebraska. She moved to the field of Management Education some years back. She is currently Associate Professor at S.P. Jain Institute of Management and Research, Mumbai. She runs a managerial skill development programme for MBA participants at the Institute and has designed a course on feminist issues in the corporate world using movies based on real life issues as case studies.

Anuradha Rajan has been working in the field of Gender and Development for the last 15 years. Her engagement with this sector began with the Mahila Samakhya Programme in Karnataka and Andhra Pradesh, followed by a teaching stint at TISS, Mumbai. Her work on violence against women began and deepened with her seven year association with International Center for Research on Women, where she was initially the Country Representative and then the Country Director. She has published several papers and articles on violence against women. She was nominated to the National Integration Council by the Government of India in 2005.

Shramajibee Mahila Samity was founded in 1995 as a union of female agricultural workers; it has grown to become a mass organisation of rural working women and many other women's organisations in West Bengal. Its work on violence against women has resulted in a series of strategies to counter ineffectual laws, an apathetic and understaffed police, and an overworked judiciary. It operates under the assumption that community pressure can act as an effective deterrent to violence against women. They make it clear through their interventions that they are not women organising to threaten male authority, but are opposed to male values and customs that harm women.

Sonal Shukla has an M.A. in Literature and Aesthetics and an M.Ed. with comparative education as a special area. She has been a teacher–educator and has worked in Gandhian institutions before getting involved full-time in the Indian women's movement as an activist and writer from the late 1970s. She has been a founding member of Forum Against Oppression of Women and of the Women's Centre in Mumbai. Her's was the first feminist column in Gujarati, which was published for 20 years in newspapers. Her writings in English have been published in various journals and as chapters in books and anthologies. She has produced two documentaries on women from the Indian freedom movement. For the last 10 years, she has been working on issues of girls who live in poor neighbourhoods in cities. Currently, she is Director of Vacha, a women's resource centre in Mumbai.

Sita Vanka is currently a Faculty at the School of Management Studies, University of Hyderabad. After a brilliant academic career as a student in her college and University, she received her Ph.D. from the Osmania University, Hyderabad, for her study on 'Women and Educational Management'. She started her career at the Osmania University and later worked at the Institute of Public Enterprise, Hyderabad. She is a teacher, trainer, consultant and researcher in the areas of human resource management, women's studies and general management. Having travelled widely, she has published and presented papers in national and international journals. As a research supervisor, she has guided M.Phil and Ph.D research scholars.

Index

adivasi 58, 64, 68
   decision-making systems 66
   groups 60
      conflicts 65
   impoverishment 67
   structural changes 5
   recently settled 61
   rituals 59
   settlement 57
   tribal societies 55
   women 59, 63, 67
ailments, occupation related 38
Andhra Pradesh District Poverty Initiatives Project (APDPIP) 209, 210, 214
arbitration 132, 151
arbitrator 144–46
authorship 77

basic needs, deprivation of 155
behaviour patterns 6
Bhagavad Gita 106
bhajans 88
bhaktas 77
boy's clubs, and masculinity 192, 194, 199, 203

business 193, 201

capital 2
caste 157–59
child labour 212, 213
child marriage 124, 171
collective representation 141
colonies, working class 50
communal riots in Mumbai, 1992 29
communication
   between the spectator and the performer 107
   skills 221
Communist Party of India 29
community
   beliefs and norms 172
   ostracism 153
   friendship and 199
   identities 29
   local non-*adivasi* 62
   loyalty 42
   norms and attitudes 130
   participation and ownership 139
   sanctions 153
   taboos and norms 177
   will 145

conciliation 116, 124
conflict
　within family 203
　between father and son 203
　intra-household 7
　of interest between men and women 5
　on overtime 47
　and responsibility 145
　resolution 120
conjugal rights 120
contract, patriarchal 45
crime
　against human rights 16
　against women 128, 160, 161
cross-gendering 104

Dalna 78
dance movement 100
dance-drama 99
democracy
　belief in 164
　as a concept 8, 66
　domestic 15, 185, 189, 204
　within the family 124
　and governance 8–12
deprivation 171, 184, 185
desertions 31
Dhaka Declaration for Eradication of Poverty, 1993 210
discrimination 12, 13, 14, 16
dispute
　between groups 158
　family 13, 117, 124
　parties to a 117
　resolution 137, 151, 153, 176
　settlement 121, 151
divorce 115, 124
domestic violence 128, 130, 152, 155, 175, 187
　in family 128
　in India 129
　normalcy of, within families 12
　objective of studying 131–32
　private and personal issue of 137
　public and community-based responses to 136
dowry 124, 158
District Poverty Initiatives Project (DPIP) 219

economic hardships 30
education
　cuts 44
　for girls 212
　free primary 36
　school children's 37
egalitarianism 199
Employment Guarantee Scheme 157
Employment 34, 48, 49, 51
empowerment 66, 179, 207–08, 215, 216, 222–23
expenditure
　reduction 36
　reduction strategies 45
　　allocations for education 36
　　cuts in non-essentials 34–36
　　through food cuts 39–41
　　unhealthy adjustments 37–39

family 113, 114
　business 190, 192, 200, 203
　domesticity and 190
　extended 10, 41, 158
　　patrilineal South Asian 10
　of relatives 114
　support towards the 195
gender
　equity in, conceptualising 215–17

Index

institution of 5, 118, 125
joint 11, 119
law 117, 124
loyalty 7
male-headed 9
matrimonial 165
medicalisation of 115
power differentials 115
natal 7, 11
non-democratic 4, 7
nuclear 9, 10, 32
privacy 115
problems 116
significance of 114
social patterns of 98
and society 175–79
sociology 121
status of women within 158
structure 10
system 115
ties 41
various views 113–16
family courts 115–16, 118, 123
in Andhra Pradesh 116–25
conciliatory approach 124
functioning of 117, 120, 122
involvement of women as judges in 125
purpose behind 120
reasons for approaching 117
success of 125
system 122
usefulness and the effectiveness of 121
working of 121
Family Courts Act (1984) 117, 118, 121
fathering 200, 204
femininity 221
feminism 60
film songs 87, 89

financial crisis 37
folk music 83, 85
folk song 76–77, 85
as anonymous literature 76–78
definition of 76
feminist 7
Gujarati 75–76
UP 90
women's 78, 89
folk tunes 90
friendship 203, 204

gambling 36
Ganatantrik Mahila Samity 159
garba 76, 80
community 85
festivals 85
Gujarati 81
khadi propagation 83
nationalist 83
songs 80, 85
with the story of Jallianwala Bagh 83
for women 83
gender
concerns 211–14
discrimination 213
equality 15, 189, 211
equity in the family 217, 222–23
inequality 186
norms 215
in performance 107–09
politics of, and feminist research 184
relations 55, 185
and relationships 138
roles, traditional knowledge about 217
socialisation 1
stereotyping 15

violence 186
and women's rights 171
gendered jobs 32
globalisation 2, 3

Hidimba, character of 98, 104
Hindu Marriage Act 173
Hindu reform movements 157
hospitalisation 38
household
    adjustments, dynamics of 43–49
    better-off 29
    budget, tightening of 37
    consumption 53
    development, and families 2
    expenditure 33
    families and 30–33
    hierarchy 51
    strategies 45
    work 42
    working class 28, 36
human capital 2, 3
human resources 4
human rights 18, 130, 220, 221
human values 219, 220

Indian People's Theatre Association (IPTA) 86
inheritance 200
injustices, perpetrator of 218
in-laws, oppressive 7
institutionalised response 132
Integrated Rural Development Programme (IRDP) 156
International Conference on Population and Development, Cairo 1994 186
International Center for Research on Women (ICRW) 155, 187
International Year of the Family 115, 121

Jana Sanghati Kendra (JSK) 161, 163
Jawahar Grameen Samriddhi Yojana (JGSY) 157
Jawahar Rozgar Yojana (JRY) 157
judges 120, 124
justice 12, 143–44

Kabir 77
Kala Jatha 218, 219
karva chouth 91–92, 95
khanawalis 42
khayana 76, 78–80, 83, 84
kinship 12, 140, 215
Kohli fisherfolk, 26
kumkum 91
Kunwarbainu Mameru 78

labour
    deployment of 34, 44
    division of 17, 196
    feminisation of 4
    sexual division of 3, 17, 46
land redistribution 157
lavni dance song 88
Left movement 157
legal system 160–61
liberalisation, of markets 2
loans 43

Mahabharata 98, 101, 102, 109
mahila panch 133, 135
Mahila Samakhya programme 133
Mahila Samity activists 167
mahila sangha 213
Maitree 160, 165
male domination 118
Mandal Samakhyas 137, 211–12
marriage 31
masculinity
    and body care 197

Index

and boy's clubs 192, 194, 199, 203
and domestic violence 187
and initiation rituals 197
as an identity 185
myths about 221
stereotypes associated with 59
*mastan*s 154
matriarchy 104
Meera 77
Men-in-Maternity programmes 186
micro-credit 186, 208
mothers-in-law 214
motherhood 102, 105, 108
Mudgal, Shubha 94
*Mumbaikar*s 26
Mumbaiya culture 30
Muslim League 29
nari adalat 131, 133, 135
  sahara sangh 131
National Crime Records Bureau 161
network
  business 201
  extended family 42
  friendship 198
  informal non-kin 42
  institutionalised support 201
  kinship 204
  social 34, 41–43, 201, 203
New Economic Reforms 25
non-governmental organisations (NGOs) 14, 56, 129, 159, 208

old people 11
one-to-one dialogues 57
open market prices 40
overtime 47

party 154, 158
Paschim Banga Ganatantrik Mahila Samity 159
patriarchy 48, 102, 103–07

Paschim Banga Khet Majoor Samity (PBKMS) 163, 170, 117
phatana 78
plantation owners 59
bhakta, poets 88
policies 215, 216
politics, electoral 29
population council programmes 186
poverty
  alleviation programmes, women's share in 157
  elimination projects 210
power-brokers 154
procurement prices 40
professionals 212
public hospitals 38

rakhi brothers 42
ration shop prices 40
relations/relationships 16
  between mothers-in-law and daughters-in-law 213
  social 41, 184
  of the woman with other female relatives 158
  within families 1, 7
    and feminist songs 94–97
  father–son 190
  intra-domestic 17
  kin 7
  male–male 190, 193
  between men and women 5
  spousal 143
reproductive health 204
research
  anthropological 201
  findings 202
  methodologies 201
  reflections on, and method 201–03

responsibilities
    family, neglect of 115
    social 130, 214
Rig Veda 114
rights
    awareness of, amongst women 160
    to be human 15
    and needs 17
    woman's 139, 145, 179
Rural Poverty Elimination Program 210

sahara sangh (SS) 133, 135
sahyogini 133, 135
saint-poets 77
sangha meetings 214
sarkhi saheli 93, 96
sarpanchs, male 96
Section 125 of the CrPC 175
Section 498A of the IPC 173, 175
Self Help Groups (SHGs) 209
self-confidence 167, 222
self-respect 103
sex role stereotyping 171
sexual harassment 29
shalishi 139, 141, 146, 154, 164, 166
    decisions of 172
    follow-up 169
    process 137, 173
    Samity 172
    in West Bengal 151–79
    and work on violence 164
Shiv Sena 29
Shramajibee Mahila Samity (SMS) 131, 136, 153, 170
sibling rivalry 103
sick people 11
social capital 2, 3, 211, 215
social change 108, 138, 223
social mobilisation 210
social norms 6, 7, 9, 142–43, 220

social problems, traditional, 114
Society for Elimination of Rural Poverty (SERP) 210, 213–14, 221
socio-cultural environment 216
socio-cultural norms 7, 16, 18
songs
    booklets of, published by Jagori 92
    feminist 7, 96
    by literary writers 83
    mehendi 85
    revolutionary 89
    sahyaba 96
    traditional 85
    wedding 78, 79
    women's movement 75–76, 86–94
South Asia Poverty Alleviation Programme (SAPAP) 210, 212
Special Cell for Women and Children 129
structural adjustment policies 4
Swarnajayanti Grameen Swarozgar Yojana (SGSY) 156
Swayam 161

tadipar 26
talaq 124
training for trainers 92

United Nations Fourth World Conference on Women, Beijing, 1995 186
Urban Land Ceiling and Regulation Act, 1976 27

value systems 145, 217, 221
Velugu 213, 214
Village Organisations (VOs) 211
violence 13
    within the community 146

Index

domestic (*see* domestic violence)
within a household 187
and intimidation 222
within marriage 129, 130
men's role in 187
mental 155, 174
movement against 174
needs of women facing 131
physical 155, 167, 174
Rajput celebrations of 187
at the sangha level 133
sexual 146, 155, 174
spousal 155
voices against 13
against women 129, 159, 169, 174, 177
    increase in 128
    interventions in 159–60
    intimate 128
    within marriage 130

Women Rights Protection Committees 212
women
    barren 49
    with children 49
    and legal matters 121
    exploitation of 164
    facing violence 146
    in Gujarat 76
    hierarchy among 11
    issueless 10
    in joint families 175
    limited mobility of 208
    married 42
    mobilising 223
    morbidity rate amongst 45
    paid employment of 48
    panchayats and 161–63
    poets in Gujarati 85
    professional dancers 88
    rights of 146
    reservation for 96
    role of 125
    single 47
    with sons 10
    unmarried 40
Women's Day 92
women's movement 8, 55, 56, 97, 108
    and feminist theatre 109
    in West Bengal 159, 162
    songs from 75, 76, 86, 90, 94, 96
work
    in beauty parlours 197
    gendered division of 214
    men and 191
    non-cooperation in sharing domestic 47
    relation between men and 191
worker
    contingency 48, 52
    domestic 190, 193, 203
    unpaid household 156
World Summit for Social Development 207